ISBN 978-1-330-45667-5
PIBN 10064893

1 MONTH OF
FREE
READING

at

www.ForgottenBooks.com

By purchasing this book you are eligible for one month membership to ForgottenBooks.com, giving you unlimited access to our entire collection of over 700,000 titles via our web site and mobile apps.

To claim your free month visit:

www.forgottenbooks.com/free64893

English
Français
Deutsche
Italiano
Español
Português

www.forgottenbooks.com

Mythology Photography **Fiction**
Fishing Christianity **Art** Cooking
Essays Buddhism Freemasonry
Medicine **Biology** Music **Ancient
Egypt** Evolution Carpentry Physics
Dance Geology **Mathematics** Fitness
Shakespeare **Folklore** Yoga Marketing
Confidence Immortality Biographies
Poetry **Psychology** Witchcraft
Electronics Chemistry History **Law**
Accounting **Philosophy** Anthropology
Alchemy Drama Quantum Mechanics
Atheism Sexual Health **Ancient History**
Entrepreneurship Languages Sport
Paleontology Needlework Islam
Metaphysics Investment Archaeology
Parenting Statistics Criminology
Motivational

MULOCK'S POEMS,

NEW AND OLD.

BY THE AUTHOR OF

"JOHN HALIFAX, GENTLEMAN."

ETC.

Craik, Dinah Maria (Mulock)

NEW YORK:

HURST & CO., PUBLISHERS,

122 NASSAU STREET.

1883.

DEDICATION

TO MY HUSBAND.

This under voice, for twenty years
    Still running on, a brook unheard,
With sound half laughter and half tears,—
    Is hushed at last, like autumn bird;
Carol or quiet, which is best?
    The singer or the song, preferred?
In sacred silence unconfessed
    Take both;—and not another word.

CONTENTS.

NINETEEN SONNETS.

CONTENTS.

CONTENTS.

CONTENTS.

POEMS.

PHILIP MY KING.

"Who bears upon his baby brow the round
And top of sovereignty."

OOK at me with thy large brown eyes,
  Philip my king,
 Round whom the enshadowing purple
   lies
Of babyhood's royal dignities:
Lay on my neck thy tiny hand,
With love's invisible sceptre laden;
I am thine Esther to command
Till thou shalt find a queen-handmaiden,
  Philip my king.

O the day when thou goest a wooing,
  Philip my king!
When those beautiful lips are suing,
And some gentle heart's bars undoing
Thou dost enter, love-crowned, and there
Sittest love-glorified. Rule kindly,
Tenderly, over thy kingdom fair,
For we that love, ah! we love so blindly,
  Philip my king.

Up from thy sweet mouth,—up to thy brow,
    Philip my king!
The spirit that there lies sleeping now
May rise like a giant and make men bow
As to one heaven-chosen amongst his peers;
My Saul, than thy brethren taller and fairer
Let me behold thee in future years;—
Yet thy head needeth a circlet rarer,
    Philip my king.

—A wreath not of gold but palm.   One day,
    Philip my king,
Thou too must tread, as we trod, a way
Thorny and cruel and cold and gray:
Rebels within thee and foes without
Will snatch at thy crown.   But march on, glorious,
Martyr, yet monarch; till angels shout
As thou sit'st at the feet of God victorious,
    "Philip the king!"

THOUGHTS IN A WHEAT-FIELD.

"The harvest is the end of the world, and the reapers are the angels."

N his wide fields walks the Master,
    In his fair fields, ripe for harvest,
    Where the evening sun shines slant-wise
On the rich ears heavy bending;
    Saith the Master: "It is time."
Though no leaf shows brown decadence,
And September's nightly frost-bite
Only reddens the horizon,
"It is full time," saith the Master,
    The wise Master, "It is time."

Lo, he looks. That look compelling
Brings his laborers to the harvest;
Quick they gather, as in autumn
Passage-birds in cloudy eddies
    Drop upon the seaside fields;
White wings have they, and white raiment,
White feet shod with swift obedience,
Each lays down his golden palm-branch,
And uprears his sickle shining,
    "Speak, O Master—is it time?"

O'er the field the servants hasten,
Where the full-stored ears droop downwards,
Humble with their weight of harvest:
Where the empty ears wave upward,
    And the gay tares flaunt in rows:
But the sickles, the sharp sickles,
Flash new dawn at their appearing,
Songs are heard in earth and heaven,
For the reapers are the angels,
    And it is the harvest time.

O Great Master, are thy footsteps
Even now upon the mountains?
Art thou walking in thy wheat-field?
Are the snowy-wingèd reapers
    Gathering in the silent air?
Are thy signs abroad, the glowing
Of the distant sky, blood-reddened,—
And the near fields trodden, blighted,
Choked by gaudy tares triumphant—
    Sure, it must be harvest time!

Who shall know the Master's coming?
Whether it be at dawn or sunset,
When night dews weigh down the wheat-ears,
Or while noon rides high in heaven,
    Sleeping lies the yellow field?
Only, may thy voice, Good Master,

Peal above the reapers' chorus,
And dull sound of sheaves slow falling—
"Gather all into My garner,
    For it is My harvest time."

IMMUTABLE.

"With whom is no variableness, neither shadow of turning."

AUTUMN to winter, winter into spring,
    Spring into summer, summer into fall—
    So rolls the changing year, and so we change;
    Motion so swift, we know not that we move,
Till at the gate of some memorial hour
We pause—look in its sepulchre to find
The cast-off shape that years since we called "I"—
And start, amazed. Yet on! we may not stay
To weep or laugh. All that is past, is past.
Even while we gaze, the simulated form
Drops into dust, like many-centuried corpse
At opening of a tomb.

                Alack, this world
Is full of change, change, change,—nothing but change!
Is there not one straw in life's whirling flood
To hold by, as the torrent sweeps us down,
Us, scattered leaves; eddied and broken; torn
Roughly asunder; or in smooth mid-stream
Divided each from other without pain;
Collected in what looks like union,
Yet is but stagnant chance,—stopping to rot
By the same pebble till the tide shall turn;
Then on, to find no shelter and no rest,
Forever rootless and forever lone.
O God, we are but leaves upon Thy stream,
Clouds on Thy sky. We do but move across
The silent breast of Thine infinitude
Which bears us all. We pour out day by day

Our long, brief moan of mutability
To Thine immutable—and cease.

    Yet still
Our change yearns after Thine unchangedness;
Our mortal craves Thine immortality;
Our manifold and multiform and weak
Imperfectness, requires the perfect ONE.
For Thou art ONE, and we are all of Thee;
Dropped from Thy bosom, as Thy sky drops down
Its morning dews, which glitter for a space,
Uncertain whence they fell, or whither tend,
Till the great Sun arising on his fields
Upcalls them all, and they rejoicing go.

So with like joy, O Light Eterne, we spring
Thee-ward, and leave the pleasant fields of earth,
Forgetting equally its blossomed meads
And its dry dusty paths which drank us up
Remorseless,—we, poor humble drops of dew,
That only wished to freshen a flower's breast,
And be exhaled to heaven.

    O Thou supreme
All-satisfying and immutable One,
It is enough to be absorbed in Thee
And vanish,—were it only to a voice
That through all ages with perpetual joy
Goes evermore loud crying, "God! God! God!"

FOUR YEARS.

AT the midsummer, when the hay was down,
 Said I, mournfully,—My life is at its prime,
 Yet bare lie my meadows, shorn before the time,
In my scorched woodlands the leaves are turning
  brown.
It is the hot midsummer, and the hay is down.

At the midsummer, when the hay was down,
Stood she by the streamlet, young and very fair,
With the first white bindweed twisted in her hair,—
Hair that drooped like birch-boughs,—all in her simple gown
For it was midsummer,—and the hay was down.

At the midsummer, when the hay was down,
Crept she, a willing bride, close into my breast:
Low piled the thunder-clouds had drifted to the west,—
Red-eyed out glared the sun, like knight from leaguered town,
That eve in high midsummer, when the hay was down.

It is midsummer,—all the hay is down;
Close to her bosom press I dying eyes,
Praying, "God shield thee till we meet in Paradise!"
Bless her in Love's name who was my brief life's crown,—
And I go at midsummer, when the hay is down.

THE DEAD CZAR.

AY him beneath his snows,
    The great Norse giant who in these last days
    Troubled the nations.   Gather decently
The imperial robes about him.   'T is but man—
This demi-god.   Or rather it *was* man,
And is—a little dust, that will corrupt
As fast as any nameless dust which sleeps
'Neath Alma's grass or Balaklava's vines.

No vineyard grave for him.   No quiet tomb
By river margin, where across the seas
Children's fond thoughts and women's memories come
Like angels, to sit by the sepulchre,
Saying: "All these were men who knew to count,
Front-faced, the cost of honor, nor did shrink
From its full payment: coming here to die,
They died—like men."

But this man?   Ah! for him

Funereal state, and ceremonial grand,
The stone-engraved sarcophagus, and then
Oblivion.

      Nay, oblivion were as bliss
To that fierce howl which rolls from land to land
Exulting—"Art thou fallen, Lucifer,
Son of the morning?" or condemning—"Thus
Perish the wicked!" or blaspheming,—"Here
Lies our Belshazzar, our Sennacherib,
Our Pharoah—he whose heart God hardenèd,
So that he would not let the people go."

Self-glorifying sinners! Why, this man
Was but like other men:—you, Levite small,
Who shut your saintly ears, and prate of hell
And heretics, because outside church-doors,
Your church-doors, congregations poor and small
Praise Heaven in their own way;—you, autocrat
Of all the hamlets, who add field to field
And house to house, whose slavish children cower
Before your tyrant footstep;—you, foul-tongued
Fanatic and ambitious egotist,
Who thinks God stoops from His high majesty
To lay His finger on your puny head,
And crown it,—that you henceforth may parade
Your maggotship throughout the wondering world,—
"I am the Lord's anointed!"

        Fools and blind!
This Czar, this emperor, this disthronèd corpse,
Lying so straightly in an icy calm
Grander than sovereignty, was but as ye,—
No better and no worse; —Heaven mend us all!

Carry him forth and bury him. Death's peace
Rest on his memory! Mercy by his bier
Sits silent, or says only these few words,—
"Let him who is without sin 'mongst ye all
Cast the first stone."

THE WIND AT NIGHT.

 SUDDEN blast, that through this silence black
　　　Sweeps past my windows,
Coming and going with invisible track
　　　As death or sin does,—

Why scare me, lying sick, and, save thine own,
　　　Hearing no voices?
Why mingle with a helpless human moan
　　　Thy mad rejoices?

Why not come gently, as good angels come
　　　To souls departing,
Floating among the shadows of the room
　　　With eyes light-darting,

Bringing faint airs of balm that seem to rouse
　　　Thoughts of a Far Land,
Then bending softly upon weary brows
　　　Death's poppy-garland?

O fearful blast, I shudder at thy sound,
　　　Like heathen mortal
Who saw the Three that mark life's doomèd bound
　　　Sit at his portal.

Thou mightst be laden with sad, shrieking souls,
　　　Carried unwilling
From their known earth to the unknown stream
　　　　　that rolls
　　　All anguish stilling.

Fierce wind, will the Death-angel come like thee,
　　　Soon, soon to bear me
—*Whither?* what mysteries may unfold to me,
　　　What terrors scare me?

Shall I go wand'ring on through empty space
  As on earth, lonely?
Or seek through myriad spirit-ranks one face,
  And miss that only?

Shall I not then drop down from sphere to sphere
  Palsied and aimless?
Or will my being change so, that both fear
  And grief die nameless?

Rather I pray Him who Himself is Love,
  Out of whose essence
We all proceed, and towards Him tending, move
  Back to His presence,

That even His brightness may not quite efface
  The soul's earth-features,
That the dear human likeness each may trace
  Glorified creatures;

That we may not cease loving, only taught
  Holier desiring;
More faith, more patience; with more wisdom fraught,
  Higher aspiring.

That we may do all work we left undone
  Through sad unmeetness;
From height to height celestial passing on
  Towards full completeness.

Then, strong Azrael, be thy supreme call
  Soft as spring-breezes,
Or like this blast, whose loud fiend festival
  My heart's blood freezes,

I will not fear thee. If thou safely keep
  My soul, God's giving,
And my soul's soul, I, wakening from death-sleep,
  Shall first know living.

A FABLE.

ILENT and sunny was the way
      Where Youth and I danced on together:
  So winding and embowered o'er,
We could not see one rood before.
Nevertheless all merrily
We bounded onward, Youth and I,
      Leashed closely in a silken tether:
          (Well-a-day, well-a-day!)
Ah Youth, ah Youth, but I would fain
See thy sweet foolish face again!

It came to pass, one morn of May,
      All in a swoon of golden weather,
That I through green leaves fluttering
Saw Joy uprise on Psyche wing:
Eagerly, too eagerly
We followed after,—Youth and I,—
      Till suddenly he slipped the tether.
          (Well-a-day, well-a-day!)
"Where art thou, Youth?" I cried.   In vain;
He never more came back again.

Yet onward through the devious way
      In rain or shine, I recked not whether,
Like many another maddened boy
I tracked my Psyche-wingèd Joy;
Till, curving round the bowery lane,
Lo,—in the pathway stood pale Pain,
      And we met face to face together:
          (Well-a-day, well-a-day!)
"Whence comest thou?"—and I writhed in vain—
"Unloose thy cruel grasp, O Pain!"

But he would not.   Since, day by day
    He has ta'en up Youth's silken tether
And changed it into iron bands.
So through rich vales and barren lands
Solemnly, all solemnly,
March we united, he and I;
    And we have grown such friends together
       (Well-a-day, well-a-day!)
I and this Shape, my brother Pain,
I think we'll never part again.

LABOR IS PRAYER.

LARORARE est orare :
    We, black-visaged sons of toil,
    From the coal-mine and the anvil
 And the delving of the soil,—
From the loom, the wharf, the warehouse,
    And the ever-whirling mill,
Out of grim and hungry silence
    Raise a weak voice small and shrill;—
Laborare est orare:—
    Man, dost hear us?   God, He will.

We who just can keep from starving,
    Sickly wives,—not always mild:
Trying not to curse Heaven's bounty
 When it sends another child,—
We who, worn-out, doze on Sundays
    O'er the Book we strive to read,
Cannot understand the parson
    Or the catechism and creed.
Laborare est orare:
    Then, good sooth, we pray indeed.

We, poor women, feeble-natured,
    Large of heart, in wisdom small,

Who the world's incessant battle
    Cannot understand at all,
All the mysteries of the churches,
    All the troubles of the state—
Whom child-smiles teach "God is loving,"
    And child-coffins, "God is great:"
Laborare est orare:—
    We too at His footstool wait.

Laborare est orare;
    Hear it, ye of spirit poor,
Who sit crouching at the threshold
    While your brethren force the door;
Ye whose ignorance stands wringing
    Rough hands, seamed with toil, nor dares
Lift so much as eyes to heaven,—
    Lo! all life this truth declares,
Laborare est orare:
    And the whole earth rings with prayers.

A SILLY SONG.

 HEART, my heart!" she said, and heard
        His mate the blackbird calling,
    While through the sheen of the garden green
    May rain was softly falling,—
    Aye softly, softly falling,—

The buttercups across the field
    Made sunshine rifts of splendor:
The round snow-bud of the thorn in the wood
    Peeped through its leafage tender,
    As the rain came softly falling.

"O heart, my heart!" she said and smiled,
    " There's not a tree of the valley,
Or a leaf I wis which the rain's soft kiss

Freshens in yonder alley,
Where the drops keep ever falling,—

"There's not a foolish flower i' the grass,
Or bird through the woodland calling,
So glad again of the coming of rain
As I of these tears now falling,—
These happy tears down falling."

IN MEMORIAM.

Obiit 1854.

HEAVEN rest thee
We shall go about to-day
In our festal garlands gay;
Whatsoever robes we wear
Not a trace of black be there.
Well, what matters? none is seen
On thy daisy covering green,
Or thy pure white pillow, hid
Underneath a coffin lid.
Heaven rest thee!

Heaven take thee!—
Ay, heaven only. Sleeps beneath
One who died a virgin death:
Died so slowy, day by day,
That it scarcely seemed decay,
Till this lonely churchyard kind
Opened,—and we left behind
Nothing but a little dust;—
Heaven is pitiful and just:
Heaven take thee!

Heaven keep thee:
Nevermore above the ground,

Be one relic of thee found :
Lay the turf so smooth, we crave,
None would guess it was a grave,
Save for grass that greener grows,
Or for wind that gentlier blows
All the earth o'er, from this spot
Where thou wert—and thou art not.
Heaven keep thee !

———

AN HONEST VALENTINE.

Returned from the Dead-Letter Office.

THANK ye for your kindness,
    Lady fair and wise,
    Though love's famed for blindness,
Lovers—hem! for lies.
    Courtship's mighty pretty,
        Wedlock a sweet sight ;—
    Should I (from the city,
        A plain man, Miss—) write
    Ere we spouse-and-wive it,
        Just one honest line,
    Could you e'er forgive it,
        Pretty Valentine?

    Honey-moon quite over,
        If I less should scan
    You with eye of lover
        Than of mortal man?
    Seeing my fair charmer
        Curl hair spire on spire,
    All in paper armor,
        By the parlor fire ;
    Gown that wants a stitch in
        Hid by apron fine,
    Scolding in her kitchen,—
        O fie, Valentine!

Should I come home surly
  Vexed with fortune's frown,
Find a hurly-burly,
  House turned upside down,
Servants all a-snarl, or
  Cleaning steps or stair:
Breakfast still in parlor,
  Dinner—anywhere:
Shall I to cold bacon
  Meekly fall and dine?
No,—or I'm mistaken
  Much, my Valentine.

What if we should quarrel?
  —Bless you, all folks do:—
Will you take the war ill,
  Yet half like it too?
When I storm and jangle,
  Obstinate, absurd,
Will you sit and wrangle
  Just for the last word,—
Or, while poor Love, crying,
  Upon tiptoe stands,
Ready plumed for flying,—
  Will you smile, shake hands,
And the truth beholding,
  With a kiss divine
Stop my rough mouth's scolding?—
  Bless you, Valentine!

If, should times grow harder,
  We have lack of pelf,
Little in the larder,
  Less upon the shelf;
Will you, never tearful,
  Make your old gowns do,
Mend my stockings, cheerful,
  And pay visits few?
Crave nor gift nor donor,

Old days ne'er regret,
  Seek no friend save Honor,
    Dread no foe but Debt;
Meet ill-fortune steady,
    Hand to hand with mine,
Like a gallant lady,—
    Will you, Valentine?

Then, whatever weather
    Come, or shine, or shade,
We'll set out together,
    Not a whit afraid.
Age is ne'er alarming,—
    I shall find, I ween,
You at sixty charming
    As at sweet sixteen:
Let's pray, nothing loath, dear,
    That our funeral may
Make one date serve both, dear,
    As our marriage day.
Then, come joy or sorrow,
    Thou art mine,—I thine.
So we'll wed to-morrow, -
    Dearest Valentine.

LOOKING DEATH IN THE FACE.

AY, in thy face, old fellow! Now's the time.
  The Black sea wind flaps my tent-roof, nor wakes
  These lads of mine, who take of sleep their fill,
    As if they'd thought they'd never sleep again.
Instead of—

    Pitiless Crimean blast,
How many a howling lullaby thou'lt raise
To-morrow night, all nights till the world's end,
Over some sleepers here!

                Some ?—*who ?*   Dumb Fate
Whispers in no man's ear his coming doom;
Each thinks—" not I—not I."
                    But thou, grim Death,
I hear thee on the night-wind flying abroad,
I feel thee here, squatted at our tent-door,
Invisible and incommunicable,
Pointing:
        "Hurrah ! "

                Why yell so in your sleep,
Comrade ?   Did *you* see aught ?
                Well—let him dream:
Who knows, to-morrow such a shout as this
He'll die with.   A brave lad, and very like
His sister.

    *   *   *   *   *

                So! just two hours have I lain
Freezing.   That pale white star, which came and peered
Through the tent-opening, has passed on, to smile
Elsewhere, or lost herself i' the dark—God knows.
Two hours nearer to dawn.   The very hour,
The very hour and day, a year ago,
When we light-hearted and light-footed fools
Went jingling idle swords in waltz and reel,
And smiling in fair faces.   How they'd start,
Those dainty red and white soft faces kind,
If they could but behold my visage now,
Or his—or his—or some poor faces cold
We covered up with earth last noon.

                    —There sits
The laidly Thing I felt on our tent-door
Two hours back.   It has sat and never stirred.
I cannot challenge it, or shoot it down,
Or grapple with it, as with that young Russ
Whom I killed yesterday.   (What eyes he had !—
Great limpid eyes, and curling dark-red hair,—
A woman's picture hidden in his breast,—

I never liked this fighting hand to hand),
No, it will not be met like flesh and blood,
This shapeless, voiceless, immaterial Thing.
Yet I *will* meet it. Here I sit alone,—
Show me thy face, O Death!
                  There, there. I think
I did not tremble.

            I am a young man,
Have done full many an ill deed, left undone
Many a good one: lived unto the flesh,
Not to the spirit: I would rather live
A few years more, and try if things might change.
Yet, yet I hope I do not tremble, Death;
And that thy finger pointed at my heart
But calms the tumult there.

               What small account
The All-living seems to take of this thin flame
Which we call *life*. He sends a moment's blast
Out of war's nostrils, and a myriad
Of these our puny tapers are blown out
Forever. Yet we shrink not,—we, such frail
Poor knaves, whom a spent ball can instant strike
Into eternity,—we helpless fools,
Whom a serf's clumsy hand and clumsier sword
Smiting—shall sudden into nothingness
Let out that something rare which could conceive
A universe and its God.

              Free, open-eyed,
We rush like bridegrooms to Death's grisly arms.
Surely the very longing for that clasp,
Proves us immortal. Immortality
Alone could teach this mortal how to die.
Perhaps war is but Heaven's great ploughshare, driven
Over the barren, fallow earthly fields,
Preparing them for harvest; rooting up

Grass, weeds, and flowers, which necessary fall,
That in these furrows the wise Husbandman
May drop celestial seed.
                          So let us die;
Yield up our little lives, as the flowers do;
Believing He'll not lose one single soul,—
One germ of His immortal. Naught of His
Or Him can perish; therefore let us die.

I half remember, something like to this
She says in her dear letters. So—let's die.
What, dawn? The faint hum in the trenches fails.
Is that a bell i' the mist? My faith, they go
Early to matins in Sebastopol!—
A gun!—Lads, stand to your arms; the Russ is here.

Agnes.

Kind Heaven, I have looked Death in the face,
     Help me to die.

BY THE ALMA RIVER.

ILLIE, fold your little hands;
          Let it drop, that "soldier" toy
     Look where father's picture stands,—
Father, who here kissed his boy
Not two months since,—father kind,
Who this night may— Never mind
Mother's sob, my Willie dear,
Call aloud that He may hear
Who is God of battles, say,
"O, keep father safe this day
     By the Alma river."

Ask no more, child. Never heed
     Either Russ, or Frank, or Turk,

Right of nations or of creed.
 Chance-poised victory's bloody work.
Any flag i' the wind may roll
On thy heights, Sebastopol;
Willie, all to you and me
Is that spot, where'er it be
Where he stands—no other word!
Stands—God sure the child's prayer heard—
 By the Alma river.

Willie, listen to the bells
 Ringing through the town to-day.
That's for victory. Ah, no knells
 For the many swept away,—
Hundreds—thousands! Let us weep,
We who need not,—just to keep
Reason steady in my brain
Till the morning comes again,
Till the third dread morning tell
Who they were that fought and *fell*
 By the Alma river.

Come, we'll lay us down, my child,
 Poor the bed is, poor and hard;
Yet thy father, far exiled,
 Sleeps upon the open sward,
Dreaming of us two at home:
Or beneath the starry dome
Digs out trenches in the dark,
Where he buries—Willie, mark—
Where *he buries* those who died
Fighting bravely at his side
 By the Alma river.

Willie, Willie, go to sleep,
 God will keep us, O my boy;
He will make the dull hours creep
 Faster, and send news of joy,
When I need not shrink to meet

Those dread placards in the street,
Which for weeks will ghastly stare
In some eyes— Child, say thy prayer
Once again, a different one :
Say, "O God, Thy will be done
    By the Alma river."

ROTHESAY BAY.

FU' yellow lie the corn-rigs
        Far doun the braid hillside ;
    It is the brawest harst field
Alang the shores o' Clyde,—
And I'm a puir harst-lassie
    Wha stan's the lee-lang day ·
Shearing the corn-rigs of Ardbeg
    Aboon sweet Rothesay Bay.

O I had ance a true-love,—
    Now, I hae nane ava ;
And I had three braw brithers,
    But I hae tint them a';
My father and my mither
    Sleep i' the mools this day.
I sit my lane amang the rigs,
    Aboon sweet Rothesay Bay.

It's a bonnie bay at morning,
    And bonnier at the noon,
But it's bonniest when the sun draps
    And red comes up the moon :
When the mist creeps o'er the Cumbrays,
    And Arran peaks are gray,
And the great black hills, like sleepin' kings,
    Sit grand roun' Rothesay Bay,

Then a bit sigh stirs my bosom,
    And a wee tear blin's my e'e,—

And I think o' that far Countrie
What I wad like to be!
But I rise content i' the morning
To wark while wark I may
I' the yellow harst field of Ardbeg
Aboon sweet Rothesay Bay.

LIVING:

AFTER A DEATH.

"That friend of mine who lives in God."

LIVE!
(Thus seems it we should say to our beloved,—
Each held by such slight links, so oft removed;)
And I can let thee go to the world's end,
All precious names, companion, love, spouse, friend,
Seal up in an eternal silence gray,
Like a closed grave till resurrection-day:
All sweet remembrances, hopes, dreams, desires,
Heap, as one heaps up sacrificial fires:
Then, turning, consecrate by loss, and proud
Of penury—go back into the loud
Tumultuous world again with never a moan—
Save that which whispers still, "My own, my own."
Unto the same broad sky whose arch immense
Enfolds us both like the arm of Providence:
And thus, contented, I could live or die,
With never clasp of hand or meeting eye
On this side Paradise.—While thee I see
Living to God, thou art alive to me.

O live!
And I, methinks, can let all dear rights go,
Fond duties melt away like April snow,
And sweet, sweet hopes, that took a life to weave,

Vanish like gossamers of autumn eve.
Nay, sometimes seems it I could even bear
To lay down humbly this love-crown I wear,
Steal from my palace, helpless, hopeless, poor,
And see another queen it at the door,—
If only that the king had done no wrong,
If this my palace, where I dwelt so long,
Were not defiled by falsehood entering in:—
There is no loss but change, no death but sin,
No parting, save the slow corrupting pain
Of murdered faith that never lives again.

O live!
(So endeth faint the low pathetic cry
Of love, whom death has taught love cannot die,)
And I can stand above the daisy bed,
The only pillow for thy dearest head,
There cover up forever from my sight
My own, my earthly all of earth delight;
And enter the sea cave of widowed years,
Where far, far off the trembling gleam appears
Through which thy heavenly image slipped away,
And waits to meet me at the open day.
Only to me, my love, only to me.
This cavern underneath the moaning sea;
This long, long life that I alone must tread,
To whom the living seem most like the dead,—
Thou wilt be safe out on the happy shore:
He who in God lives, liveth evermore.

IN OUR BOAT.

STARS trembling o'er us and sunset before us,
  Mountains in shadow and forests asleep;
  Down the dim river we float on forever,
Speak not, ah, breathe not,—there's peace on the
    deep.

Come not, pale Sorrow, flee till to-morrow,
  Rest softly falling o'er eyelids that weep;
While down the river we float on forever,
  Speak not, ah, breathe not,—there's peace on the deep.

As the waves cover the depths we glide over,
  So let the past in forgetfulness sleep,
While down the river we float on forever,
  Speak not, ah, breathe not,—there's peace on the deep.

Heaven shine above us, bless all that love us,
  All whom we love in thy tenderness keep!
While down the river we float on forever,
  Speak not, ah, breathe not,—there's peace on the deep.

THE RIVER SHORE.

For an old tune of Dowland's.

WALKING by the quiet river
    Where the slow tide seaward goes,
  All the cares of life fall from us,
    All our troubles find repose:
  Naught forgetting, naught regretting,
    Lovely ghosts from days no more
  Glide with white feet o'er the river,
    Smiling towards the silent shore.

So we pray in His good pleasure
    When this world we've safely trod,
  We may walk beside the river
    Flowing from the throne of God:
  All forgiving, all believing,
    Not one lost we loved before,
  Looking towards the hills of heaven
    Calmly from the eternal shore.

A FLOWER OF A DAY.

LD friend, that with a pale and pensile grace
　　Climbest the lush hedgerows, art thou back again,
　　Marking the slow round of the wond'rous
　　　　years?
Didst beckon me a moment, silent flower?

Silent?　As silent is the archangel's pen
That day by day writes our life chronicle,
And turns the page,—the half-forgotten page,
Which all eternity will never blot.

Forgotten?　No, we never do forget:
We let the years go: wash them clean with tears,
Leave them to bleach, out in the open day,
Or lock them careful by, like dead friends' clothes,
Till we shall dare unfold them without pain,—
But we forget not, never can forget.

Flower, thou and I a moment face to face—
My face as clear as thine, this July noon
Shining on both, on bee and butterfly
And golden beetle creeping in the sun—
Will pause, and, lifting up, page after page,
The many-colored history of life,
Look backwards, backwards.

　　　　　　　　　So, the volume close!
This July day, with the sun high in heaven,
And the whole earth rejoicing,—let it close.

I think we need not sigh, complain, nor rave;
Nor blush,—our doings and misdoing all
Being more 'gainst heaven than man, heaven them
　　　　does keep
With all its doings and undoings strange

Concerning us.—Ah, let the volume close:
I would not alter in it one poor line.

My dainty flower, my innocent white flower
With such a pure smile looking up to heaven,
With such a bright smile looking down on me—
(Nothing but smiles,—as if in all the world
Were no such things as thunder-storms or frosts,
Or broken petals trampled on the ground,
Or shivering leaves whirled in the wintry air
Like ghosts of last year's joys:)—my pretty flower,
I'll pluck thee—smiling too.   Not one salt drop
Shall stain thee:—if these foolish eyes are dim,
'T is only with a wondering thankfulness
That they behold such beauty and such peace,
Such wisdom and such sweetness, in God's world.

THE NIGHT BEFORE THE MOWING.

ALL shimmering in the morning shine
   And diamonded with the dew,
And quivering in the scented wind
   That thrills its green heart through,—
The little field, the smiling field,
   With all its flowers a-blowing,
How happy looks the golden field
   The day before the mowing!

Outspread 'neath the departing light,
   Twilight, still void of stars,
Save where, low westering, Venus hides
   From the red eye of Mars;
How quiet lies the silent field
   With all its beauties glowing;
Just stirring,—like a child asleep,—
   The night before the mowing.

Sharp steel, inevitable hand,
   Cut keen, cut kind!   Our field
We know full well must be laid low
   Before its wealth it yield:
Labor and mirth and plenty blest
   Its blameless death bestowing:
And yet we weep, and yet we weep,
   The night before the mowing.

––––

PASSION PAST.

ERE I a boy, with a boy's heart-beat
   At glimpse of her passing adown the street,
   Of a room where she had entered and gone,
Or a page her hand had written on,—
Would all be with me as it was before?
O no, never! no, no, never!
Never any more.

Were I a man, with a man's pulse-throb,
Breath hard and fierce, held down like a sob,
Dumb, yet hearing *her* lightest word,
Blind, until only *her* garment stirred:
Would I pour my life like wine on her floor?
No, no, never: never, never!
Never any more.

Gray and withered, wrinkled and marred,
I have gone through the fire and come out unscarred,
With the image of manhood upon me yet,
No shame to remember, no wish to forget:
But could she rekindle the pangs I bore?—
O no, never! thank God, never!
Never any more.

Old and wrinkled, withered and gray,—
And yet if her light step passed to-day,
I should see her face all faces among,

And say,—" Heaven love thee, whom I loved long!
Thou hast lost the key of my heart's door,
Lost it ever, and forever,
Ay, forevermore."

————

OCTOBER.

T is no joy to me to sit
　　On dreamy summer eves,
　　When silently the timid moon
· Kisses the sleeping leaves
And all things through the fair hushed earth
　　Love, rest—but nothing grieves.
Better I like old Autumn
　　With his hair tossed to and fro,
Firm striding o'er the stubble fields
　　When the equinoctials blow.

When shrinkingly the sun creeps up
　　Through misty mornings cold,
And Robin on the orchard hedge
　　Sings cheerily and bold,
While heavily the frosted plum
　　Drops downward on the mould;—
And as he passes, Autumn
　　Into earth's lap does throw
Brown apples gay in a game of play,
　　As the equinoctials blow.

When the spent year its carol sinks
　　Into a humble psalm,
Asks no more for the pleasure draught,
　　But for the cup of balm,
And all its storms and sunshine bursts
　　Controls to one brave calm,—
Then step by step walks Autumn,
　　With steady eyes that show
Nor grief nor fear, to the death of the year,
　　While the equinoctials blow.

MOON-STRUCK.

A FANTASY.

T is a moor
   Barren and treeless; lying high and bare
   Beneath the archèd sky.. The rushing winds
Fly over it, each with his strong bow bent
And quiver full of whistling arrows keen.

I am a woman, lonely, old, and poor.
If there be any one who watches me
(But there is none) adown the long blank wold,
My figure painted on the level sky
Would startle him as if it were a ghost,—
And like a ghost, a weary wandering ghost,
I roam and roam, and shiver through the dark,
That will not hide me. O for but one hour,
One blessed hour of warm and dewy night,
To wrap me like a pall—with not an eye
In earth or heaven to pierce the black serene.
Night, call ye this? No night; no dark—no rest—
A moon-ray sweeps down sudden from the sky,
And smites the moor—

              Is't thou, accursèd Thing,
Broad, pallid, like a great woe looming out—
Out of its long-sealed grave, to fill all earth
With its dead, ghastly smile? Art there again,
Round, perfect, large, as when we buried thee,
I and the kindly clouds that heard my prayers?
I'll sit me down and meet thee face to face,
Mine enemy?—Why didst thou rise upon
My world—my innocent world, to make me mad?
Wherefore shine forth, a tiny tremulous curve
Hung out in the gray sunset beauteously,
To tempt mine eyes—then nightly to increase
Slow orbing, till thy full, blank, pitiless stare
Hunts me across the world?

                                 No rest—no dark.
Hour after hour that passionless bright face
Climbs up the desolate blue.   I will press down
The lids on my tired eyeballs—crouch in dust
And pray.
     —Thank God, thank God!—a cloud has hid
My torturer.   The night at last is free:
Forth peep in crowds the merry twinkling stars.
Ah, we'll shine out, the little silly stars
And I; we'll dance together across the moor,
They up aloft—I here.   At last, at last
We are avengèd of our adversary!

The freshening of the night air feels like dawn.
Who said that I was mad?   I will arise,
Throw off my burthen, march across the wold
Airily—Ha! what, stumbling?   Nay, no fear—
I am used unto the dark, for many a year
Steering companionless athwart the waste
To where, deep hid in valleys of white mist,
The pleasant home-lights shine.   I will but pause,
Turn round and gaze—
                                 O miserable me!
The cloud-bank overflows: sudden outpour
The bright white moon-rays—ah!   I drown, I drown,
And o'er the flood, with steady motion, slow
It walketh—my inexorable Doom.

No more: I shall not struggle any more:
I will lie down as quiet as a child,—
I can but die.
                    There, I have hid my face:
Stray travelers passing o'er the silent wold
Would only say, "She sleeps."

                                 Glare on, my Doom;
I will not look at thee: and if at times
I shiver, still I neither weep nor moan:
Angels may see, I neither weep nor moan,

Was that sharp whistling wind the morning breeze
That calls the stars back to the fold of heaven?
I am very cold.—And yet there is a change.
Less fiercely the sharp moonbeams smite my brain,
My heart beats slower, duller; soothing rest
Like a soft garment binds my shuddering limbs.—
If I looked up now, should I see it still
Gibbeted ghastly in the hopeless sky?—
No!

    It is very strange: all things seem strange:
Pale spectral face, I do not fear thee now:
Was't this mere shadow which did haunt me once
Like an avenging fiend?—Well, we fade out
Together: I'll nor dread nor curse thee more.

How calm the earth seems! and I know the moor
Glistens with dew-stars. I will try and turn
My poor face eastward. Close not, eyes! That light
Fringing the far hills, all so fair—so fair,
Is it not dawn? I am dying, but 'tis dawn.
"Upon the mountains I behold the feet
Of my Beloved: let us forth to meet"—
Death.

    This is death. I see the light no more;
I sleep.

    But like a morning bird my soul
Springs singing upward, into the deeps of heaven
Through world on world to follow Infinite Day.

A STREAM'S SINGING.

 HOW beautiful is Morning!
How the sunbeams strike the daisies,
  And the kingcups fill the meadow
    Like a golden-shielded army
    Marching to the uplands fair;—

I am going forth to battle,
And life's uplands rise before me,
And my golden shield is ready,
And I pause a moment, timing
My heart's pæan to the waters,
As with cheerful song incessant
    Onwards runs the little stream;
Singing ever, onward ever,
    Boldly runs the merry stream.

O how glorious is Noon-day!
With the cool large shadows lying
Underneath the giant forest,
The far hill-tops towering dimly
    O'er the conquered plains below;—
I am conquering—I shall conquer
In life's battle-field impetuous:
And I lie and listen dreamy
To a double-voiced, low music,—
Tender beech trees sheeny shiver
Mingled with the diapason
    Of the strong, deep, joyful stream,
Like a man's love and a woman's;
    So it runs—the happy stream!

O how grandly cometh Even,
Sitting on the mountain summit,
Purple-vestured, grave, and silent,
Watching o'er the dewy valleys,
    Like a good king near his end:—
I have labored, I have governed;
Now I feel the gathering shadows
Of the night that closes all things:
And the fair earth fades before me,
And the stars leap out in heaven,
While into the infinite darkness
    Solemn runs the steadfast stream—
Onward, onward, ceaseless, fearless,
    Singing runs the eternal stream.

A REJECTED LOVER

YOU "never loved me," Ada.   These slow words,
Dropped softly from your gentle woman-tongue
Out of your true and kindly woman-heart,
Fell, piercing into mine like very swords
The sharper for their kindness.   Yet no wrong
Lies to your charge, nor cruelty, nor art,—
Ev'n while you spoke, I saw the tender tear-drop start.

You "never loved me."   No, you never knew,
You, with youth's morning fresh upon your soul,
What 't is *to love:* slow, drop by drop, to pour
Our life's whole essence, perfumed through and through
With all the best we have or can control
For the libation—cast it down before
Your feet—then lift the goblet, dry for evermore.

I shall not die as foolish lovers do :
A man's heart beats beneath this breast of mine,
The breast where—Curse on that fiend-whispering
" *It might have been !* "—Ada, I will be true
Unto myself—the self that worshipped thine :
May all life's pain, like these few tears that spring
For me, glance off as rain-drops from my white dove's
.wing !

May you live long, some good man's bosom-flower
And gather children round your matron knees :
So, when all this is past, and you and I
Remember each our youth-days as an hour
Of joy—or anguish, one, serene, at ease,
May come to meet the other's steadfast eye,
Thinking, "He loved me well !" clasp hands, and so pass by.

A LIVING PICTURE.

NO, I'll not say your name. I have said it now,
 As you mine, first in childish treble, then
 Up through a score and more familiar years
Till baby-voices mock us. Time may come
When your tall sons look down on our white hair,
Amused to hear us call each other thus,
And question us about the old, old days,
The far-off days, the days when we were young.

How distant do they seem, and yet how near!
Now, as I lie and watch you come and go,
With garden basket in your hand; in gown
Just girdled, and brown curls that girl-like fall,
And straw hat flapping in the April breeze,
I could forget this lapse of years—start up
Laughing—"Come, let's go play!"
       Well-a-day, friend
Our play-days are all done.

      Still, let us smile:
For as you flit about your garden here
You look like this spring morning; on your lips
An unseen bird sings snatches of gay tunes,
While, an embodied music, moves your step,
Your free, wild, springy step, like Atala,
Or Pocahontas, careless child o' the sun—
Those Indian beauties I compare you to—
I, still your praiser,—
      Nay, nay, I'll not praise,
Fair seemeth fairest, ignorant 'tis fair:
That light incredulous laugh is worth a world!
That laugh, with childish echoes.
      So then, fade,
Mere dream. Come, true and sweet reality:

Come, dawn of happy wifehood, motherhood,
Ripening to perfect noon !   Come, peaceful round
Of simple joys, fond duties, gladsome cares,
When each full hour drops bliss with liberal hand,
Yet leaves to-morrow richer than to-day.

Will you sit here ?   the grass is summer-warm.
Look at those children making daisy-chains,
So did we too, do you mind ?   That eldest lad,
He has your very mouth.   Yet, you will have 't
His eyes are like his father's ?   Perhaps so :
They could not be more dark and deep and kind.
Do you know, this hour I have been fancying you
A poet's dream, and almost sighed to think
There was no poet to praise you—
                              Why, you're flown
After those mad elves in the flower-beds there,
Ha—ha—you're no dream now.
                              Well, well—so best !
My eyelids droop content o'er moistened eyes :
I would not have you other than you are.

LEONORA.

EONORA, Leonora,
    How the word rolls—*Leonora*—
    Lion-like, in full-mouthed sound,
  Marching o'er the metric ground
  With a tawny tread sublime—
  So your name moves, Leonora,
  Down my desert rhyme.

  So you pace, young Leonora,
  Through the alleys of the wood,
  Head erect, majestic, tall,
  The fit daughter of the Hall :
  Yet with hazel eyes declined,

And a voice like summer wind,
And a meek mouth, sweet and good,
Dimpling ever, Leonora,
In fair womanhood.

How those smiles dance, Leonora,
As you meet the pleasant breeze
Under your ancestral trees:
For your heart is free and pure
As this blue March sky o'erhead,
And in the life-path you tread,
All the trees are budding, sure,
All the primroses are springing,
All the birds begin their singing—
'T is your spring-time, Leonora,
May it long endure.

But it *will* pass, Leonora:
And the silent days must fall
When a change comes over all:
When the last leaf downward flitters,
And the last, last sunbeam glitters
On the terraced hillside cool,
On the peacocks by the pool:
When you'll walk along these alleys
With no lightsome foot that dallies
With the violets and the moss,—
But with quiet steps and slow,
And grave eyes that earthward grow,
And a matron-heart inured
To all women have endured,—
Must endure and ever will,
All the joy and all the ill,
All the gain and all the loss,—
Can you cheerfully lay down
Careless girlhood's flowery crown,
And thus take up, Leonora,
Womanhood's meek cross?

Ay! your eyes shine, Leonora,
Warm, and true, and brave, and kind:
And although I nothing know
Of the maiden heart below,
I in them good omens find.
Go, enjoy your present hours
Like the birds and bees and flowers
And may summer days bestow
On you just so much of rain,
Blessed baptism of pain!
As will make your blossoms grow.
May you walk, as through life's road
Every noble woman can,—
With a pure heart before God,
And a true heart unto man:
Till with this same smile you wait
For the opening of the Gate
That shuts earth from mortal eyes ;
Till at last, with peaceful heart,
All contented to depart,
Leaving children's children playing
In these woods you used to stray in,
You may enter, Leonora
Into Paradise.

PLIGHTED.

INE to the core of the heart, my beauty!
  Mine, all mine, and for love, not duty :
  Love given willingly, full and free,
Love for love's sake—as mine to thee.
  Duty's a slave that keeps the keys,
But Love, the master, goes in and out
Of his goodly chambers with song and shout,
  Just as he please—just as he please.

Mine, from the dear head's crown, brown-golden,
To the silken foot that's scarce beholden ;
Give to a few friends hand or smile,
Like a generous lady, now and awhile,
    But the sanctuary heart, that none dare win
Keep holiest of holiest evermore :
The crowd in the aisles may watch the door
    The high-priest only enters in.

Mine, my own, without doubts or terrors,
With all thy goodnesses, all thy errors,
Unto me and to me alone revealed,
"A spring shut up, a fountain sealed."
    Many may praise thee—praise mine as thine,
Many may love thee—I'll love them too ;
But thy heart of hearts, pure, faithful, and true,
    Must be mine, mine wholly, and only mine.

Mine!—God, I thank Thee that Thou hast given
Something all mine on this side heaven :
Something as much myself to be
As this my soul which I lift to Thee :
    Flesh of my flesh, bone of my bone,
Life of my life, whom Thou dost make
Two to the world for the world's work's sake—
    But each unto each, as in Thy sight, *one*.

MORTALITY.

"And we shall be changed."

E dainty mosses, lichens gray,
    Pressed each to each in tender fold,
And peacefully thus, day by day,
    Returning to their mould ;

Brown leaves, that with aerial grace
  Slip from your branch like birds a-wing,
Each leaving in the appointed place
  Its bud of future spring ;—

If we, God's conscious creatures, knew
  But half your faith in our decay,
We should not tremble as we do
  When summoned clay to clay.

But with an equal patience sweet
  We should put off this mortal gear,
In whatsoe'er new form is meet
  Content to reappear.

Knowing each germ of life He gives
  Must have in Him its source and rise,
Being that of His being lives
  May change, but never dies.

Ye dead leaves, dropping soft and slow,
  Ye mosses green and lichens fair,
Go to your graves, as I will go,
  For God is also there.

LIFE RETURNING.

After war-time.

O LIFE, dear life, with sunbeam finger touching
    This poor damp brow, or flying freshly by
    On wings of mountain wind, or tenderly
In links of visionary embraces clutching
  Me from the yawning grave—
Can I believe thou yet hast power to save ?

I see thee, O my life, like phantom giant
  Stand on the hill-top, large against the dawn,

Upon the night-black clouds a picture drawn
Of aspect wonderful, with hope defiant,
  And so majestic grown
I scarce discern the image as my own.

Those mists furl off, and through the vale resplendent
  I see the pathway of my years prolong:
  Not without labor, yet for labor strong:
Not without pain, but pain whose touch transcendent
  By love's divinest laws
Heart unto heart, and all hearts upwards, draws.

O life, O love, your diverse tones bewildering
  Make silence, like two meeting waves of sound;
  All cruel echoes of the past are drowned:
I dream of wifely white arms, lisp of children—
  Never of ended wars,
Save kisses sealing honorable scars.

No more of battles! save the combat glorious
  To which all earth and heaven may witness stand;
  The sword of the Spirit taking in my hand
I shall go forth, since in new fields victorious
  The King yet grants that I
His servant live, or His good soldier die.

MY FRIEND.

Y Friend wears a cheerful smile of his own,
  And a musical tongue has he;
  We sit and look in each other's face,
  And are very good company.
A heart he has, full warm and red
  As ever a heart I see;
And as long as I keep true to him,
  Why, he'll keep true o me.

When the wind blows high and the snow falls fast
  And we hear the wassailers' roar—

My Friend and I, with a right good-will
    We bolt the chamber door:
I smile at him and he smiles at me
    In a dreamy calm profound,
Till his heart leaps up in the midst of him
    With a comfortable sound.

His warm breath kisses my thin gray hair
    And reddens my ashen cheeks;
He knows me better than you all know,
    Though never a word he speaks:—
Knows me as well as some had known
    Were things—not as things be.
But hey, what matters? my Friend and I
    Are capital company.

At dead of night, when the house is still,
    He opens his pictures fair:
Faces that are, that used to be,
    And faces that never were:
My wife sits sewing beside my hearth,
    My little ones frolic wild,
Though—Lillian's married these twenty years,
    And I never had a child.

But hey, what matters? when those who laugh
    May weep to-morrow, and they
Who weep be as those that wept not—all
    Their tears long wiped away.
I shall burn out, like you, my Friend,
    With a bright warm heart and bold,
That flickers up to the last—then drops
    Into quiet ashes cold.

And when you flicker your last on me,
    In the old man's elbow-chair,
Or—something easier still, where we
    Lie down, to arise up fair

And young, and happy—why then, my Friend,
  Should other friends ask of me,
Tell them I lived and loved and died
  In the best of all company.

A VALENTINE.

YE are twa laddies unco gleg,
    An' blithe an' bonnie:
  As licht o' heel as Anster's Meg;—
Gin ye 'd a lassie's favor beg,
I' faith she couldna stir a peg
    Ance lookin' on ye!

He 's a douce wiselike callant—Jim,
    Of wit aye ready.
Cuts aff ane's sentence, 't ither's limb,
An' whiles he 's daft and whiles he 's grim,
But brains?—wha's got the like o' him
    In 's wee bit heidie?

Dear laddie wi' the curlin' hair,
    Gentlest of ony:
That gies kind looks an' speeches fair
To dour auld wives as lassies rare,—
I ken a score o' lads an' mair,
    But nane like Johnnie!

And gin ye learn the way to woo,
    Hae sweethearts mony,
O laddie, never say ye loe
An' gie fause coin for siller true;
A lassie's sair heart 's naething new,—
    Mind ye that, Johnnie.

An' dinna change your luve too fast
    For ilk face bonnie,

Lest waefu' want track wilfu' waste,
And a' your youthfu' years lang past,
Ye get the crookit stick at last,
    Ochone, puir Johnnie!

But callants baith, tak tent, and when
    Bright e'en hae won ye,
Tak each your jo—and keep her—then
Be faithfu' as ye 're fond, ye ken,
Or—gang your gate like honest men,
    Young Jim and Johnnie.

Sae when auld Time his crookit claw
    Sall lay upon ye,
And, Jim, your feet that dance like snaw
Are no the lightest in the ha',
An' a' your curly haffets fa',
    My winsome Johnnie,—

May each his ain warm ingle view,
    Cosie as ony:
A gudewife sonsie, leal and true,
O' bonnie dochters not a few,
An' lads—sic lads as ye 're the noo—
    Dear Jim and Johnnie!

GRACE OF CLYDESIDE.

AH, little Grace of the golden locks,
    The hills rise fair on the shores of Clyde.
    As the merry waves wear out these rocks
She wears my heart out, glides past and mocks:
    But heaven's gate ever stands open wide.

The boat goes softly along, along,
    Like a river of life glows the amber Clyde;
Her voice floats near me like angels' song,—

Ah, sweet love-death, but thy pangs are strong!
    Though heaven's gate ever stands open wide.

We walk by the shore and the stars shine bright,
    But coldly, above the solemn Clyde:
Her arm touches mine—her laugh rings light—
ONE hears my silence: His merciful night
    Hides me—*Can* heaven be open wide?

I ever was but a dreamer, Grace:
    As the gray hills watch o'er the sunny Clyde,
Standing afar, each in his place,
I watch your young life's beautiful race,
    Apart—until heaven be opened wide.

And sometimes when in the twilight balm
    The hills grow purple along the Clyde,
The waves flow softly and very calm,
I hear all nature sing this one psalm,
    That "heaven's gate ever stands open wide."

So, happy Grace, with your spirit free,
    Laugh on! life is sweet on the banks of Clyde;
This is no blame unto thee or me;
Only God saw it could not be,
    Therefore His heaven stands open wide.

TO A BEAUTIFUL WOMAN.

"A daughter of the gods: divinely tall,
    And most divinely fair."

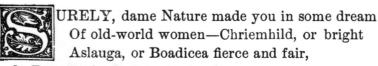

URELY, dame Nature made you in some dream
    Of old-world women—Chriemhild, or bright
    Aslauga, or Boadicea fierce and fair,
Or Berengaria as she rose, her lips
Yet ruddy from the poison that anoints
Her memory still, the queen of queenly wives.

I marvel, who will crown you wife, you grand
And goodly creature! who will mount supreme
The empty chariot of your maiden heart,
Curb the strong will that leaps and foams and chafes
Still masterless, and guide you safely home
Unto the golden gate, where quiet sits
Grave Matronhood, with gracious, loving eyes.

What eyes you have, you wild gazelle o' the plain,
You fierce hind of the forest! now they flash,
Now glow, now in their own dark down-dropt shade
Conceal themselves a moment, as some thought,
Too brief to be a feeling, flits across
The April cloudland of your careless soul—
There—that light laugh—and 't is full sun—full day.

Would I could paint you, line by line, ere Time
Touches the gorgeous picture! your ripe mouth,
Your white arched throat, your stature like to Saul's
Among his brethren, yet so fitly framed
In such harmonious symmetry, we say
As of a cedar among common trees
Never " How tall!" but only "O how fair!"

Who made you fair? moulded you in the shape
That poets dream of; sent you forth to men,
His caligraph inscribed on every curve
Of your brave form?

                         Is it written on your soul?
—I know not.
                    Woman, upon whom is laid
Heaven's own sign-manual, Beauty, mock heaven not!
Reverence thy loveliness—the outward type
Of things we understand not, nor behold
But as in a glass, darkly; wear it thou
With awful gladness, grave humility,
That not contemns, nor boasts, nor is ashamed,
But lifts its face up prayerfully to heaven,—
" Thou who hast made me, make me worthy Thee."

MARY'S WEDDING.

February 25th, 1851.

YOU are to be married, Mary;
    This hour as I wakeful lie
    In the dreamy dawn of the morning,
Your wedding hour draws nigh;
Miles off you are rising, dressing,
    Your bridemaidens gay among,
In the same old house we played in,—
    You and I, when we were young.

Your bridemaids—they were our playmates:
    Those known rooms, every wall,
Could speak of our childish frolics,
    Loves, jealousies, great and small:
Do you mind how pansies changed we
    And smiled at the word " forget " ?—
'T was a girl's romance: yet somehow
    I have kept my pansy yet.

Do you mind our poems written
    Together? our dreams of fame—
And of love—how we 'd share all secrets
    When that sweet mystery came?
It is no mystery, now, Mary;
    It was unveiled, year by year,
Till—this is your marriage morning;
    And I rest quiet here.

I cannot call up your face, Mary,
    The face of the bride to-day:
You have outgrown my knowledge,
    The years have so slipped away.
I see but your girlish likeness,
    Brown eyes and brown falling hair;—
God knows, I did love you dearly,
    And was proud that you were fair.

Many speak my name, Mary,
    While yours in home's silence lies:
The future I read in toil's guerdon,
    You will read in your children's eyes:
The past—the same past with either—
    Is to you a delightsome scene,
But I cannot trace it clearly
    For the graves that rise between.

I am glad you are happy, Mary!
    These tears, could you see them fall,
Would show, though you have forgotten,
    I have remembered all.
And though my cup may be empty
    While yours is all running o'er,
Heaven keep you its sweetness, Mary,
    Brimming for evermore.

BETWEEN TWO WORLDS.

Parting for Australia.

ERE sitting by the fire
    I aspire, love, I aspire—
    Not to that "other world" of your fond
        dreams,
    But one as nigh and nigher,
Compared to which your real, unreal seems.

    Together as to-night
    In our light, love, in our light
Of reunited joy appears no shade:
    From this our hope's reached height
All things are possible and level made.

    Therefore we sit and view—
    I and you, love, I and you—
That wondrous valley o'er southern seas,

Where in a country new
You will make for me a sweet nest of ease ;

Where I, your poor tired bird,
(Nothing stirred ?   Love, nothing stirred ?)
May fold her wings and be no more distrest :
Where troubles may be heard
Like outside winds at night which deepen rest.

Where in green pastures wide
We'll abide, love, we'll abide,
And keep content our patriarchal flocks,
Till at our aged side
Leap our young brown-faced shepherds of the rocks.

Ah, tale that's easy told !
(Hold my hand, love, tighter hold.)
What if this face of mine, which *you* think fair—
If it should ne'er grow old,
Nor matron cap cover this maiden hair ?

What if this silver ring
(Loose it clings, love, yet does cling :)
Should ne'er be changed for any other ? nay,
This very hand I fling
About your neck should—   Hush ! to-day's to-day :

To-morrow is—ah, whose ?
You'll not lose, love, you'll not lose
This hand I pledged, if never a wife's hand
For tender household use
Led by yours fearless into a far, far land.

Kiss me and do not grieve ;
I believe, love, I believe
That he who holds the measure of our days,
And did thus strangely weave
Our opposite lives together, to His praise—

He never will divide
Us so wide, love, us so wide;
But will, what'er befalls us, clearly snow
That those in Him allied
In life or death are nearer than they know.

———

COUSIN ROBERT.

COUSIN ROBERT, far away
   Among the lands of gold,
How many years since we two met?—
You would not like it told.

O cousin Robert, buried deep
   Amid your bags of gold—
I thought I saw you yesternight
   Just as you were of old.

You own whole leagues—I half a rood
   Behind my cottage door;
You have your lacs of gold rupees,
   And I my children four;

Your tall barques dot the dangerous seas,
   My "ship's come home"—to rest
Safe anchored from the storms of life
   Upon one faithful breast.

And it would cause no start or sigh,
   Nor thought of doubt or blame,
If I should teach our little son
   His cousin Robert's name.—

That name, however wide it rings,
   I oft think, when alone,
I rather would have seen it graved
   Upon a churchyard stone—

Upon the white sunshining stone
 Where cousin Alick lies:
Ah, sometimes, woe to him that lives!
 Happy is he that dies!

O Robert, Robert, many a tear—
 Though not like tears of old—
Drops, thinking of your face so loved,
 Your hand's remembered fold;

A young man's face, so like our two
 Dead mothers' faces fair:
A young man's hand, so firm to clasp,
 So resolute to dare.

I thought you good—I wished you great;
 You were my hope, my pride:
To know you good, to make you great
 I once had happy died.

To tear the plague-spot from your heart,
 Place honor on your brow,
See old age come in crownèd peace—
 I almost would die now!

Would give—all that's now mine to give—
 To have you sitting there,
The cousin Robert of my youth—
 Though beggar'd, with gray hair

O Robert, Robert, some that live
 Are dead, long ere they are old;
Better the pure heart of our youth
 Than palaces of gold;

Better the blind faith of our youth
 Than doubt, which all truth braves;
Better to mourn, God's children dear,
 Than laugh, the Devil's slaves.

O Robert, Robert, life is sweet,
   And love is boundless gain :
Yet if I mind of you, my heart
   Is stabbed with sudden pain :

And as in peace this Christmas eve
   I close our quiet doors,
And kiss " good-night " on sleeping heads—
   Such bonnie curls,—like yours :

I fall upon my bended knees
   With sobs that choke each word ;—
"On those who err and are deceived
   Have mercy, O good Lord ! "

AT LAST.

OWN, down like a pale leaf dropping,
   Under an autumn sky,
My love dropped into my bosom
   Quietly, quietly.

There was not a ray of sunshine
   And not a sound in the air,
As she trembled into my bosom—
   My love, no longer fair.

All year round in her beauty
   She dwelt on the tree-top high :
She danced in the summer breezes,
   She laughed to the summer sky.

I lay so low in the grass-dews,
   She sat so high above,
She never wist of my longing,
   She never dreamed of my love.

But when winds laid bare her dwelling,
   And her heart could find no rest,
I called—and she fluttered downward
   Into my faithful breast.

I know that my love is fading ;
   I know I cannot fold
Her fragrance from the frost-blight,
   Her beauty from the mould :

But a little, little longer
   She shall contented lie,
And wither away in the sunshine
   Silently, silently.

Come when thou wilt, grim Winter,
   My year is crowned and blest
If when my love is dying
   She die upon my breast.

THE AURORA ON THE CLYDE

September, 1850.

AH me, how heavily the night comes down,
   Heavily, heavily :
Fade the curved shores, the blue hills' serried throng,
The darkening waves we oared in light and song ;
Joy melts from us as sunshine from the sky ;
   And Patience with sad eye
Takes up her staff and drops her withered crown.

Our small boat heaves upon the heaving river,
   Wearily, wearily :
The flickering shore-lights come and go by fits ;
Towering 'twixt earth and heaven dusk silence sits,
Death at her feet ; above, infinity ;
   Between, slow drifting by,
Our tiny boat, like life, floats onward ever.

Pale, mournful hour,—too early night that falls
    Drearily, drearily,
Come not so soon! Return, return, bright day,
Kind voices, smiles, blue mountains, sunny bay!
In vain! Life's dial cannot backward fly :
    The dark time comes. Low lie,
And listen, soul. Oft in the night, God calls.

    *   *   *   *   *   *

Light, light on the black river! How it gleams,
    Solemnly, solemnly!
Like troops of pale ghosts on their pensive march,
Treading the far heavens in a luminous arch,
Each after each : phantasms serene and high
    From that eternity
Where all earth's sharpest woes grow dim as dreams.

Let us drink in the glory, full and whole,
    Silently, silently :
Gaze, till it lulls all pain, all vain desires :—
See now, that radiant bow of pillared fires
Spanning the hills like dawn, until they lie
    In soft tranquility,
And all night's ghastly glooms asunder roll.

Look, look again! the vision changes fast,
    Gloriously, gloriously :
That was heaven's gate with its illumined road,
But this *is* heaven; the very throne of God
Hung with flame curtains of celestial dye
    Waving perpetually,
While to and fro innumerous angels haste.

I see no more the stream, the boat that moves
    Mournfully, mournfully :
And we who sit, poor prisoners of clay .
It is not night, it is immortal day,
Where the One Presence fills eternity,
    And each, His servant high,
Forever praises and forever loves.

O soul, forget the weight that drags thee down,
   Deathfully, deathfully :
Know thyself. As this glory wraps thee round,
Let it melt off the chains that long have bound
Thy strength. Stand free before thy God and cry—
   "My Father, here am I :
Give to me as Thou wilt—first cross, then crown."

AN AURORA BOREALIS.

Roslin Castle.

 STRANGE soft gleam, O ghostly dawn
   That never brightens unto day;
 Ere earth's mirk pale once more be drawn
Let us look out beyond the gray.

It is just midnight by the clock—
   There is no sound on glen or hill,
The moaning linn adown its rock
   Leaps, but the woods lie dark and still.

Austere against the kindling sky
   Yon broken turret blacker grows;
Harsh light, to show remorselessly
   Ruins night hid in kind repose!

Nay, beauteous light, nay, light that fills
   The whole heaven like a dream of morn,
As waking upon northern hills
   She smiles to find herself new-born,—

Strange light, I know thou wilt not stay,
   That many an hour must come and go
Before the pale November day
   Break in the east, forlorn and slow.

Yet blest one gleam—one gleam like this,
  When all heaven brightens in our sight,
And the long night that was and is
  And shall be, vanishes in light:

O blest one hour like this! to rise
  And see grief's shadows backward roll;
While bursts on unaccustomed eyes
  The glad Aurora of the soul.

AT THE LINN-SIDE.

Roslin.

LIVING, living water,
    So busy and so bright,
  Aye flashing in the morning beams,
    And sounding through the night;
O golden-shining water—
    Would God that I might be
A vocal message from His mouth
    Into the world, like thee!

O merry, merry water,
    Which nothing e'er affrays;
And as it pours from rock to rock
    Nothing e'er stops or stays;
But past cool heathery hollows
    And gloomy pools it flows;
Past crags that fain would shut it in
    Leaps through—and on it goes.

O fresh'ning, sparkling water,
    O voice that's never still,
Though winter lays her dead-white hand
    On brae and glen and hill;

Though no leaf's left to flutter
    In woods all mute and hoar,
Yet thou, O river, night and day
    Thou runnest evermore.

No foul thing can pollute thee;
    Thy swiftness casts aside
All ill, like a good heart and true,
    However sorely tried.
O living, living water,
    So fresh and bright and free—
God lead us through this changeful world
    Forever pure, like thee!

A HYMN FOR CHRISTMAS MORNING.

1855.

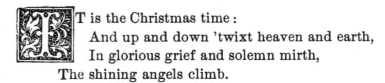T is the Christmas time:
    And up and down 'twixt heaven and earth,
    In glorious grief and solemn mirth,
The shining angels climb.

And unto everything
That lives and moves, for heaven, on earth,
With equal share of grief and mirth,
The shining angels sing:—

"Babes new-born, undefiled,
In lowly hut, or mansion wide—
Sleep safely through this Christmas-tide
When Jesus was a child.

"O young men, bold and free,
In peopled town, or desert grim,
When ye are tempted like to Him,
'The man Christ Jesus' see.

·" Poor mothers, with your hoard
Of endless love and countless pain-
Remember all her grief, her gain,
The Mother of the Lord.

" Mourners, half blind with woe,
Look up!   One standeth in this place,
And by the pity of His face
The Man of Sorrows know.

"Wanderers in far countrie,
O think of Him who came, forgot,
To His own. and they received Him not—
Jesus of Galilee.

" O all ye who have trod
The wine-press of affliction, lay
Your hearts before His heart this day—
Behold the Christ of God ! "

A PSALM FOR NEW YEAR'S EVE.

1855.

 FRIEND stands at the door :
In either tight-closed hand
Hiding rich gifts, three hundred and three score :
Waiting to strew them daily o'er the land
Even as seed the sower.
Each drops he, treads it in and passes by :
It cannot be made fruitful till it die.

O good New Year, we clasp
This warm, shut hand of thine,
Loosing forever, with half sigh, half gasp,

That which from ours falls like dead fingers' twine:
Ay, whether fierce its grasp
Has been, or gentle, having been, we know
That it was blessed: let the Old Year go.

O New Year, teach us faith!
The road of life is hard:
When our feet bleed and scourging winds us scathe,
Point thou to Him whose visage was more marred
Than any man's; who saith
"Make straight paths for your feet"—and to the op-
          prest—
"Come ye to Me, and I will give you rest."

Yet hang some lamp-like hope
Above this unknown way,
Kind year, to give our spirits freér scope
And our hands strength to work while it is day.
But if that way must slope
Tombward, O bring before our fading eyes
The lamp of life, the Hope that never dies.

Comfort our souls with love,—
Love of all human kind;
Love special, close—in which like sheltered dove
Each weary heart its own safe nest may find;
And love that turns above
Adoringly; contented to resign
All loves, if need be, for the Love Divine.

Friend, come thou like a friend,
And whether bright thy face,
Or dim with clouds we cannot comprehend,—
We'll hold out patient hands, each in his place,
And trust thee to the end.
Knowing thou leadest onwards to those spheres
Where there are neither days nor months nor years,

FAITHFUL IN VANITY-FAIR.

Suggested by one of David Scott's illustrations of " Pilgrim's Progress."

I.

THE great human whirlpool—'t is seething and seeth-
        ing:
    On! No time for shrieking out—scarcely for
        breathing:
All toiling and moiling, some feebler, some bolder,
But each sees a fiend-face grim over his shoulder:
    Thus merrily live they in Vanity-fair.

The great human caldron—it boils ever higher:
Some drowning, some sinking; while some, stealing nigher
Athirst, come and lean o'er its outermost verges,
Or touch, as a child's feet touch, timorous, the surges—
    One plunge—lo! more souls swamped in Vanity-fair.

Let's live while we live; for to-morrow all's over:
Drink deep, drunkard bold; and kiss close, maddened
        lover;
Smile, hypocrite, smile; it is no such hard labor,
While each stealthy hand stabs the heart of his neighbor—
    Faugh! Fear not: we've *no* hearts in Vanity-fair.

The mad crowd divides and then soon closes after:
Afar towers the pyre. Through the shouting and laughter
" What new sport is this?" gasps a reveller, half turning.—
" One Faithful, meek fool, who is led to the burning,
    He cumbered us sorely in Vanity-fair.

" A dreamer, who held every man for a brother;
A coward, who, smit on one cheek, gave the other;
A fool, whose blind soul took as truth all our lying,
    Too simple to live, so best fitted for dying;
    Sure, such are best swept out of Vanity-fair."

II.

Silence! though the flames arise and quiver:
Silence! though the crowd howls on forever:
Silence! Through this fiery purgatory
God is leading up a soul to glory.

See, the white lips with no moans are trembling,
Hate of foes or plaint of friends' dissembling;
If sighs come—his patient prayers outlive them,
"Lord—these know not what they do. Forgive them !"

Thirstier still the roaring flames are glowing;
Fainter in his ear the laughter growing;
Brief will last the fierce and fiery trial,
Angel welcomes drown the earth denial.

Now the amorous death-fires, gleaming ruddy,
Clasp him close.   Down drops the quivering body,
While through harmless flames ecstatic flying
Shoots the beauteous soul.   This, this is *dying.*

Lo, the opening sky with splendor rifted,
Lo, the palm-branch for his hands uplifted:
Lo, the immortal chariot, cloud-descending,
And its legioned angels close attending.

Let his poor dust mingle with the embers
While the crowds sweep on and none remembers:
Saints unnumbered through the Infinite Glory,
Praising God, recount the martyr's story.

HER LIKENESS.

 GIRL, who has so many wilful ways
    She would have caused Job's patience to
        forsake him;
Yet is so rich in all that's girlhood's praise,
Did Job himself upon her goodness gaze,
    A little better she would surely make him,

Yet is this girl I sing in naught uncommon,
  And very far from angel yet, I trow.
Her faults, her sweetnesses, are purely human;
Yet she's more lovable as simple woman
  Than any one diviner that I know.

Therefore I wish that she may safely keep
  This womanhede, and change not, only grow;
From maid to matron, youth to age, may creep,
And in perennial blessedness, still reap
  On every hand of that which she doth sow.

ONLY A DREAM.

"I waked—she fled: and day brought back my night."

ETHOUGHT I saw thee yesternight,
    Sit by me in the olden guise,
  The white robes and the palm foregone.
Weaving instead of amaranth crown,
  A web of mortal dyes.

I cried, "Where hast thou been so long?"
  (The mild eyes turned and mutely smiled:)
"Why dwellest thou in far-off lands?
What is that web within thy hands?"
  —"I work for thee, my child."

I clasped thee in my arms and wept;
  . I kissed thee oft with passion wild:
I poured fond questions, tender blame;
Still thy sole answer was the same,—
  "I work for thee, my child."

"Come and walk with me as of old."
  Then camest thou, silent as before;
We passed along that churchyard way
We used to tread each Sabbath day,
  Till one trod earth no more.

I felt thy hand upon my arm,
　Beside me thy meek face I saw,
Yet through the sweet familiar grace
A something spiritual could trace
　That left a nameless awe.

Trembling I said "Long years have passed
　Since thou wert from my side beguiled;
Now thou 'rt returned and all shall be
As was before."—Half-pensively
　Thou answered'st—"Nay, my child."

I pleaded sore: "Hadst thou forgot
　The love wherewith we loved of old,—
The long sweet days of converse blest,—
The nights of slumber on thy breast;—
　Wert thou to me grown cold?"

There beamed on me those eyes of heaven
　That wept no more, but ever smiled;
"Love only *is* love in that Home
Where I abide—where, till thou come,
　I work for thee, my child."

If from my sight thou passedst then,
　Or if my sobs the dream exiled,
I know not: but in memory clear
I seem these strange words still to hear,
　"*I work for thee, my child.*"

———

TO MY GODCHILD ALICE.

ALICE, Alice, little Alice,
　My new-christened baby Alice,
　　Can there ever rhymes be found
To express my wishes for thee
In a silvery flowing, worthy

Of that silvery sound?
Bonnie Alice, Lady Alice,
  Sure, this sweetest name must be
A true omen to thee, Alice,
  Of a life's long melody.

Alice, Alice, little Alice,
Mayst thou prove a golden chalice,
  Filled with holiness like wine:
With rich blessings running o'er
Yet replenished evermore
  From a fount divine:
Alice, Alice, little Alice,
  When this future comes to thee,
In thy young life's brimming chalice
  Keep some drops of balm for me!

Alice, Alice, little Alice,
Mayst thou grow a goodly palace,
  Fitly framed from roof to floor,
Pure unto the inmost centre,
While high thoughts like angels enter
  At the open door:
Alice, Alice, little Alice,
  When this beauteous sight I see,
In thy woman-heart's wide palace
  Keep one nook of love for me.

Alice, Alice, little Alice,—
Sure the verse halts out of malice
  To the thoughts it feebly bears,
And thy name's soft echoes, ranging
From quaint rhyme to rhyme, are changing
  Into silent prayers.
God be with thee, little Alice,
  Of His bounteousness may He
Fill the chalice, build the palace,
  Here, unto eternity!

NINETEEN SONNETS.

RESIGNING.

> "Poor heart, what bitter words we speak,
>   When God speaks of resigning!"

CHILDREN, that lay their pretty garlands by
　　So piteously, yet with a humble mind;
　　Sailors, who, when their ship rocks in the wind,
Cast out her freight with half-averted eye,
Riches for life exchanging solemnly,
Lest they should never gain the wished-for shore;—
Thus we, O Father, standing Thee before,
Do lay down at Thy feet without a sigh
Each after each our precious things and rare,
Our dear heart-jewels and our garlands fair.
Perhaps Thou knewest that the flowers would die,
And the long-voyaged hoards be found but dust:
So took'st them, while unchanged.   To Thee we trust
For incorruptible treasure: Thou art just.

SAINT ELIZABETH OF BOHEMIA.

> "Would that we two were lying
>   Beneath the churchyard sód,
> With our limbs at rest in the green earth's breast,
>   And our souls at home with God."
>
> KINGSLEY'S *Saint's Tragedy.*

I.

I NEVER lay me down to sleep at night
　But in my heart I sing that little song:
　The angels hear it as, a pitying throng,
They touch my burning lids with fingers bright

As moonbeams, pale, impalpable, and light ;
And when my daily pious tasks are done,
And all my patient prayers said one by one,
God hears it.   Seems it sinful in His sight
That round my slow burnt-offering of quenched will
One quivering human sigh creeps wind-like still ?
That when my orisons celestial fail
Rises one note of natural human wail ?
Dear lord, spouse, hero, martyr, saint ! erelong,
I trust, God will forgive my singing that poor song.

II.

A YEAR ago I bade my little son
Bear upon pilgrimage a heavy load
Of alms ; he cried, half-fainting on the road,
" Mother, O mother, would the day were done ! "
Him I reproved with tears, and said, " Go on !
Nor pause nor murmur till thy task be o'er."—
Would not God say to me the same, and more ?
I will not sing that song.   Thou, dearest one,
Husband—no, brother !—stretch thy steadfast hand
And let mine grasp it.   Now, I also stand,
My woman weakness nerved to strength like thine ;
We'll quaff life's aloe-cup as if 't were wine
Each to the other ; journeying on apart,
Till at heaven's golden doors we two leap heart to
        heart.

A MARRIAGE-TABLE.

W. H. L. and F. R.

HERE was a marriage-table where One sate
        Haply, unnoticed, till they craved His aid :
        Thenceforward does it seem that He has made
All virtuous marriage-tables consecrate :
And so, at this, where without pomp or state

We sit, and only say, or mute, are fain
To wish the simple words " God bless these twain ! "
I think that he who " in the midst " doth wait
Oft-times, would not abjure our prayerful cheer,
But, as at Cana, list with gracious ear
To us, beseeching, that the Love divine
May ever at their household table sit,
Make all His servants who encompass it,
And change life's bitterest waters into wine.

MICHAEL THE ARCHANGEL.

A Statuette.

I.

M Y white archangel, with thy steadfast eyes
 Beholding all this empty ghost-filled room,
 Thy clasped hands resting on the sword of doom,
Thy firm, close lips, not made for human sighs
Or smiles, or kisses sweet, or bitter cries,
But for divine exhorting, holy song
And righteous counsel, bold from seraph tongue.
Beautiful angel, strong as thou art wise,
Would that thy sight could make me wise and strong !
Would that this sheathèd sword of thine, which lies
Stonily idle, could gleam out among
The spiritual hosts of enemies
That tempting shriek— "Requite thou wrong with
  wrong."
Lama Sabachthani,—How long, how long.

II.

MICHAEL, the leader of the hosts of God,
Who warred with Satan for the body of him
Whom, living, God had loved—If cherubim
With cherubim contended for one clod

Of human dust, for forty years that trod
The gloomy desert of Heaven's chastisement,
Are there not ministering angels sent
To battle with the devils that roam abroad,
Clutching our living souls? "The living, still
The living, they shall praise Thee!"—Let some great
Invisible spirit enter in and fill
The howling chambers of hearts desolate;
With looks like thine, O Michael, strong and wise,
My white archangel with the steadfast eyes.

I.

BEATRICE TO DANTE.

"Guardami ben. Ben son, ben son."*

EGARD me well: I am thy love, thy love;
  Thy blessing, thy delight, thy hope, thy peace
  Thy joy above all joys that break and cease
When their full waves in widest circles move:
Thy bird of comfort, thine eternal dove,
Whom thou didst send out of thy mournful breast
To flutter back and point thee to thy rest:
Thine angel, who forgets her crown star-wove
To come to thee with folded woman-hands
Pleading,—"Look on me, Beatrice stands
Before thee; by the Triune Light divine
Undazzled, still beholds thy human face,
And is more happy in this happy place
That thou alone art hers and she is thine."

II.

DANTE TO BEATRICE.

I SEE thee, gliding towards me with slow pace
Across the azure fields of Paradise,

* Suggested by a statue of Beatrice, bearing this motto.

Where thine each footstep makes a star arise.
So from this heart's once void but infinite space
Each strange sweet touch of thy celestial grace
In the old mortal life, struck out some spark
To light the world, though all my heaven lay dark.
O Beatrice, cypresses enlace
My laurels: none have grown save tear-bedewed—
Salt tears that sank into the earth unviewed,
And sprang up green to form a crown of bays.
Take it! At thy dear feet I lay my all,
What men my honors, virtues, glories, call:
I lived, loved, suffered, sung—for thy sole praise.

A QUESTION.

I.

SOUL, spirit, genius—which thou art—that whence
    I know not, rose upon this mortal frame
    Like the sun o'er the mountains, all aflame,
Seen large through mists of childish innocence,
And year by year with me uptravelling thence,
As hour by hour the day-star, madest aspire
My nature, interpenetrate with fire
It felt but understood not—strong, intense,
Wisdom with folly mixed, and gold with clay;—
Soul, thou hast journeyed with me all this way.
Oft hidden and o'erclouded, oft arrayed
In scorching splendors that my earth-life burned,
Yet ever unto thee my true life turned,
For, dim, or clear, 'twas thou my daylight made.

II.

SOUL, dwelling oft in God's infinitude,
And sometimes seeming no more part of me—
This *me*, worms' heritage—than that sun can be
Part of the earth he has with warmth imbued,—

Whence camest thou? whither ˎgoest thou? I, sub-
    dued
With awe of mine own being—thus sit still,
Dumb, on the summit of this lonely hill,
Whose dry November-grasses dew-bestrewed
Mirror a million suns—That sun, so bright,
Passes, as thou must pass, Soul, into night:
Art thou afraid, who solitary hast trod
A path I know not, from a source to a bourne,
Both which I know not? fear'st thou to return
Alone, even as thou camest, *alone*, to God?

ANGEL FACES.

"And with the dawn those angel faces smile
That I have loved long since, and lost awhile."

I.

SHALL not paint them.   God them sees, and I:
No other can, nor need.   They have no form,
I may not close with human kisses warm
Their eyes which shine afar or from on high,
But never will shine nearer till I die.
How long, how long!   See, I am growing old;
I have quite ceased to note in my hair's fold
The silver threads that there in ambush lie;
Some angel faces bent from heaven would pine
To trace the sharp lines graven upon mine;
What matter? in the wrinkles ploughed by care
Let age tread after, sowing immortal seeds;
All this life's harvest yielded, wheat or weeds,
Is reaped, methinks! at last my little field lies bare.

II.

But in the night time, 'twixt me and the stars,
The angel faces still come glimmering by;
No death-pale shadow, no averted eye
Marking the inevitable doom that bars

Me from them.   Not a cloud their aspect mars;
And my sick spirit walks with them hand in hand
By the cool waters of a pleasant land:
Sings with them o'er again, without its jars,
The psalm of life, that ceased, as one by one
Their voices, dropping off, left mine alone
With dull monotonous wail to grieve the air.
O solitary love, thou art so strong,
I think God will have pity on thee erelong,
And take thee where thou'lt find those angel faces fair

SUNDAY MORNING BELLS.

FROM the near city comes the clang of bells:
  Their hundred jarring diverse tones combine
  In one faint misty harmony, as fine
As the soft note yon winter robin swells.—
What if to Thee in Thine Infinity
These multiform and many colored creeds
Seem but the robe man wraps as masquers' weeds
Round the one living truth Thou givest him—Thee?
What if these varied forms that worship prove,
Being heart-worship, reach Thy perfect ear
But as a monotone, complete and clear,
Of which the music is, through Christ's name, Love?
Forever rising in sublime increase
To "Glory in the Highest,—on earth peace?"

CŒUR DE LION:

Marochetti's Statue in the Great Exhibition of 1851.

I.

RICHARD the Lion-hearted, crowned serene
  With the true royalty of noble man;
  Seated in stone above the praise or ban
Of these mixed crowds who come and gaping lean

As if to see what the word "king" might mean
In those old times. Behold! what need that rim
Of crown 'gainst this blue sky, to signal him
A monarch, of the monarchs that have been,
And, perhaps, are not?—Read his destinies
In the full brow o'er-arching kingly eyes,
In the strong hands, grasping both rein and sword,
In the close mouth, so sternly beautiful;—
Surely, a man who his own spirit can rule;
Lord of himself, therefore his brethren's lord.

II.

"*ORichard, O mon roi.*" So minstrels sighed.
The many-centuried voice dies faint away
Amidst the turmoil of our modern day.
How know we but these green-wreathed legends hide
An ugly truth that never could abide
In this our living world's far purer air?—
Nevertheless, O statue, rest thou there,
Our Richard, of all chivalry the pride;
Or if not the true Richard, still a type
Of the old regal glory, fallen, o'er-ripe,
And giving place to better blossoming:
Stand—imaging the grand heroic days;
And let our little children come and gaze,
Whispering with innocent awe—"This *was* a King."

GUNS OF PEACE.

Sunday Night, March 30th, 1856.

GHOSTS of dead soldiers in the battle slain,
    Ghosts of dead heroes dying nobler far,
    In the long patience of inglorious war,
Of famine, cold, heat, pestilence, and pain,—
All ye whose loss makes our victorious gain—
This quiet night, as sounds the cannon's tongue

Do ye look down the trembling stars among
Viewing our peace and war with like disdain?
Or wiser grown since reaching your new spheres,
Smile ye on those poor bones ye sowed as seed
For this our harvest, nor regret the deed?—
Yèt lift one cry with us to Heavenly ears—
"Strike with Thy bolt the next red flag unfurled,
And make all wars to cease throughout the world."

DÁVID'S CHILD.

—"Is the child dead?"—And they answered, "He is dead."

N face of a great sorrow like to death
How do we wrestle night and day with tears;
How do we fast and pray; how small appears
The outside world, while, hanging on some breath
Of fragile hope, the chamber where we lie
Includes all space.—But if sudden at last
The blow falls; or by incredulity
Fond led, we—never having one thought cast
Towards years where "the child" was not—see it die,
And with it all our future, all our past,—
We just look round us with a dull surprise:
For lesser pangs we had filled earth with cries
Of wild and angry grief that would be heard:—
But when the heart is broken—not a word.

A WORD IN SEASON.

HIS is a day the Lord hath made."—Thus spake
The good religious heart, unstained, unworn,
Watching the golden glory of the morn.—
Since, on each happy day that came to break
Like sunlight o'er this silent life of mine,
Yea, on each beauteous morning I saw shine,

I have remembered these your words, rejoiced
And been glad in it.   So, o'er many-voiced
Tumultuous harmonies of tropic seas,
Which chant an everlasting farewell grand
Between ourselves and you and the old land,
Receive this token : many words chance-sown
May oftentimes have taken root and grown,
To bear good fruit perennially, like these.

AUGUST THE SIXTH.

H. G. de W.

HIS day when upon French soil you were born,
   My baby feet were trampling English daisies :
   The world had neither said a word of praises
Nor turned a frowning face on us, that morn :
Now, we know both.   Our summer's half out-worn,
And the next change will be to autumn mild.
But yet I read in your soft eyes "the child,"
And feel it in my own heart without scorn
Even as if you and I, who all these years
Lived unknown each to the other, with clasp'd hands
And girlish voices innocent of tears,
Went singing in our tongue of diverse lands
The song of life together.   So may we
Sing it—unsilenced—to eternity.

THE PATH THROUGH THE SNOW.

ARE and sunshiny, bright and bleak,
   Rounded cold as a dead maid's cheek,
   Folded white as a sinner's shroud,
Or wandering angel's robes of cloud.—

Well I know, well I know
Over the fields the path through the snow.

Narrow and rough it lies between
Wastes where the wind sweeps, biting keen
Every step of the slippery road
Marks where some weary foot has trod;
     Who 'll go, who 'll go
After the rest on the path through the snow?

They who would tread it must walk alone,
Silent and steadfast—one by one:
Dearest to dearest can only say,
"My heart! I'll follow thee all the way,
     As we go, as we go,
Each after each on this path through the snow."

It may be under that western haze
Lurks the omen of brighter days;
That each sentinel tree is quivering
Deep at its core with the sap of spring,
     And while we go, while we go,
Green grass-blades pierce thro' the glittering snow.

It may be the unknown path will tend
Never to any earthly end,
Die with the dying day obscure,
And never lead to a human door:
     That none know who did go
Patiently once on this path through the snow.

No matter, no matter! the path shines plain;
These pure snow-crystals will deaden pain;
Above, like stars in the deep blue dark,
Eyes that love us look down and mark.
     Let us go, let us go,
Whither heaven leads in the path thro' the snow.

THE PATH THROUGH THE CORN.

AVY and bright in the summer air,
    Like a pleasant sea when the wind blows
        fair,
And its roughest breath has scarcely curled
The green highway to a distant world,—
Soft whispers passing from shore to shore,
As from hearts content, yet desiring more—
    Who feels forlorn,
Wandering thus down the path through the corn

A short space since, and the dead leaves lay
Mouldering under the hedgerow gray,
Nor hum of insect, nor voice of bird,
O'er the desolate field was ever heard
Only at eve the pallid snow
Blushed rose-red in the red sun-glow;
    Till, one blest morn,
Shot up into life the young green corn.

Small and feeble, slender and pale,
It bent its head to the winter gale,
Harkened the wren's soft note of cheer,
Hardly believing spring was near:
Saw chestnuts bud out and campions blow,
And daisies mimic the vanished snow
    Where it was born,
On either side of the path through the corn.

The corn, the corn, the beautiful corn,
Rising wonderful, morn by morn:
First, scarce as high as a fairy's wand,
Then, just in reach of a child's wee hand,
Then growing, growing, tall, brave and strong:
With the voice of new harvests in its song;
    While in fond scorn
The lark out-carols the whispering corn.

A strange, sweet path, formed day by day,
How, when, and wherefore, we cannot say,
No more than of our life-paths we know,
Whither they lead us, why we go;
Or whether our eyes shall ever see
The wheat in the ear or the fruit on the tree;
  Yet, who's forlorn?—
He who watered the furrows can ripen the corn.

THE GOOD OF IT.

A Cynic's Song.

SOME men strut proudly, all purple and gold,
  Hiding queer deeds 'neath a cloak of good
    fame;
I creep along, braving hunger and cold,
  To keep my heart stainless as well as my name;
    So, so, where is the good of it?

Some clothe bare Truth in fine garments of words,
  Fetter her free limbs with cumbersome state:
With me, let me sit at the lordliest boards,
  "I love" means *I love*, and "I hate" means *I hate*,
    But, but, where is the good of it?

Some have rich dainties and costly attire,
  Guests fluttering round them and duns at the door:
I crouch alone at my plain board and fire,
  Enjoy what I pay for and scorn to have more.
    Yet, yet, where is the good of it?

Some gather round them a phalanx of friends,
  Scattering affection like coin in a crowd;
I keep my heart for the few that heaven sends,
  Where they'll find their names writ when I lie in my
    shroud.
    Still, still, where is the good of it?

Some toy with love, lightly come, lightly go,
  A blithe game at hearts, little worth, little cost:—
I staked my whole soul on one desperate throw,
  A life 'gainst an hour's sport. We played; and I—
      lost.
    Ha, ha, such was the good of it!

MORAL: ADDED ON HIS DEATH-BED.

TURN the Past's mirror backward. Its shadows removed,
  The dim confused mass becomes softened, sublime:
I have worked—I have felt—I have lived—I have loved,
  And each was a step towards the goal I now climb:
    Thou, God, Thou sawest the good of it.

MINE.

For a German Air.

O HOW my heart is beating as her name I keep re
      peating,
    And I drink up joy like wine:
O how my heart is beating as her name I keep repeat-
      ing,
    For the lovely girl is mine!
She's rich, she's fair, beyond compare,
Of noble mind, serene and kind—
And how my heart is beating as her name I keep repeat-
      ing,
    For the lovely girl is mine

O how my heart is beating as her name I keep repeat-
     - ing,
    In a music soft and fine;
O how my heart is beating as her name I keep repeating,
    For the girl I love is mine.

She owns no lands, has no white hands,
Her lot is poor, her life obscure ;—
Yet how my heart is beating as her name I keep repeat-
    ing,
   ~For the girl I love is mine !

———

A GHOST AT THE DANCING.

 WIND-SWEPT tulip-bed—a colored cloud
    Of butterflies careening in the air—
    A many-figured arras stirred to life,
And merry unto midnight music dumb—
So the dance whirls.   Do any think of thee
    Amiel, Amiel ?

Friends greet each other—countless rills of talk
Meander round, scattering a spray of smiles.
Surely—the news was false.   One minute more
And thou wilt stand here, tall and quiet-eyed,
Shakespearian beauty in thy pensive face,
    Amiel, Amiel.

Many here knew and loved thee—I nor loved,
Scarce knew—yet in thy place a shadow glides,
And a face shapes itself from empty air,
Watching the dancers, grave and quiet-eyed—
Eyes that now see the angels evermore,
    Amiel, Amiel.

On just such night as this, 'midst dance and song,
I bade thee carelessly a light good by—
"Good-by" — saidst thou ; "A happy journey
    home ! "
Was the unseen death-angel at thy side,
Mocking those words—"*A happy journey home*,"
    Amiel, Amiel ?

Ay, we play fool's play still; thou hast gone home.
While these dance here, a mile hence o'er thy grave
Drifts the deep New Year snow. The wondrous gate
We spoke of, thou hast entered; I without
Grope ignorant still—thou dost its secrets know,
    Amiel, Amiel.

What if, thus sitting where we sat last year,
Thou camest, took'st up our broken thread of talk,
And told'st of that new Home, which far I view,
As children, wandering on through wintry fields,
Mark on the hill the father's window shine,
    Amiel, Amiel?

No. We shall see thy pleasant face no more;
Thy words on earth are ended.   Yet thou livest;
'Tis we who die.—I too, one day shall come,
And, unseen, watch these shadows, quiet-eyed—
Then flit back to thy land, the living land,
    Amiel, Amiel.

MY CHRISTIAN NAME.

Y Christian name, my Christian name,
    I never hear it now:
    None have the right to utter it,
  'Tis lost, I scarce know how.
My worldly name the world speaks loud;
    Thank God for well-earned fame!
But silence sits at my cold hearth,—
    I have no household name.

My Christian name, my Christian name,
    It has an uncouth sound;
My mother chose it out of those
    In Bible pages found:
Mother, whose accents made half sweet
    What else I held in shame,

Dost thou remember up in heaven
    My poor lost Christian name?

Brothers and sisters, mockers oft
    Of the quaint name I bore,
Would I could leap back years, to hear
    Ye shout it out once more!
One speaks it still in written lines,
    The last fraternal claim:
But the wide seas between us drown
    Its sound—my Christian name.

I had a long dream once. *Her* voice
    Might breathe the homely word,
And make it music—as love makes
    Any name, said or heard.
O, dumb, dumb lips!—O, silent heart!
    Though it is no one's blame:
Now while I live I'll never hear
    Her speak my Christian name.

God send her bliss, and send me rest!
    If her white footsteps calm
Should track my bleeding feet, God make
    To them each blood-drop balm!
Peace—peace. O mother, put thou forth
    Thine elder, holier claim,
And the first word I hear in heaven
    May be my Christian name.

———

A DEAD BABY.

LITTLE soul, for such brief space that entered
    In this little body straight and chilly,
    Little life that fluttered and departed,
Like a moth from out a budding lily,
Little being, without name or nation,
Where is now thy place among creation?

Little dark-lashed eyes, that never opened,
  Little mouth, by earthly food ne'er tainted,
Little breast, that just once heaved, and settled
  To eternal slumber, white and sainted,—
Child, shall I in future children's faces
See some pretty look that thine retraces?

Is this thrill that strikes across my heart-strings
  And in dew beneath my eyelid gathers,
Token of the bliss thou might'st have brought me,
  Dawning of the love they call a father's?
Do I hear through this still room a sighing
Like thy spirit to me its author crying?

Whence didst come and whither take thy journey,
  Little soul, of me and mine created?
Must thou lose us, and we thee, forever,
  O strange life, by minutes only dated?
Or new flesh assuming, just to prove us,
In some other babe return and love us?

Idle questions all : yet our beginning
  Like our ending, rests with the Life-sender,
With whom naught is lost, and naught spent vainly :
  Unto Him this little one I render.
Hide the face—the tiny coffin cover :
So, our first dream, our first hope—is over.

———

FOR MUSIC.

ALONG the shore, along the shore
  I see the wavelets meeting :
  But thee I see—ah, nevermore,
For all my wild heart's beating.
The little wavelets come and go,
The tide of life ebbs to and fro,
  Advancing and retreating :

But from the shore, the steadfast shore,
  The sea is parted never:
And mine I hold thee evermore,
  Forever and forever.

Along the shore, along the shore,
  I hear the waves resounding,
But thou wilt cross them nevermore
  For all my wild heart's bounding:
The moon comes out above the tide
And quiets all the waters wide
  Her pathway bright surrounding;
While on the shore, the dreary shore,
  I walk with weak endeavor;
I have thy love's light evermore,
  Forever and forever.

THE CANARY IN HIS CAGE.

SING away, ay, sing away,
  Merry little bird,
  Always gayest of the gay,
Though a woodland roundelay
  You ne'er sung nor heard;
Though your life from youth to age
Passes in a narrow cage.

Near the window wild birds fly,
  Trees are waving round:
Fair things everywhere you spy
Through the glass pane's mystery,
  Your small life's small bound:
Nothing hinders your desire
But a little gilded wire.

Like a human soul you seem
  Shut in golden bars:

Placed amidst earth's sunshine-stream,
Singing to the morning beam,
   Dreaming 'neath the stars;
Seeing all life's pleasures clear,—
But they never can come near.

Never! Sing, bird-poet mine,
   As most poets do;—
Guessing by an instinct fine
At some happiness divine
   Which they never knew.
Lonely in a prison bright
Hymning for the world's delight.

Yet, my birdie, you're content
   In your tiny cage:
Not a carol thence is sent
But for happiness is meant—
   Wisdom pure as sage:
Teaching, the true poet's part
Is to sing with merry heart.

So, lie down, thou peevish pen,
   Eyes, shake off all tears;
And my wee bird, sing again:
I'll translate your song to men
   In these future years.
"Howso'er thy lot's assigned,
Meet it with a cheerful mind."

CONSTANCY IN INCONSTANCY.

AN OLD MAN'S CONFESSION.

SHE has a large still heart—this lady of mine,
(Not mine, i' faith! nor would I that she
    were:)
She walks this world of ours like Grecian nymph,

Pure with a marble pureness, moving on
Among the herd of men, environed round
With native airs of deep Olympian calm.
I have a great love for that lady 'of mine:
I like to watch her motions, trick of face,
And turn of thought, when speaking high and wise
The tengue of gods, not men.   Ay, every day,
And twenty times a day, I start to catch
Some look or gesture of familiar mould,
And then my panting soul leans forth to her
Like some sick traveller who astonied sees
Gliding across the distant twilight fields—
His lovely, lost, beloved memory-fields—
The shadowy people of an earlier world.
I have a friend, how dearly liked, heart-warm,
Did I confess, sure she and all would smile :
I watch her as she steals in some dull room
That brightens at her entrance—slow lets fall
A word or two of wise simplicity,
Then goes, and at her going all seems dark.
Little she knows this : little thinks each brow
Lightens, each heart grows purer 'neath her eyes,
Good, honest eyes—clear, upward, righteous eyes,
That look as if they saw the dim unseen,
And learnt from thence their deep compassionate
        calm.
Why do I precious hold this friend of mine?
Why in our talks, our quiet fireside talks,
When we, two earnest travellers through the dark,
Grasp at the guiding threads that homeward lead,
Seems it another soul than hers looks out
From these her eyes ?—until I ofttimes start
And quiver, as when some soft ignorant hand
Touches the barb hid in a long-healed wound.
Yet still no blame, but thanks to thee, dear friend,
Ay, even when we wander back at eve,
Thy careless arm loose linked within my own—
The same height as I gaze down—nay, the hair

Her very color—fluttering 'neath the stars—
The same large stars which lit that earlier world.
I have another love—whose dewy looks
Are fresh with life's young dawn.   I prophesy
The streak of light now trembling on the hills
Will broaden out into a glorious day.
Thou sweet one, meek as good, and good as fair,
Wise as a woman, harmless as a child,
I love thee well!   And yet not thee, not thee,
God knows—*they* know who sit among the stars.
As one whose sun was darkened before noon,
Creeps patiently along the twilight lands,
Sees glow-worms, meteors, or tapers kind
Of an hour's burning, stops awhile to mark,
Thanks heaven for them, but never calls them day—
So love I these, and more.   Yet thou, my sun,
Who rose, leaped to thy zenith, sat there throned,
And made the whole earth day—look, if thou canst,
Out of thy veilèd glory, and behold
How all these lesser lights but come and go,
Mere reflexes of thee.   Be it so!   I keep
My face unto the eastward, where thou stand'st—
I *know* thou stand'st—behind the purpling hills,
And I shall wake and find morn in the world.

BURIED TO-DAY.

February 23, 1858.

URIED to-day.
  When the soft green buds are bursting
      out,
    And up on the south wind comes a shout
Of village boys and girls at play
  In the mild spring evening gray.

Taken away
    Sturdy of heart and stout of limb,
    From eyes that drew half their light from him,
And put low, low, underneath the clay,
In his spring—on this spring day.

Passes away
    All the pride of boy-life begun,
    All the hope of life yet to run ;
Who dares to question when One saith "Nay
Murmur not—only pray.

Enters to-day
    Another body in churchyard sod,
    Another soul on the life in God.
His Christ was buried—yet lives alway :
Trust Him, and go your way,

———

THE MILL.

For an Irish Tune.

WINDING and grinding
        Round goes the mill :
    Winding and grinding
    Should never stand still.
Ask not if neighbor
    Grind great or small :
Spare not *your* labor,
    Grind *your* wheat all.
Winding and grinding round goes the mill :
Winding and grinding should never stand still.

    Winding and grinding
        Work through the day,
    Grief nèver minding—
        Grind it away!

What though tears dropping
Rust as they fall?
Have no wheel stopping—
Work comforts all.
Winding and grinding round goes the mill :
Winding and grinding should never stand still.

NORTH WIND.

OUD wind, strong wind, sweeping o'er the moun-
tains,
Fresh wind, free wind, blowing from the
sea,
Pour forth thy vials liks streams from airy fountains,
Draughts of life to me.

Clear wind, cold wind, like a Northern giant,
Stars brightly threading thy cloud-driven hair,
Thrilling the blank night with thy voice defiant,
Lo! I meet thee there.

Wild wind, bold wind, like a strong-armed angel,
Clasp me and kiss me with thy kisses divine ;
Breathe in this dulled ear thy secret sweet evangel—
Mine—and only mine.

Fierce wind, mad wind, howling o'er the nations,
Knew'st thou how leapeth my heart as thou goest
by ;
Ah, thou wouldst pause awhile in a sudden patience
Like a human sigh.

Sharp wind, keen wind, cutting as word-arrows,
Empty thy quiverful! pass by! What is 't to thee,
That in some mortal eyes life's whole bright circle nar-
rows,
To one misery!

Loud wind, strong wind, stay thou in the mountains,
  Fresh wind, free wind, trouble not the sea.
Or lay thy deathly hand upon my heart's warm foun-
    tains,
  That I hear not thee.

NOW AND AFTERWARDS.

" Two hands upon the breast and labor is past."
          —RUSSIAN PROVERB.

WO hands upon the breast,
  And labor 's done ;
  Two pale feet crossed in rest—
The race is won ;
Two eyes with coin-weights shut,
  And all tears cease ;
Two lips where grief is mute,
  Anger at peace " ;—
So pray we oftentimes, mourning our lot
God in his kindness answereth not.

" Two hands to work addrest
  Aye for His praise ;
Two feet that never rest
  Walking His ways ;
Two eyes that look above
  Through all their tears ;
Two lips still breathing love,
  Not wrath, nor fears ; "
So pray we afterwards, low on our knees ;
Pardon those erring prayers !   Father, hear
    these !

A SKETCH.

"Emelie, that fayrer was to seene
Than is the lilye on hys stalke grene. . . .
Uprose the sun and uprose Emelie."

OST thou thus love me, O thou beautiful?
So beautiful, that by thy side I seem
Like a great dusky cloud beside a star:
Yet thou creep'st e'er its edges, and it rests
On its lone path, the slow deep-hearted cloud—
That opes a rift and lets thee enter in:
And with thy beauty shining on its breast,
Feels no more its own blackness—*thou* art fair.

Dost thou thus love me, O thou all beloved,
In whose large store the very meanest coin
Would out-buy my whole wealth?   Yet here thou
   comest
Like a kind heiress from her purple and down
Uprising, who for pity cannot sleep,
But goes forth to the stranger at her gate—
The beggared stranger at her beauteous gate—
And clothes and feeds; scarce blest till she has blest.

Dost thou thus love me, O thou pure of heart,
Whose very looks are prayers?   What couldst thou see
In this forsaken pool by the yew-wood's side,
To sit down at its bank, and dip thy hand,
Saying, "It is so clear!"—And lo, erelong
Its blackness caught the shimmer of thy wings,
Its slimes slid downward from thy stainless palm,
Its depths grew still that there thy form might rise.

O beautiful!   O well-beloved!   O rich
In all that makes my need!   I lay me down
I' the shadow of thy love, and feel no pain.
The cloud floats on, thee glittering on its breast,

The beggar wears thy purple as his own :
The noisome waves, made calm, creep to thy feet
Rejoicing that they yet can image thee,
And beyond thee, God's heaven, thick-sown with
    stars.

THE UNKNOWN COUNTRY.

To a German Air.

"WHERE is the unknown country ? "
    I whispered sad and slow,—
"The strange and awful country
    To which I soon must go, must go.
    To which I soon must go ? "

Out of the unknown country
    A voice sang soft and low :—
"O pleasant is that country
    And sweet it is to go, to go,
    And sweet it is to go.

"Along the shining country
    The peaceful rivers flow ;
And in that wondrous country
    The tree of life does grow, does grow,
    The tree of life does grow."

Ah, then into that country
    Of which I nothing know,
The everlasting country,
    With willing heart I go, I go,
    With willing heart I go.

A CHILD'S SMILE.

"For I say unto you, that in heaven their angels do always behold the face of my Father which is in heaven."

CHILD'S smile—nothing more;
   Quiet, and soft, and grave, and seldom seen;
   Like summer lightning o'er,
Leaving the little face again serene.

I think, boy well-beloved,
Thine angel, who did grieve to see how far
Thy childhood is removed
From sports that dear to other children are,

On this pale cheek has thrown
The brightness of his countenance, and made
A beauty like his own—
That, while we see it, we are half afraid,

And marvel, will it stay?
Or, long ere manhood, will that angel fair,
Departing some sad day,
Steal the child-smile and leave the shadow care?

Nay, fear not. As is given
Unto this child the father watching o'er,
His angel up in heaven
Beholds Our Father's face for evermore.

And he will help him bear
His burthen, as his father helps him now;
So may he come to wear
That happy child-smile on an old man's brow.

VIOLETS.

SENT IN A LITTLE BOX.

ET them lie, yes, let them lie,
　　They'll be dead to-morrow:
　Lift the lid up quietly
As you'd lift the mystery
　Of a shrouded sorrow.

Let them lie, the fragrant things,
　Their sweet souls thus giving:
Let no breezes' ambient wings,
And no useless water-springs
　Lure them into living.

They have lived—they live no more:
　Nothing can requite them
For the gentle life they bore
And up-yielded in full store
　While it did delight them.

Yet, poor flowers, not sad to die
　In the hand that slew ye,
Did ye leave the open sky,
And the winds that wandered by,
　And the bees that knew ye.

Giving up a small earth place,
　And a day of blooming,
Here to lie in narrow space,
Smiling in this sickly face,
　This dull air perfuming?

O my pretty violets dead,
　Coffined from all gazes,
We will also smiling shed

Out of our flowers witherèd
Perfume of sweet praises.

And as ye, for this poor sake,
Love with life are buying,
So, I doubt not, ONE will make
All our gathered flowers to take
Richer scent through dying.

EDENLAND.

For Music.

YOU remember where in starlight
We two wandered hand in hand,
While the night-flowers poured their per-
fume,
And night-airs the still earth fanned ?—
There I, walking yester even,
Felt like a ghost in Edenland.

I remember all you told me,
Looking up as we did stand,
While my heart poured out its perfume,
Like the night-flowers in your hand;
And the path where we two wanderèd
Seemed not like earth but Edenland.

Now the stars shine paler, colder
Night-flowers die without your hand;
Yet my spirit walks beside you
Everywhere, unsought, unbanned.
And I wait till we shall wander
Under the stars of Edenland.

THE HOUSE OF CLAY.

HERE was a house, a house of clay,
　　Wherein the inmate sat all day,
　　　Merry and poor ;
For Hope sat with her, heart to heart,
　　Fond and kind, fond and kind,
Vowing he never would depart,—
　　Till all at once he changed his mind :
"Sweetheart, good by !"　He slipped away
　　And shut the door.

But Love came past, and, looking in,
With smile that pierced like sunbeam thin
　　Through wall, roof, floor,
Stood in the midst of that poor room,
　　Grand and fair, grand and fair,
Making a glory out of gloom :—
　　Till at the window mocked grim Care :
Love sighed ; "All lose, and nothing win ?"—
　　He shut the door.

Then o'er the close-barred house of clay
Kind clematis and woodbine gay
　　Crept more and more ;
And bees hummed merrily outside,
　　Loud and strong, loud and strong,
The inner silentness to hide,
　　The patient silence all day long ;
Till evening touched with finger gray
　　The bolted door.

Most like, the next step passing by
Will be the Angel's, whose calm eye
　　Marks rich, marks poor :
Who, fearing not, at any gate
　　Stands and calls, stands and calls ;

At which the inmate opens straight,—
    Whom, ere the crumbling clay-house falls,
He takes in kind arms silently,
    And shuts the door.

WINTER MOONLIGHT.

OUD-VOICED night, with the wild wind
    blowing
      Many a tune;
Stormy night, with white rain-clouds going
    Over the moon;
Mystic night, that each minute changes,
Now as blue as the mountain-ranges
    Far, far away;
Now as black as a heart where strange is
    Joy, night or day.

Wondrous moonlight, unlike all moonlights
    Since I was born;
That on a hundred, bright as moonlights,
    Looks in slow scorn,—
Moonlights where the old vine-leaves quiver,
Moonlights shining on vale and river,
    Where old paths lie;
Moonlights—Night, blot their like forever
    Out of the sky!

Hail, new moonlight, fierce, wild, and stormy,
    Wintry and bold!
Hail, sharp wind, that can strengthen, warm me,
    Though ne'er so cold!
Not chance-driven this deluge rages,
ONE doth pour out and ONE assuages;
    Under His hand
Drifting, Noah-like, into the ages
    I shall touch land.

THE PLANTING.

*"I said unto my little son, who was watching tearfully a tree he had
planted.—'Let it alone: it will grow while you are sleeping.'"*

LANT it safe and sure, my child,
  Then cease watching and cease weep-
   ing;
 You have done your utmost part:
 Leave it with a quiet heart:
  It will grow while you are sleeping.

"But, O father," says the child,
  With a troubled face up-creeping,
"How can I but think and grieve
When the fierce wind comes at eve
  Tearing it—and I lie sleeping!

"I have loved my young tree so!
  In each bud seen leaf and floweret,
Watered it each day with prayers,
Guarded it with many cares,
  Lest some canker should devour it.

"O good father," sobs the child,
  "If I come in summer's shining
And my pretty tree be dead,
How the sun will scorch my head,
  How I shall sit lorn, repining!

"Rather let me, evermore,
  An incessant watch thus keeping,
Bear the cold, the storm, the frost,
That my treasure be not lost—
  Ay, bear aught—but idle sleeping."

Sternly said the father then,
  "Who art thou, child, vainly grieving?

Canst *thou* send the balmy dews,
Or the rich sap interfuse
    Through the dead trunk, inly living?

"Canst thou bid the heavens restrain
    Natural tempests for thy praying?
Canst thou bend one tender shoot,
Urge the growth of one frail root,
    Keep one leaflet from decaying?

"If it live to bloom all fair,
    Will it praise *thee* for its blossom?
If it die, will any plaints
Reach thee, as with kings and saints
    Drops it the cold earth's bosom?

"Plant it—all thou canst!—with prayers;
    It is safe 'neath His sky's folding
Who the whole earth compasses,
Whether we watch more or less,
    His wide eye all things beholding.

"Should He need a goodly tree
    For the shelter of the nations,
He will make it grow: if not,
Never yet His love forgot
    Human love, and faith, and patience.

"Leave thy treasure in His hand—
    Cease all watching and all weeping:
Years hence, men its shade may crave,
And its mighty branches wave
    Beautiful above thy sleeping."

If his hope, tear-sown, that child
    Garnered after joyful reaping,
Know I not: yet unawares
Gleams this truth through many cares,
    "*It will grow while thou art sleeping.*"

SITTING ON THE SHORE.

HE tide has ebbed away :
    No more wild dashings 'gainst the adamant
        rocks,
Nor swayings amidst sea-weed false that mocks
    The hues of gardens gay :
    No laugh of little wavelets at their play :
No lucid pools reflecting heaven's clear brow—
Both storm and calm alike are ended now.

    The rocks sit gray and lone :
The shifting sand is spread so smooth and dry,
That not a tide might ever have swept by
    Stirring it with rude moan :
    Only some weedy fragments idly thrown
To rot beneath the sky, tell what has been :
But Desolation's self has grown serene.

    Afar the mountains rise,
And the broad estuary widens out,
All sunshine ; wheeling round and round about
    Seaward, a white bird flies.
    A bird ?   Nay, seems it rather in these eyes
A spirit, o'er Eternity's dim sea
Calling—"Come thou where all we glad souls be."

    O life, O silent shore,
Where we sit patient ; O great sea beyond
To which we turn with solemn hope and fond,
    But sorrowful no more :
    A little while, and then we too shall soar
Like white-winged sea-birds into the Infinite Deep :
Till then, Thou, Father—wilt our spirits keep.

EUDOXIA.

FIRST PICTURE.

 SWEETEST my sister, my sister that sits in the sun,
   Her lap full of jewels, and roses in showers on her
      hair;
Soft smiling and counting her riches up slow, one by one,
Cool-browed, shaking dew from her garlands—those garlands so
      fair,
Many gasp, climb, snatch, struggle, and die for—*her* every-day
      wear!
O beauteous my sister, turn downwards those mild eyes of
      thine,
Lest they stab with their smiling, and blister or scorch where
      they shine.

Young sister who never yet sat for an hour in the cold,
Whose cheek scarcely feels half the roses that throng to caress,
Whose light hands hold loosely these jewels and silver and gold,
Remember thou those in the world who forever on press
In perils and watchings, and hunger and nakedness,
While thou sit'st content in the sunlight that round thee doth
      shine
Take heed! these have long borne their burthen—now lift thou
      up thine.

Be meek—as befits one whose cup to the brim is love-crowned,
While others in dry dust drop empty—What, what canst thou
      know
Of the wild human tide that goes sweeeping eternally round
The isle where thou sit'st pure and calm as a statue of snow,
Around which good thoughts like kind angels continually go?
Be pitiful. *Whose* eyes once turned from the angels to shine
Upon publicans, sinners? O sister, 't will not pollute thine,
Who, even-eyed, looks on His children, the black and the fair,
The loved and the unloved, the tempted, untempted—marks all,
And metes—not as man metes? If thou with weak tender hand
      dare

To take up His balances—say where His justice should fall,
Far better be Magdalen dead at the gate of thy hall—
Dead, sinning, and loving, and contrite, and pardoned, to shine
Midst the saints high in heaven, than thou, angel sister of mine !

EUDOXIA.

SECOND PICTURE.

 DEAREST my sister, my sister who sits by th
　　　hearth,
　　With lids softly drooping, or lifted up saintly an
　　　calm,
With household hands folded, or opened for help and for balm,
And lips, ripe and dewy, or ready for innocent mirth,—
Thy life rises upwards to heaven every day like a psalm
Which the singer sings sleeping, and waked, would half wonder-
　　　ing say—
" I sang not.　Nay, how could I sing thus ?—I only do pray."

O gentlest my sister, who walks in at every dark door
Whether bolted or open, unheedful of welcome or frown ;
But entering silent as sunlight, and there sitting down,
Illumines the damp walls and shines pleasant shapes on the
　　floor,
And unlocks dim chambers where low lies sad Hope, without
　　crown,
Uplifts her from sackcloth and ashes and black mourning weeds,
Re-crowns and re-clothes her.—Then, on to the next door that
　　needs.

O blessed my sister, whose spirit so wholly dost live
In loving, that even the word "loved," with its rapturous
　　sound,
Rings faintly, like earth-tunes when angels are hymning around :
Whose eyes say : " Less happy methinks to receive than to
　　give."—

So whatsoever we give, may One give to thee without bound,
All best gifts—all dearest gifts—whether His right hand do close
Or open—He holds it forever above thee;—He knows!

EUDOXIA.

THIRD PICTURE.

SILENT my sister, who stands by my side at the
 shore,
Back gazing with me on those waves which we
 mortals call years,
That rose, grew, and threatened, and climaxed, and broke, and
 were o'er,
While we still sit watching and watching, our cheeks free from
 tears —
O sister, with looks so familiar, yet strange, flitting by,
Say, say, hast thou been to those dead years as faithful as I?

Have they cast at thy feet also, jewels and whitening bones,
Gold, silver, and wreck-wood, dank sea-weed and treasures of
 cost?
Hast thou buried thy dead, sought thy jewels 'midst shingle and
 stones,
And learnt how the lost is the found, and the found is the lost?
Or stood with clear eyes upturned placid 'twixt sorrow and
 mirth,
As asking deep questions that cannot be answered on earth?—

I know not. Who knoweth? Our own souls we scarcely do
 know,
And none knows his brother's. Who judges, contemns, or be-
 wails,
Or mocketh, or praiseth? In this world's strange vanishing
 show,
The one truth is *loving*. O sister, the dark cloud that veils
All life, lets this rift through to glorify future and past.
" Love ever—love only—love faithfully—love to the last."

BENEDETTA MINELLI.

I.

THE NOVICE.

T is near morning.   Ere the next night fall
    I shall be made the bride of heaven.   Then
       home
To my still marriage chamber I shall come,
And spouseless, childless, watch the slow years crawl.

These lips will never meet a softer touch
    Than the stone crucifix I kiss; no child
    Will clasp this neck.   Ah, virgin-mother mild,
Thy painted bliss will mock me overmuch.

This is the last time I shall twist the hair
    My mother's hand wreathed, till in dust she lay:
    The name, her name, given on my baptism-day,
This is the last time I shall ever bear.

O weary world, O heavy life, farewell!
    Like a tired child that creeps into the dark
    To sob itself asleep, where none will mark,—
So creep I to my silent convent cell.

Friends, lovers whom I loved not, kindly hearts
    Who grieve that I should enter this still door,
    Grieve not.   Closing behind me evermore,
Me from all anguish, as all joy, it parts.

Love, whom alone I loved; who stand'st far off,
    Lifting compassionate eyes that could not save,
    Remember, this my spirit's quiet grave
Hides me from worldly pity, worldly scoff.

'Twas less thy hand than Heaven's which came between,
    And dashed my cup down.   See, I shed no tears:

And if I think at all of vanished years,
'Tis but to bless thee, dear, for what has been.

My soul continually does cry to thee;
  In the night-watches ghost-like stealing out
  From its flesh tomb, and hovering thee about;
So live that I in heaven thy face may see!

Live, noble heart, of whom this heart of mine
  Was half unworthy.   Build up actions great,
  That I down looking from the crystal gate
Smile o'er our dead hopes urned in such a shrine.

Live, keeping aye thy spirit undefiled,
  That, when we stand before our Master's feet,
  I with an angel's love may crown complete
The woman's faith, the worship of the child.

Dawn, solemn bridal morn; ope, bridal door;
  I enter.   My vowed soul may Heaven now take;
  My heart its virgin spousal for thy sake;
O love, keeps sacred thus forevermore.

II.

THE SISTER OF MERCY.

IS it then so?—Good friends, who sit and sigh
    While I lie smiling, are my life's sands run?
    Will my next matins, hymned beyond the sun,
  Mingle with those of saints and martyrs high?

Shall I with these my gray hairs turned to gold,
  My aged limbs new clad in garments white,
  Stand all transfigured in the angels' sight,
Singing triumphantly that moan of old,—

Thy will be done?   It was done.   O my God,
  Thou know'st, when over grief's tempestuous sea
  My broken-wing d soul fled home to Thee,
I writhed, but never murmured at Thy rod.

It fell upon me, stern at first, then soft
  As parent's kisses, till the wound was healed;
  And I went forth a laborer in Thy field:—
They best can bind who have been bruisèd oft.

And Thou wert pitiful.   I came heart-sore,
  And drank Thy cup because earth's cups ran dry:
  Thou slew'st me not for that impiety,
But madest the draught so sweet, I thirst no more.

I came for silence, heavy rest, or death:
  Thou gavest instead life, peace, and holy toil:
  My sighing lips from sorrow didst assoil,
And fill with righteous thankfulness each breath.

Therefore I praise Thee, who didst shut Thine ears
  Unto my misery: doing Thy will, not mine:
  That to this length of days Thy hand divine,
My feet from falling kept, mine eyes from tears.

Sisters, draw near.   Hear my last words serene:
  When I was young I walked in mine own ways,
  Worshipped—not God: sought not alone His praise
So he cut down my gourd while it was green.

And then He o'er me threw His holy shade,
  That though no other mortal plants might grow,
  Mocking the beauty that was long laid low,
I dwelt in peace, and His commands obeyed.

I thank Him for all joy and for all pain:
  For healèd pangs, for years of calm content:
  For blessedness of spending and being spent
In His high service where all loss is gain.

I bless Him for my life and for my death ,
　　But most, that in my death my life is crowned,
　　Since I see there, with angels gathering round,
My angel.　Ay, love, thou hast kept thy faith,

I mine.　The golden portals will not close
　　Like those of earth, between us.　Reach thy hand !
　　No *miserere* sisters.　Chant out grand
Te Deum laudamus.　Now,—'t is all repose.

A DREAM OF DEATH.

 HERE　shall　we　sail　to-day ? "—Thus said, me·
　　　thought,
　　　A voice, that only I shall hear in dreams :
And on we glided without mast or oar,
A wondrous boat upon a wondrous sea.

Sudden, the shore curved inward to a bay,
Broad, calm, with gorgeous sea-weeds waving slow
Beneath the water, like rich thoughts that stir
In the mysterious deep of poets' hearts.

So still, so fair, so rosy in the dawn
Lay that bright sea : yet something seemed to breathe,
Or in the air, or from the whispering waves,
Or from that voice, as near as one's own soul,

" *There was a wreck last night.*"　A wreck ?　then
　　　where
The ship, the crew ?—The all-entombing wave
On which is writ nor name nor chronicle
Laid itself o'er them with smooth crystal smile.

" *Yet was the wreck last night.*"　And gazing down
Deep down below the surface, we were ware
Of ghastly faces with their open eyes
Uplooking to the dawn they could not see.

One moved with moving sea-weeds : one lay prone,
The tinted fishes gliding o'er his breast ;
One, caught by floating hair, rocked quietly
Upon his reedy cradle, like a child.

" The wreck has been "—said the melodious voice,
" Yet all is peace. The dead, that, while we slept,
Struggled for life, now sleep and fear no storms :
O'er them let us not weep when heaven smiles."

So we sailed on above the diamond sands,
Bright sea-flowers, and white faces stony calm,
Till the waves bore us to the open main,
And the great sun arose upon the world.

A DREAM OF RESURRECTION.

O heavenly beautiful it lay,
    It was less like a human corse
    Than that fair shape in which perforce
A lost hope clothes itself away.

The dream showed very plain : the bed
    Where that known unknown face reposed,—
    A woman's face with eyelids closed,
A something precious that was dead ;

A something, lost on this side life,
    By which the mourner came and stood,
    And laid down, ne'er to be indued,
All flaunting robes of earthly strife ;

Shred off, like votive locks of hair,
    Youth's ornaments of pride and strength,
    And cast them in their golden length
The silence of her bier to share.

No tears fell,—but with gazings long
   Lorn memory tried to print that face
   On the heart's ever-vacant place,
With a sun-finger, sharp and strong.—

Then kisses, dropping without sound,
   And solemn arms wound round the dead,
   And lifting from the natural bed
Into the coffin's strange new bound.

Yet still no farewell, or belief
   In death, no more than one believes
   In some dread truth that sudden weaves
The whole world in a shroud of grief.

And still unanswered kisses; still
   Warm clingings to the image cold
   With an incredulous faith's close fold
Creative in its fierce " *I will.*"

Hush,—hush! the marble eyelids move,
   The kissed lips quiver into breath:
   Avaunt, thou mockery of Death!
Avaunt!—we are conquerors, I and Love.

Corpse of dead Hope, awake, arise,
   A living Hope that only slept
   Until the tears thus overwept
Had washed the blindness from our eyes.

Come back into the upper day:
   Pluck off these cerements.   Patient shroud,
   We'll wrap thee as a garment proud
Round the fair shape we thought was clay.

Clasp, arms; cling, soul; eyes, drink anew
   The beauty that returns with breath:
   Faith, that out-loved this trance-like death,
May see this resurrection too.

ON THE CLIFF-TOP.

ACE upward to the sky
    Quiet I lie :
    Quiet as if the finger of God's will
Had bade this human mechanism "be still!"
And sent the intangible essence, this strange *I*,
All wondering forth to His eternity.

Below, the sea's sound, faint
    As dying saint
Telling of gone-by sorrows long at rest :
Above, the fearless sea-gull's shimmering breast
Painted a moment on the dark blue skies—
A hovering joy, that while I watch it flies.

Alike unheeded now
    Old griefs, and thou
Quick-wingéd Joy, that like a bird at play
Pleasest thyself to visit me to-day .
On the cliff-top, earth dim and heaven clear,
My soul lies calmly, above hope—or fear.

But not—(do Thou forbid
    Whose stainless lid
Wept tears at Lazarus' grave, and looking down
Afar off, upon Solyma's doomed town.)
Ah, not above *love*—human yet divine—
Which, Thee seen first, in Thee sees all of Thine!

Is 't sunset ?   The keen breeze
    Blows from the seas :
And at my side a pleasant vision stands
With her brown eyes and kind extended hands.
Mary ?—Come, Dear, we'll go down full fain
From the cliff-top to the busy world again.

EVENING GUESTS.

F in the silence of this lonely eve
With the street-lamps faint flickering on the wall
An angel were to say to me—"Believe!
It shall be granted.   Call!"—whom should I call?

And then I were to see thee gliding in
With thy pale robe that in long empty fold
Lies in my keeping; and my fingers, thin
As thine were once, to feel in thy safe hold:

I should fall weeping on thy neck, and say,
"I have so suffered since—since"—But my tears
Would cease, remembering how thou count'st thy day:
A day of God that is a thousand years

Then what are these long weeks, months, years of
mine
Measured by thy sublime infinitude?
What my whole life, when myriad lives divine
May wait us, leading each to a higher good!

I lose myself—I faint—Beloved—best—
Sit in thy older dear humanity
Near me awhile, my head upon thy breast—
And then, O! take me back to heaven with thee.

———

Should I call thee?   Ah no, I would not call:
But if, by some invisible spirit led,
I heard outside the door thy footstep's fall,
Entering—Ah 't would be life unto the dead!

And then I, smiling with a deep content,
Would give thee the old welcome, long unknown:
And 'stead of friends' kind accents daily sent
To cheer me, I should hear thine own—thine own

Thou, too, like the beloved guest late gone
　　Wouldst sit and clasp my feeble hand in thine:
'T would grieve thee to know why it grew so wan,
　　Therefore I would smile on and make no sign.

And thou, soft speaking in that pleasant voice,
　　Perchance with a compassionate tremble stirred
Wouldst change my dull grief into full rejoice,
　　Healing my hurts with each balm-dropping word.

So, talking of things meet for thee and me;
　　Affection, strong as life, serene as death:
Solemn as that desired eternity
　　Where I shall find thee, who wert my soul's breath,—

Upon this crownèd eve of many eves
　　Thou knowest,—one half my life and all its lore
Would climax like a breaking wave.　Who grieves
　　Though it should break, and cease, and be no more?

AFTER SUNSET.

REST—*rest*—four little letters, one short word,
　　Enfolding an infinitude of bliss—
　　Rest is upon the earth.　The heavy clouds
Hang poised in silent ether, motionless,
Seeking nor sun nor breeze.　No restless star
Thrills the sky's gray-robed breast with pulsing rays,
The night's heart has throbbed out.
　　　　　　　　　No grass blade stirs,
No downy-wingèd moth comes flittering by
Caught by the light—Thank God, there is no light,
No open-eyed, loud-voiced, quick-motioned light,
Nothing but gloom and rest.
　　　　　　　　　A row of trees
Along the hill horizon, westward, stands
All black and still, as if it were a rank
Of fallen angels, melancholy met

Before the amber gate of Paradise—
The bright shut gate, whose everlasting smile
Deadens despair to calm.
                O, better far
Better than bliss is rest ! If suddenly
Those burnished doors of molten gold, steel-barred,
Which the sun closed behind him as he went
Into his bridal chamber—were to burst
Asunder with a clang, and in a breath
God's mysteries were revealed—His kingdom came—
The multitudes of heavenly messengers
Hastening throughout all space—the thunder quire
Of praise—the obedient lightnings' lambent gleam
Around the unseen Throne—should I not sink
Crushed by the weight of such beatitudes,
Crying. " Rest, give me only rest, thou God !
Hide me within the hollow of Thy hand
In some dark corner of the universe,
Thy bright, full, busy universe, that blinds,
Deafens, and racks, and tortures—Give but *rest !* "

O for a soul-sleep, long and deep and still !
To lie down quiet after the sad day,
Dropping all pleasant flowers from the numbed hands,
Bidding good-night to all companions dear,
Drawing the curtains on this darkened world,
Closing the eyes, and with a patient sigh
Murmuring " Our Father "—fall on sleep, till dawn !

THE GARDEN-CHAIR.

TWO PORTRAITS.

 PLEASANT picture, full of meanings deep,
      Old age, calm sitting in the July sun,
      On withered hands half leaning—feeble hands,
That after their life-labors, light or hard,
Their girlish broideries, their marriage-ringed

Domestic duties, their sweet cradle cares,
Have dropped into the quiet-folded ease
Of fourscore years.   How peacefully the eyes
Face us!   Contented, unregretful eyes,
That carry in them the whole tale of life
With its one moral—"Thus all was—thus best."
Eyes now so near unto their closing mild
They seem to pierce direct through all that maze,
As eyes immortal do.

    Here—Youth.   She stands
Under the roses with elastic foot
Poised to step forward; eager-eyed, yet grave
Beneath the mystery of the unknown To-come,
Though longing for its coming.   Firm prepared
(So say the lifted head and close, sweet mouth)
For any future: though the dreamy hope
Throned on her girlish forehead, whispers fond,
"Surely they err who say that life is hard;
Surely it shall not be with me as these."

God knows: He only.   And so best, dear child,
Thou woman-statured, sixteen-year-old child,
Meet bravely the impenetrable Dark
Under thy roses.   Bud and blossom thou
Fearless as they—if thou art planted safe,
Whether for gathering or for withering, safe
In the King's garden.

AN OLD IDEA.

 REAM of my life, dull, placid river, flow!
I have no fear of the ingulfing seas:
Neither I look before me nor behind,
But, lying mute with wave-dipped hand, float on.

It was not always so.   My brethren, see
This oar-stained, trembling palm.   It keeps the sign

Of youth's mad wrestling with the waves that drift
Immutably, eternally along.

I would have had them flow through fields and
    flowers,
Giving and taking freshness, perfume, joy;
It winds through—here.   Be silent, O my soul!
—The finger of God's wisdom drew its line.

So I lean back and look up to the stars,
And count the ripples circling to the shore,
And watch the solemn river rolling on
Until it widen to the open seas.

PARABLES.

> "Hold every mortal joy
> With a loose hand."

E clutch our joys as children do their flowers;
    We look at them, but scarce believe them
        ours,
Till our hot palms have smirched their colors rare
And crushed their dewy beauty unaware.
But the wise Gardener, whose they were, comes by
At hours when we expect not, and with eye
Mournful yet sweet, compassionate though stern,
Takes them.
        Then in a moment we discern
By loss, what was possession, and, half-wild
With misery, cry out like angry child:
"O cruel! thus to snatch my posy fine!"
He answers tenderly, "Not thine, but mine,"
And points to those stained fingers which do prove
Our fatal cherishing, our dangerous love;
At which we, chidden, a pale silence keep;
Yet evermore must weep, and weep, and weep.

So on through gloomy ways and thorny brakes,
Quiet and slow, our shrinking feet he takes
Led by the soilèd hand, which, laved in tears,
More and more clean beneath his sight appears.
At length the heavy eyes with patience shine—
"I am content.   Thou took'st but what was thine."

And then he us his beauteous garden shows,
Where bountiful the Rose of Sharon grows:
Where in the breezes opening spice-buds swell,
And the pomegranates yield a pleasant smell :
While to and fro peace-sandalled angels move
In the pure air that they—not we—call Love :
An air so rare and fine, our grosser breath
Cannot inhale till purified by death.
And thus we, struck with longing joy, adore,
And, satisfied, wait mute without the door,
Until the gracious Gardener maketh sign,
"Enter in peace.   All this is mine—and thine."

LETTICE.

 SAID to Lettice, our sister Lettice,
      While drooped and glistened her eye-lash
         brown,
"Your man's a poor man, a cold and dour man,
   There's many a better about our town."
She smiled securely—"He loves me purely :
   A true heart's safe, both in smile or frown ;
And nothing harms me while his love warms me,
   Whether the world go up or down."

"He comes of strangers, and they are rangers,
   And ill to trust, girl, when out of sight :
Fremd folk may blame ye, and e'en defame ye,—
   A gown oft handled looks seldom white."
She raised serenely her eyelids queenly,—

"My innocence is my whitest gown;
No harsh tongue grieves me while he believes me,
    Whether the world go up or down."

"Your man's a frail man, was ne'er a hale man,
    And sickness knocketh at every door,
And death comes making bold hearts cower, break-
        ing—"
Our Lettice trembled;—but once, no more:
"If death should enter, smite to the centre
    Our poor home palace, all crumbling down,
He cannot fright us, nor disunite us,
    Life bears Love's cross, death brings Love's crown."

————

A SPIRIT PRESENT.

F, coming from that unknown sphere
        Where I believe thou art,—
    The world unseen which girds our world
    So close, yet so apart,—
Thy soul's soft call unto my soul
    Electrical could reach,
And mortal and immortal blend
    In one familiar speech,—

What wouldst thou say to me? wouldst ask
    Of things which did befall?
Or close this chasm of cruel years
    Between us—knowing all?
Wouldst love me—thy pure eyes seeing what
    God only saw beside?
O, love me! 'T was so hard to live,
    So easy to have died.

If, while the dizzy whirl of life
    A moment pausing stayed,
I face to face with thee could stand,

I would not be afraid :
Not though from heaven to heaven thy feet
　　In glad ascent have trod,
While mine took through earth's miry ways
　　Their solitary road.

We could not lose each other.　World
　　On world piled ever higher
Would part like banked clouds, lightning-cleft
　　By our two souls' desire.
Life ne'er divided us ; death tried,
　　But could not ; Love's voice fine
Called luring through the dark—then ceased,
　　And I am wholly thine.

A　WINTER　WALK.

E never had believed, I wis,
　　　At primrose time when west winds stole
　　　Like thoughts of youth across the soul,
In such an altered time as this,

When if one little flower did peep
　　Up through the brown and sullen grass,
　　We should just look on it, and pass
As if we saw it in our sleep.

Feeling as sure as that this ray
　　Which cottage children call the sun,
　　Colors the pale clouds one by one,—
Our touch would make it drop to clay.

We never could have looked, in prime
　　Of April, or when July trees
　　Shook full-leaved in the evening breeze,
Upon the face of this pale time,

Still, soft, familiar; shining bleak
  On naked branches, sodden ground,
  Yet shining—as if one had found
A smile upon a dead friend's cheek,

Or old friend, lost for years, had strange
  In altered mien come sudden back,
  Confronting us with our great lack—
Till loss seemed far less sad than change.

Yet though, alas! Hope did not see
  This winter skeleton through full leaves,
  Out of all bareness Faith perceives
Possible life in field and tree.

In bough and trunk the sap will move,
  And the mould break o'er springing flowers;
  Nature revives with all her powers,
But only nature;—never love.

So, listlessly with linkèd hands
  Both Faith and Hope glide soft away;
  While in long shadows, cool and gray,
The sun sets o'er the barren lands.

"WILL SAIL TO-MORROW."

THE good ship lies in the crowded dock,
    Fair as a statue, firm as a rock:
    Her tall masts piercing the still blue air,
Her funnel glittering white and bare,
Whence the long soft line of vapory smoke
Betwixt sky and sea like a vision broke,
Or slowly o'er the horizon curled
Like a lost hope fled to the other world:
    She sails to-morrow,—
    Sails to-morrow.

Out steps the captain, busy and grave,
With his sailor's footfall, quick and brave,
His hundred thoughts and his thousand cares,
And his steady eye that all things dares:
Though a little smile o'er the kind face dawns
On the loving brute that leaps and fawns,
And a little shadow comes and goes,
As if heart or fancy fled—where, who knows?
    He sails to-morrow:
    Sails to-morrow.

To-morrow the serried line of ships
Will quick close after her as she slips
Into the unknown deep once more:
To-morrow, to-morrow, some on shore
With straining eyes shall desperate yearn—
"This is not parting? return—return!"
Peace, wild-wrung hands! hush, sobbing breath!
Love keepeth its own through life and death;
    Though she sails to-morrow—
    Sails to-morrow.

Sail, stately ship; down Southampton water
Gliding fair as old Nereus' daughter:
Christian ship that for burthen bears
Christians, speeded by Christian prayers;
All kind angels follow her track!
Pitiful God, bring the good ship back!
All the souls in her forever keep
Thine, living or dying, awake or asleep:
    Then sail to-morrow!
    Ship, sail to-morrow!

AT EVEN-TIDE.

C. N.—Died April, 1857.

HAT spirit is it that doth pervade
 The silence of this empty room?
 And as I lift my eyes, what shade
Glides off and vanishes in gloom?

I could believe this moment gone,
 A known form filled that vacant chair,
That those kind eyes upon me shone
 I never shall see anywhere!

The living are so far away:
 But *thou*—thou seemest strangely near;
Knowest all my silent heart would say,
 Its peace, its pain, its hope, its fear.

And from thy calm supernal height,
 And wondrous wisdom newly won,
Smilest upon our poor delight,
 And petty woe beneath the sun.

From all this coil thou hast slipped away,
 As softly as a cloud departs
Along the hillside purple gray—
 Into the heaven of patient hearts.

Nothing here suffered, nothing missed,
 Will ever stir from its repose
The death-smile on her lips unkissed,
 Who all things loves and all things knows.

And I, who, ignorant and weak,
 Of love so helpless—quick to pain,
With restless longing ever seek
 The unattainable in vain,

Find it strange comfort thus to sit
 While the loud world unheeded rolls,
And clasp, ere yet the fancy flit,
 A friend's hand from the land of souls.

A DEAD SEA-GULL.

Near Liverpool.

ACK-LUSTRE eye, and idle wing,
  And smirchèd breast that skims no more,
  White as the foam itself, the wave—
Hast thou not even a grave
Upon the dreary shore,
Forlorn, forsaken thing?

Thou whom the deep seas could not drown,
Nor all the elements affright,
Flashing like thought across the main,
 Mocking the hurricane,
Screaming with shrill delight
When the great ship went down.

Thee not thy beauty saved, nor mirth,
Nor daring, nor thy humble lot,
One among thousands—in quick haste
Fate clutched thee as she passed;
Dead—how, it matters not:
Corrupting, earth to earth.

And not a league from where it lies
Lie bodies once as free from stain,
And hearts as gay as this sea-bird's,
Whom all the preachers' words
Will ne'er make white again,
Or from the dead to rise.

Rot, pretty bird, in harmless clay:—
We sing too much poetic woes;
Let us be doing while we can:
Blessed the Christian man
Who on life's shore seeks those
Dying of soul decay.

LOOKING EAST.

In January, 1858.

LITTLE white clouds, why are you flying
  Over the sky so blue and cold ?
Fair faint hopes, why are you lying
Over my heart like a white cloud's fold ?

Slender green leaves, why are you peeping
  Out of the ground where the snow yet lies ?
Toying west wind, why are you creeping
  Like a child's breath across my eyes ?

Hope and terror by turns consuming,
  Lover and friend put far from me,—
What should I do with the bright spring, coming
  Like an angel over the sea ?

Over the cruel sea that parted
  Me from mine own, and rolls between ;—
Out of the woful east, whence darted
  Heaven's full quiver of vengeance keen.

Day teaches day, night whispers morning—
  " Hundreds are weeping their dead, while thou
Weeping thy living—Rise, be adorning
  Thy brows, unwidowed, with smiles."—But how ?

'O' had he married me !—unto anguish,
  Hardship, sickness, peril, and pain ;
That on my breast his head might languish
  In lonely jungle or scorching plain ;

O, had we stood on some rampart gory,
  Till he—ere Horror behind us trod—
Kissed me, and killed me—so, with his glory
  My soul went happy and pure to God !

Nay, nay, Heaven pardon me! me, sick-hearted,
　Living this long, long life-in-death:
Many there are far wider parted
　Who under one roof-tree breathe one breath.

But we that *loved*—whom one word half broken
　Had drawn together close soul to soul
As lip to lip—and it was not spoken,
　Nor may be while the world's ages roll.

I sit me down with my tears all frozen:
　I drink my cup, be it gall or wine:
For I know, if he lives, I am his chosen—
　I know, if he dies, that he is mine.

If love in its silence be greater, stronger
　Than million promises, sighs, or tears—
I will wait upon Him a little longer
　Who holdeth the balance of our years.

Little white clouds, like angels flying,
　Bring the spring with you across the sea—
Loving or losing, living or dying,
　Lord, remember, remember me!

———

OVER THE HILLS AND FAR AWAY.

 LITTLE bird flew my window by,
　'Twixt the level street and the level sky,
　The level rows of houses tall,
The long low sun on the level wall;
And all that the little bird did say
Was, "Over the hills and far away."

A little bird sang behind my chair,
From the level line of corn-fields fair,
The smooth green hedgerow's level bound

Not a furlong off—the horizon's bound,
And the level lawn where the sun all day
Burns :—" Over the hills and far away."

A little bird sings above my bed,
And I know if I could but lift my head
I would see the sun set, round and grand,
Upon level sea and level sand,
While beyond the misty distance gray
Is " Over the hills and far away."

I think that a little bird will sing
Over a grassy mound, next spring,
Where something that once was *me*, ye 'll leave
In the level sunshine, morn and eve :
But I shall be gone, past night, past day,
Over the hills and far away.

TOO LATE.

"Douglas, Douglas, tendir and treu."

COULD ye come back to me Douglas, Douglas,
    In the old likeness that I knew,
  I would be so faithful, so loving, Douglas,
Douglas, Douglas, tender and true.

Never a scornful word should grieve ye,
    I'd smile on ye sweet as the angels do ;—
Sweet as your smile on me shone ever,
    Douglas, Douglas, tender and true.

O to call back the days that are not !
    My eyes were blinded, your words were few
Do you know the truth now up in heaven,
    Douglas, Douglas, tender and true ?

I never was worthy of you, Douglas ;
  Not half worthy the like of you :
Now all men beside seem to me like shadows—
  I love *you*, Douglas, tender and true.

Stretch out your hand to me, Douglas, Douglas,
  Drop forgiveness from heaven like dew ;
As I lay my heart on your dead heart, Douglas,
  Douglas, Douglas, tender and true.

LOST IN THE MIST.

THE thin white snow-streaks pencilling
  That mountain's shoulder gray,
  While in the west the pale green sky
Smiled back the dawning day,
Till from the misty east the sun
  Was of a sudden born
Like a new soul in Paradise—
  How long it seems since morn !

One little hour, O round red sun,
  And thou and I shall come
Unto the golden gate of rest,
  The open door of home :
One little hour, O weary sun,
  Delay the threatened eve
Till my tired feet that pleasant door
  Enter and never leave.

Ye rooks that fly in slender file
  Into the thick'ning gloom,
Ye'll scarce have reached your grim gray tower
  Ere I have reached my home ;
Plover, that thrills the solitude
  With such an eerie cry,
Seek you your nest ere night-fall comes,
  As my heart's nest seek I.

O light, light heart and heavy feet,
　　Patience a little while!
Keep the warm love-light in these eyes,
　　And on these lips the smile :
Out-speed the mist, the gathering mist
　　That follows o'er the moor!—
The darker grows the world without
　　The brighter seems that door.

O door, so close yet so far off ;
　　O mist that nears and nears!
What, shall I faint in sight of home ?
　　Blinded—but not with tears—
'T is but the mist, the cruel mist,
　　Which chills this heart of mine :
These eyes, too weak to see that light—
　　It has not ceased to shine.

A little further, further yet :
　　The white mist crawls and crawls ;
It hems me round, it shuts me in
　　Its great sepulchral walls :
No earth—no sky—no path—no light—
　　A silence like the tomb :
O me, it is too soon to die—
　　And I was going home !

A little further, further yet :
　　My limbs are young,—my heart—
O heart, it is not only life
　　That feels it hard to part :
Poor lips, slow freezing into calm,
　　Numbed hands that helpless fall,
And, a mile off, warm lips, fond hands,
　　Waiting to welcome all !

I see the pictures in the room,
　　The figures moving round,
The very flicker of the fire
　　Upon the patterned ground :

O that I were the shepherd-dog
  That guards their happy door!
Or even the silly household cat
  That basks upon the floor!

O that I sat one minute's space
  Where I have sat so long!
O that I heard one little word
  Sweeter than angel's song!
A pause—and then the table fills,
  The harmless mirth brims o'er;
While I—O *can* it be God's will?—
  I die, outside the door.

My body fails—my desperate soul
  Struggles before it go:
The bleak air 's full of voices wild,
  But not the voice I know;
Dim shapes come wandering through the dark:
  With mocking, curious stares,
Faces long strange peer glimmering by—
  But not one face of theirs.

Lost, lost, and such a little way
  From that dear sheltering door!
Lost, lost, out of the loving arms
  Left empty evermore!
His will be done. O, gate of heaven,
  Fairer than earthly door,
Receive me! Everlasting arms,
  Enfold me evermore!

And so, farewell   *   *   *   *   *
               What is this touch
  Upon my closing eyes?
My name, too, that I thought to hear
  Next time in Paradise?
Warm arms—close lips—O, saved, saved, saved!
  Across the deathly moor
Sought, found—and yonder through the night
  Shineth the blessed door.

SEMPER FIDELIS.

"Mine own familiar friend, in whom I trusted."

HINK you, had we two lost fealty, something would not
      as I sit
  With this book upon my lap here, come and over-
      shadow it?
Hide with spectral mists the pages, under each familiar leaf
Lurk, and clutch my hand that turns it with the icy clutch of
      grief?

Think you, were we twain divided, not by distance, time, or
      aught
That the world calls separation, but we smile at, better taught,
That I should not feel the dropping of each link you did un-
      twine
Clear as if you sat before me with your true eyes fixed on
      mine?

That I should not, did you crumble as the other false friends
      do
To the dust of broken idols, know it without sight of you,
By some shadow darkening daylight in the fickle skies of
      spring,
By foul fears from household corners crawling over everything?

If that awful gulf were opening which makes two, however
      near,
Parted more than we were parted, dwelt we in each hemis-
      phere,—
Could I sit here, smiling quiet on this book within my hand,
And while earth was cloven beneath me, feel no shock nor un-
      derstand?

No, you cannot, could not alter. No, my faith builds safe on
      yours,

Rock-like; though the winds and waves howl, its foundation
      still endures:
By a man's will—"See, I hold thee: mine thou art, and mine
      shalt be."
By a woman's patience—"Sooner doubt I my own soul than
      thee."

So, Heaven mend us! we'll together once again take counsel
      sweet;
Though this hand of mine drops empty, that blank wall my
      blank eyes meet:
Life may flow on: men be faithless,—ay, forsooth, and women
      too!
ONE is true; and as He liveth, I believe in truth—and *you.*

ONE SUMMER MORNING.

T is but a little while ago:
    The elm-leaves have scarcely begun to drop
      away;
The sunbeams strike the elm-trunk just where they
      struck that day—
    Yet all seems to have happened long ago.

    And the year rolls round, slow, slow:
Autumn will fade to winter and winter melt in spring,
New life return again to every living thing.
    Soon, this will have happened long ago.

    The bonnie wee flowers will blow;
The trees will re-clothe themselves, the birds sing out
      amain,—
But never, never, never will the world look again
    As it looked before this happened—long ago!

MY LOVE ANNIE.

OFT of voice and light of hand
 As the fairest in the land—
 Who can rightly understand
  My love Annie?

Simple in her thoughts and ways,
True in every word she says,—
 Who shall even dare to praise
  My love Annie?

Midst a naughty world and rude
Never in ungentle mood;
Never tired of being good—
  My love Annie.

Hundreds of the wise and great
Might o'erlook her meek estate;
But on her good angels wait,
  My love Annie.

Many or few the loves that may
Shine upon her silent way,—
God will love her night and day,
  My love Annie.

SUMMER GONE.

MALL wren, mute pecking at the last red plum
  Or twittering idly at the yellow boughs
  Fruit-emptied, over thy forsaken house,—
Birdie, that seems to come
Telling, we too have spent our little store,
Our summer 's o'er;

Poor robin, driven in by rain-storms wild
    To lie submissive under household hands
    With beating heart that no love understands,
And scarèd eye, like a child
Who only knows that he is all alone
And summer's gone;

Pale leaves, sent flying wide, a frightened flock
    On which the wolfish wind bursts out, and tears
    Those tender forms that lived in summer airs
Till, taken at this shock,
They, like weak hearts when sudden grief sweeps by,
Whirl, drop, and die :—

All these things, earthy, of the earth—do tell
    This earth's perpetual story ; we belong
    Unto another country, and our song
Shall be no mortal knell ;
Though all the year's tale, as *our* years run fast
Mourns, "summer's past."

O love immortal, O perpetual youth,
    Whether in budding nooks it sits and sings
    As hundred poets in a hundred springs,
Or, slaking passion's drouth,
In wine-press of affliction, ever goes
Heavenward, through woes :

O youth immortal —O undying love !
    With these by winter fireside we'll sit down
    Wearing our snows of honor like a crown ;
And sing as in a grove,
Where the full nests ring out with happy cheer,
" Summer is here."

Roll round, strange years ; swift seasons, come and go;
    Ye leave upon us but an outward sign ;
    Ye cannot touch the inward and divine,
Which God alone does know ;

There sealed till summers, winters, all shall cease
In His deep peace.

Therefore uprouse ye winds and howl your will;
    Beat, beat, ye sobbing rains on pane and door;
    Enter, slow-footed age, and thou, obscure,
Grand Angel—not of ill;
Healer of every wound, where'er thou come,
Glad, we'll go home.

THE VOICE CALLING.

IN the hush of April weather,
    With the bees in budding heather,
    And the white clouds floating, floating,
        and the sunshine falling broad
   While my children down the hill
   Run and leap, and I sit still,—
Through the silence, through the silence art Thou call-
      ing, O my God?

    Through my husband's voice that prayeth,
    Though he knows not what he sayeth,
Is it Thou who in Thy Holy Word hast solemn words
      for me?
    And when he clasps me fast,
    And smiles fondly o'er the past,
And talks, hopeful, of the future—Lord, do I hear
      only Thee?

    Not in terror nor in thunder
    Comes Thy voice, although it sunder
Flesh from spirit, soul from body, human bliss from
      human pain:
    All the work that was to do,
    All the joys so sweet and new
Which Thou shewed'st me in a vision—Moses-like—
      and hid'st again.

From this Pisgah, lying humbled,
The long desert where I stumbled,
And the fair plains I shall never reach, look equal,
    clear and far:
On this mountain-top of ease
Thou wilt bury me in peace;
While my tribes march onward, onward, unto Canaan
    and war.

In my boy's loud laughter ringing,
In the sigh more soft than singing
Of my baby girl that nestles up unto this mortal
    breast,
After every voice most dear
Comes a whisper—" Rest not here."
And the rest Thou art preparing, is it best, Lord, is
    it best?

" Lord, a little, little longer! "
Sobs the earth-love, growing stronger:
He will miss me, and go mourning through his sol-
    itary days.
And heaven were scarcely heaven
If these lambs which Thou hast given
Were to slip out of our keeping and be lost in the
    world's ways.

Lord, it is not fear of dying
Nor an impious denying
Of Thy will, which forevermore on earth, in heaven,
    be done:
But the love that desperate clings
Unto these my precious things
In the beauty of the daylight, and the glory of the
    sun.

.Ah, Thou still art calling, calling,
With a soft voice unappalling:

And it vibrates in far circles through the everlasting
      years ;
  When Thou knockest, even so !
  I will arise and go.—
What, my little ones, more violets?—Nay, be patient
      —mother hears.

———

THE WREN'S NEST.

TOOK the wren's nest ;—
    Heaven forgive me !
    Its merry architects so small
Had scarcely finished their wee hall,
That, empty still, and neat and fair,
Hung idly in the summer air.
The mossy walls, the dainty door,
Where Love should enter and explore,
And Love sit carrolling outside,
And Love within chirp multiplied ;—
    I took the wren's nest ;—
    Heaven forgive me !

How many hours of happy pains
Through early frosts and April rains,
How many songs at eve and morn
O'er springing grass and greening corn,
What labors hard through sun and shade
Before the pretty house was made !
One little minute, only one,
And she 'll fly back, and find it—gone !
    I took the wren's nest :
    Bird, forgive me !

Thou and thy mate, sans let, sans fear,
Ye have before you all the year,
And every wood holds nooks for you,

In which to sing and build and woo;
One piteous cry of birdish pain—
And ye 'll begin your life again,
Forgetting quite the lost, lost home
In many a busy home to come.—
But I ?—Your wee house keep I must
Until it crumble into dust.
　　　I took the wren's nest:
　　　God forgive me !

A CHRISTMAS CAROL.

TUNE—"God rest ye, merry gentlemen."

OD rest ye, merry gentlemen: let nothing you dismay,
　　For Jesus Christ, our Saviour, was born on Christmas-
　　　　day.
The dawn rose red o'er Bethlehem, the stars shone
　　through the gray,
When Jesus Christ, our Saviour, was born on Christmas-
　　day.

God rest ye, little children; let nothing you affright,
For Jesus Christ, your Saviour, was born this happy
　　　　night ;
Along the hills of Galilee the white flocks sleeping lay,
When Christ, the Child of Nazareth, was born on Christ-
　　mas-day.

God rest ye, all good Christians ; upon this blessed morn
The Lord of all good Christians was of a woman born :
Now all your sorrows He doth heal, your sins He takes
　　　· away ;
For Jesus Christ, our Saviour was born on Christmas-day.

THE MOTHER'S VISITS.

From the French.

LONG years ago she visited my chamber,
    Steps soft and slow, a taper in her hand;
    Her fond kiss she laid upon my eyelids,
  Fair as an angel from the unknown land:
Mother, mother, is it thou I see?
Mother, mother, watching over me.

And yesternight I saw her cross my chamber,
    Soundless as light, a palm-branch in her hand;
    Her mild eyes she bent upon my anguish,
    Calm as an angel from the blessed land;
Mother, mother, is it thou I see?
Mother, mother, art thou come for me?

A GERMAN STUDENT'S FUNERAL HYMN.

"Thou shalt call, and I will answer Thee: Thou wilt have a desire to the work of Thine hands."

WITH steady march across the daisy meadow,
    And by the churchyard wall we go;
    But leave behind, beneath the linden shadow,
  One, who no more will rise and go:
Farewell, our brother, here sleeping in dust,
Till thou shalt wake again, wake with the just.

Along the street where neighbor nods to neighbor,
    Along the busy street we throng,
Once more to laugh, to live and love and labor,—
    But he will be remembered long:

Sleep well, our brother, though sleeping in dust;
Shalt thou not rise again—rise with the just?

Farewell, true heart and kindly hand, left lying
   Where wave the linden branches calm;
'Tis his to live, and ours to wait for dying,
   We win, while he has won, the palm;
Farewell, our brother! But one day, we trust,
Call—he will answer Thee, God of the just.

WESTWARD HO!

WE should not sit us down and sigh,
   My girl, whose brow undimmed appears,
   Whose steadfast eyes look royally
Backwards and forwards o'er the years—

The long, long years of conquered time,
   The possible years unwon, that slope
Before us in the pale sublime
   Of lives that have more faith than hope.

We dare not sit us down and dream
   Fond dreams, as idle children do:
My forehead owns too many a seam,
   And tears have worn their channels through

Your poor thin cheeks, which now I take
   'Twixt my two hands, caressing. Dear,
A little sunshine for my sake!
   Although we're far on in the year.

Though all our violets long are dead,
   The primrose lost from fields we knew,
Who knows what harvests may be spread
   For reapers brave like me and you?

Who knows what bright October suns
  May light up distant valleys mild,
Where as our pathway downward runs
  We see Joy meet us like a child

Who, sudden, by the roadside stands,
  To kiss the travellers' weary brows,
And lead them through the twilight lands
  Safely unto their Father's house.

So, we'll not dream, nor look back, dear!
  But march right on, content and bold,
To where our life sets, heavenly clear,
  Westward, behind the hills of gold.

OUR FATHER'S BUSINESS:

HOLMAN HUNT'S PICTURE OF "CHRIST IN THE TEMPLE."

 CHRIST-CHILD, Everlasting, Holy One,
Sufferer of all the sorrow of this world,
Redeemer of the sin of all this world,
Who by Thy death brought'st life into this world,—
O Christ, hear us!

This, this is *Thou.*   No idle painter's dream
Of aureoled, imaginary Christ,
Laden with attributes that make not God;
But Jesus, son of Mary; lowly, wise,
Obedient, subject unto parents, mild,
Meek—as the meek that shall inherit earth,
Pure—as the pure in heart that shall see God.

O infinitely human, yet divine!
Half clinging childlike to the mother found,
Yet half repelling—as the soft eyes say,
"How is it that ye sought me?   Wist ye not
That I must be about my Father's business?"
As in the Temple's splendors mystical,
Earth's wisdom hearkening to the all-wise One,
Earth's closest love clasping the all-loving One,
He sees far off the vision of the cross,
The Christ-like glory and the Christ-like doom.

Messiah!   Elder Brother, Priest and King,
The Son of God, and yet the woman's seed;
Enterer within the veil; Victor of death,
And made to us first fruits of them that sleep;

Saviour and Intercessor, Judge and Lord,—
All that we know of Thee, or knowing not
Love only, waiting till the perfect time
When we shall know even as we are known—
O Thou Child Jesus, Thou dost seem to say
By the soft silence of these heavenly eyes
(That rose out of the depths of nothingness
Upon this limner's reverent soul and hand)
We too should be about our Father's business—
O Christ, hear us!

Have mercy on us, Jesus Christ, our Lord!
The cross Thou borest still is hard to bear;
And awful even to humblest follower
The little that Thou givest each to do
Of this Thy Father's business; whether it be
Temptation by the devil of the flesh,
Or long-linked years of lingering toil obscure,
Uncomforted, save by the solemn rests
On mountain-tops of solitary prayer;
Oft ending in the supreme sacrifice,
The putting off all garments of delight,
And taking sorrow's kingly crown of thorn,
In crucifixion of all self to Thee,
Who offeredst up Thyself for all the world.
O Christ, hear us!

Our Father's business:—unto us, as Thee,
The whole which this earth-life, this hand-breadth span
Out of our everlasting life that lies
Hidden with Thee in God, can ask or need.
Outweighing all that heap of petty woes—
To us a measure huge—which angels blow
Out of the balance of our total lot,
As zephyrs blow the winged dust away.

O Thou who wert the Child of Nazareth,
Make us see only this, and only Thee,

Who camest but to do thy Father's will,
And didst delight to do it.　Take Thou then
Our bitterness of loss,—aspirings vain,
And anguishes of unfulfilled desire,
Our joys imperfect, our sublimed despairs,
Our hopes, our dreams, our wills, our loves, our all,
And cast them into the great crucible
In which the whole earth, slowly purified,
Runs molten, and shall run—the Will of God.
O Christ, hear us !

AN AUTUMN PSALM FOR 1860.

In Largo Bay.

"He that goeth forth weeping, bearing precious seed, shall doubtless
come again rejoicing, bringing his sheaves with him."

NO shadow o'er the silver sea,
　　That as in slumber heaves,
　　No cloud on the September sky,
　　No blight on any leaves,
As the reaper comes rejoicing,
　　Bringing in his sheaves.

Long, long and late the spring delayed,
　　And summer, dank with rain,
Hung trembling o'er her sunless fruit,
　　And her unripened grain ;
And, like a weary, hopeless life,
　　Sobbed herself out in pain.

So the year laid her child to sleep,
　　Her beauty half expressed ;
Then slowly, slowly cleared the skies,

And smoothed the seas to rest,
And raised the fields of yellowing corn
   O'er Summer's buried breast;

Till Autumn counterfeited Spring
   With such a flush of flowers,
His fiery-tinctured garlands more
   Than mocked the April bowers,
And airs as sweet as airs of June
   Brought on the twilight hours.

O holy twilight, tender, calm!
   O star above the sea!
O golden harvest, gathered in
   With late solemnity,
And thankful joy for gifts nigh lost
   Which yet so plenteous be;—

Although the rain-cloud wraps the hill,
   And sudden swoop the leaves,
And the year nears his sacred end,
   No eye weeps—no heart grieves:
For the reaper came rejoicing,
   Bringing in his sheaves.

IN THE JUNE TWILIGHT.

Suggested by Noel Paton's Picture of "The Silver Cord Loosed."

N the June twilight, in the soft gray twilight,
   The yellow sun-glow trembling through the rainy
      eve,
As my love lay quiet, came the solemn fiat,
   "All these things forever—*forever*—thou must leave."

My love she sank down quivering, like a pine in tempest shiver-
   ing—

"I have had so little happiness as yet beneath the sun :
I have called the shadow sunshine, and the merest frosty moon
  shine
 I have, weeping, blessed the Lord for, as if daylight had be_
  gun ;

" Till He sent a sudden angel, with a glorious sweet evangel,
 Who turned all my tears to pearl-gems, and crowned *me*—so
  little worth ;
Me !—and through the rainy even changed my poor earth into
  heaven,
 Or, by wondrous revelation, brought the heavens down to
  earth.

"O the strangeness of the feeling !—O the infinite revealing—
 To think how God must love me to have made me so content !
Though I would have served Him humbly, and patiently, and
  dumbly,
 Without any angel standing in the pathway that I went.' "

In the June twilight—in the lessening twilight—
 My love cried from my bosom an exceeding bitter cry :
"Lord, wait a little longer, until my soul is stronger,—
 O, wait till Thou hast taught me to be content to die."

Then the tender face, all woman, took a glory superhuman,
 And she seemed to watch for something, or see some I could
  not see :
From my arms she rose full statured, all transfigured, queenly
  featured—
 "As Thy will is done in heaven, so on earth still let it be." –

   * * * * * * *

I go lonely, I go lonely, and I feel that earth is only
 The vestibule of palaces whose courts we never win :
Yet I see my palace shining, where my love sits, amaranths
  twining,
 And I know the gates stand open, and I shall enter in.

A MAN'S WOOING.

YOU said, last night, you did not think
 In all the world of men
Was one true lover—true alike
 In deed and word and pen :—

One knightly lover, constant as
 The old knights, who sleep sound :
Some women said you, there might be—
 Not one man faithful found :

Not one man, resolute to win,
 Or, winning, firm to hold
The woman, among women—sought
 With steadfast love and bold.

Not one whose noble life and pure
 Had power so to control
To tender humblest loyalty
 Her free, but reverent soul,

That she beside him took her place
 Both sovereign and slave ;
In faith unfettered, homage true,
 Each claiming what each gave.

And then you dropped your eyelids white,
 And stood in maiden bloom
Proud, calm :—unloving and unloved
 Descending to the tomb.

I let you speak and ne'er replied ;
 I watched you for a space,
Until that passionate glow, like youth,
 Had faded from your face.

No anger showed I—nor complaint :
  My heart's beats shook no breath,
Although I knew that I had found
  Her, who brings life or death ;

The woman, true as life or death ;
  The love, strong as these twain,
Against which seas of mortal fate
  Beat harmlessly in vain.

" Not one true man : " I hear it still,
  Your voice's clear cold sound,
Upholding all your constant swains
  And good knights underground.

" Not one true lover ; "—Woman, turn ;
  I love you.   Words are small ;
'T is life speaks plain : In twenty years
  Perhaps you may know all.

I seek you.   You alone I seek :
  All other women, fair,
Or wise, or good, may go their way,
  Without my thought or care.

But you I follow day by day,
  And night by night I keep
My heart's chaste mansion lighted, where
  Your image lies asleep.

Asleep ! If e'er to wake, He knows
  Who Eve to Adam brought,
As you to me : the embodiment
  Of boyhood's dear sweet thought,

And youth's fond dream, and manhood's hope,
  That still half hopeless shone ;
Till every rootless vain ideal
  Commingled into one,—

You; who are so diverse from me,
　And yet as much my own
As this my soul, which, formed apart,
　Dwells in its bodily throne;—

Or rather, for *that* perishes,
　As these our two lives are
So strangely, marvellously drawn
　Together from afar;

Till week by week and month by month
　We closer seem to grow,
As two hill streams, flushed with rich rain,
　Each into the other flow.

I swear no oaths, I tell no lies,
　Nor boast I never knew
A love-dream—we all dream in youth—
　But waking, I found *you,*

The real woman, whose first touch
　Aroused to highest life
My real manhood.　Crown it then,
　Good angel, friend, love, wife!

Imperfect as I am, and you,
　Perchance, not all you seem,
We two together shall bind up
　Our past's bright, broken dream.

We two together shall dare look
　Upon the years to come,
As travelers, met in far countrie,
　Together look towards home.

Come home!　The old tales were not false,
　Yet the new faith is true;
Those saintly souls who made men knights,
　Were women such as you.

For the great love that teaches love
　　Deceived not, ne'er deceives:
And she who most believes in man
　　Makes him what she believes.

Come! If you come not, I can wait;
　　My faith, like life, is long;
My will—not little; my hope much:
　　The patient are the strong.

Yet come, ah come! The years run fa
　　And hearths grow swiftly cold—
Hearts too: but while blood beats in mine
　　It holds you and will hold.

And so before you it lies bare,—
　　Take it or let it lie,
It is an honest heart; and yours
　　To all eternity.

———

THE CATHEDRAL TOMBS.

"Post tempestatem tranquillitas."
Epitaph in Ely Cathedral.

HEY lie, with upraised hands, and feet
　　Stretched like dead feet that walk no more,
And stony masks oft human sweet,
　　As if the olden look each wore,
Familiar curves of lip and eye,
Were copied by some fond memory.

All waiting: the new-coffined dead,
　　The handful of mere dust that lies
Sarcophagused in stone and lead
　　Under the weight of centuries:
Knight, cardinal, bishop, abbess mild,
With last week's buried year-old child.

After the tempest cometh peace,
  After long travail sweet repose;
These folded palms, these feet that cease
  From any motion, are but shows
Of—what? *What* rest? *How* rest they? *Where*?
  The generations naught declare.

Dark grave, unto whose brink we come,
  Drawn nearer by all nights and days;
Each after each, thy solemn gloom
  We pierce with momentary gaze,
Then go, unwilling or content,
The way that all our fathers went.

Is there no voice or guiding hand
  Arising from the awful void,
To say, "Fear not the silent land;"
  Would He make aught to be destroyed?
Would He? or can He? What know we
Of Him who is Infinity?

Strong Love, which taught us human love,
  Helped us to follow through all spheres
Some soul that did sweet dead lips move,
  Lived in dear eyes in smiles and tears,
Love—once so near our flesh allied,
That "Jesus wept" when Lazarus died;—

Eagle-eyed Faith that can see God,
  In worlds without and heart within;
In sorrow by the smart o' the rod,
  In guilt by the anguish of the sin:
In everything pure, holy, fair,
God saying to man's soul, "I am there;"—

These only, twin-archangels, stand
  Above the abyss of common doom,
These only stretch the tender hand
  To us descending to the tomb,

Thus making it a bed of rest,
With spices and with odors drest.

So, like one weary and worn, who sinks
  To sleep beneath long faithful eyes,
Who asks no word of love, but drinks
  The silence which is paradise—
We only cry—"Keep tender ward,
And give us good rest, O good Lord!"

————

WHEN GREEN LEAVES COME AGAIN.

SONG.

HEN green leaves come again, my love,
  —When green leaves come again,—
  Why put on such a cloudy face,
When green leaves come again?

"Ah, this spring will be like the last,
  Of promise false and vain;
And summer die in winter's arms
  Ere green leaves come again.

"So slip the seasons—and our lives:
  'T is idle to complain:
But yet I sigh, I scarce know why,
  When green leaves come again."

Nay, lift up thankful eyes, my sweet!
  Count equal, loss and gain:
Because, as long as the world lasts,
  Green leaves *will* come again.

For, sure as earth lives under snows,
  And Love lives under pain,
'T is good to sing with everything,
  "When green leaves come again."

THE FIRST WAITS.

A MEDITATION FOR ALL.

SO, Christmas is here again!—
    While the house sleeps, quiet as death,
    'Neath the midnight moon comes the Waits'
        shrill tune,
And we listen and hold our breath.

The Christmas that never was—
    On this foggy November air,
With clear pale gleam, like the ghost of a dream,
    It is painted everywhere.

The Christmas that might have been—
    It is borne in the far-off sound,
Down the empty street, with the tread of feet
    That lie silent underground.

The Christmas that yet may be—
    Like the Bethlehem star, leads kind :
Yet our life slips past, hour by hour, fast, fast,
    Few before—and many behind.

The Christmas we have and hold,
    With a tremulous tender strain,
Half joy, half fears—Be the psalm of the years,
    " Grief passes, blessings remain ! "

The Christmas that sure will come,
    Let us think of, at fireside fair ;—
When church bells sound o'er one small green mound,
    Which the neighbors pass to prayer.

The Christmas that God will give,—
    Long after all these are o'er,
When is day nor night, for the LAMB is our Light,
    And we live forevermore.

DAY BY DAY.

VERY day has its dawn,
    Its soft and silent eve,
      Its noontide hours of bliss or bale;—
Why should we grieve?

Why do we heap huge mounds of years
    Before us and behind,
And scorn the little days that pass
    Like angels on the wind?

Each turning round a small sweet face
    As beautiful as near;
Because it is so small a face
    We will not see it clear:

We will not clasp it as it flies,
    And kiss its lips and brow:
We will not bathe our wearied souls
    In its delicious Now.

And so it turns from us, and goes
    Away in sad disdain :
Though we would give our lives for it,
    It never comes again.

Yet, every day has its dawn,
    Its noontide and its eve:
Live while we live, giving God thanks—
    He will not let us grieve.

ONLY A WOMAN.

"She loves with love that cannot tire:
And if, ah, woe! she loves alone,
Through passionate duty love flames higher,
As grass grows taller round a stone."

COVENTRY PATMORE.

O, the truth's out. I'll grasp it like a snake,—
It will not slay me. My heart shall not break
Awhile, if only for the children's sake.

For his too, somewhat. Let him stand unblamed;
None say, he gave me less than honor claimed,
Except—one trifle scarcely worth being named—

The *heart*. That's gone. The corrupt dead might be
As easily raised up, breathing—fair to see,
As he could bring his whole heart back to me.

I never sought him in coquettish sport,
Or courted him as silly maidens court,
And wonder when the longed-for prize falls short.

I only loved him—any woman would:
But shut my love up till he came and sued,
Then poured it o'er his dry life like a flood.

I was so happy I could make him blest!
So happy that I was his first and best,
As he mine—when he took me to his breast.

Ah me! if only then he had been true!
If for one little year, a month or two,
He had given me love for love, as was my due!

Or had he told me, ere the deed was done,
He only raised me to his heart's dear throne—
Poor substitute—because the queen was gone!

O, had he whispered, when his sweetest kiss
Was warm upon my mouth in fancied bliss,
He had kissed another woman even as this,—

It were less bitter!   Sometimes I could weep
To be thus cheated, like a child asleep:—
Were not my anguish far too dry and deep.

So I built my house upon another's ground;
Mocked with a heart just caught at the rebound—
A cankered thing that looked so firm and sound.

And when that heart grew colder—colder still,
I, ignorant, tried all duties to fulfil,
Blaming my foolish pain, exacting will,

All—anything but him.   It was to be:
The full draught others drink up carelessly
Was made this bitter Tantalus-cup for me.

I say again—he gives me all I claimed,
I and my children never shall be shamed:
He is a just man—he will live unblamed.

Only—O God, O God, to cry for bread,
And get a stone!   Daily to lay my head
Upon a bosom where the old love's dead!

Dead?—Fool!   It never lived.   It only stirred
Galvanic, like an hour-cold corpse.   None heard:
So let me bury it without a word.

He'll keep that other woman from my sight.
I know not if her face be foul or bright;
I only know that it was his delight—

As his was mine: I only know he stands
Pale, at the touch of their long-severed hands,
Then to a flickering smile his lips commands,

Lest I should grieve, or jealous anger show.
He need not.   When the ship's gone down, I trow,
We little reck whatever wind may blow.

And so my silent moan begins and ends.
No world's laugh or world's taunt, no pity of friends
Or sneer of foes with this my torment blends.

None knows—none heeds.   I have a little pride;
Enough to stand up, wife-like, by his side,
With the same smile as when I was a bride.

And I shall take his children to my arms;
They will not miss these fading, worthless charms;
Their kiss—ah! unlike his—all pain disarms.

And haply, as the solemn years go by,
He will think sometimes with regretful sigh,
The other woman was less true than I.

A "MERCENARY" MARRIAGE.

SHE moves as light across the grass
      As moves my shadow large and tall;
    And like my shadow, close yet free,
The thought of her aye follows me,
      My little maid of Moreton Hall.

No matter how or where we loved,
      Or when we'll wed, or what befall;
I only feel she's mine at last,
I only know I'll hold her fast,
      Though to dust crumbles Moreton Hall.

Her pedigree—good sooth, 't is long!
      Her grim sires stare from every wall;
And centuries of ancestral grace
Revive in her sweet girlish face,
      As meek she glides through Moreton Hall.

Whilst I have—nothing ; save, perhaps,
  Some worthless heaps of idle gold,
And a true heart—the which her eye
Through glittering dross spied, womanly,
  Therefore they say *her* heart was sold!

I laugh—she laughs—the hills and vales
  Laugh as we ride 'neath chestnuts tall,
Or start the deer that silent graze,
And look up, large-eyed, with soft gaze,
  At the fair maid of Moreton Hall ;—

We let the neighbors talk their fill,
  For life is sweet, and love is strong,
And two, close knit in marriage ties,
The whole world's shams may well despise—
  Its folly, madness, shame, and wrong.

We are not proud, with a fool's pride,
  Nor cowards—to be held in thrall
By pelf or lineage, rank or lands :—
One honest heart, two honest hands,
  Are worth far more than Moreton Hall.

Therefore, we laugh to scorn—we two—
The bars that weaker souls appal :
I take her hand and hold it fast—
Knowing she'll love me to the last—
  My dearest maid of Moreton Hall.

OVER THE HILLSIDE.

Reichip. 1864.

FAREWELL.   In dimmer distance
  I watch your figures glide,
Across the sunny moorland,
  The brown hillside ;

Each momently up rising
  Large, dark against the sky,
Then—in the vacant moorland,
  Alone sit I.

Within the unknown country
  Where some lost footsteps pass,
What beauty decks the heavens
  And clothes the grass !

Over the mountain shoulder
  What glories may unfold !
Though I see but the mountain
  Bleak, bare and cold,—

And the pale road, slow winding
  To where, each after each,
They slipped away—ah, whither ?
  I cannot reach.

And if I call, what answers ?
  Only 'twixt earth and sky
Like wail of parting spirit,
  The curlew's cry.

*   *   *

Yet, sunny is the moorland,
  . And soft the pleasant air,
And little flowers like blessings,
  Grow everywhere.

While, over all, the mountain
  Stands sombre, calm, and still,
Immutable and steadfast,
  As the One Will.

Which, done on earth, in heaven
  Eternally confessed
By men and saints and angels,
  Be ever blest !

Under its infinite shadow
  (Safer than light of ours!)
I'll sit me down a little,
  And gather flowers.

Then I will rise and follow
  After the setting day,
Without one wish to linger,—
  The appointed way.

THE UNFINISHED BOOK.

TAKE it, reader, idly passing,
  This, like other idle lines;
  Take it, critic, great at classing
Subtle genius and its signs:
But, O reader, be thou dumb;
Critic, let no sharp wit come;
For the hand that wrote and blurred
Will not write another word;
And the soul you scorn or prize,-
Now than angels is more wise.

Take it, heart of man or woman,
  This unfinished broken strain,
Whether it be poor and common
  Or the noblest work of brain;
Let that good heart only sit
Now in judgment over it
Tenderly, as we would read,—
Any one, of any creed,
Any churchyard passing by,—
"Sacred to the Memory."

Wholly sacred: even as lingers
  Final word, or last look cast,

Or last clasp of life-warm fingers,
　Which we knew not was the last.
Or, as we apart do lay,
　The day after funeral-day,
Their dear relies, great and small,
Who need nothing—yet win all :
All the best we had and have,
Buried in one silent grave.

All our highest aspirations,
　And our closest love of loves ;
Our most secret resignations,
　Our best work that man approves,
Yet which jealously we keep,
In our mute heart's deepest deep.
So of this poor broken song
Let no echoes here prolong :
For the singer's voice is known
In the heaven of heavens alone.

TWILIGHT IN THE NORTH.

1864.

" Until the day break and the shadows flee away."

 THE long northern twilight between the day and the
　　　night,
When the heat and the weariness of the world are
　　　ended quite :
When the hills grow dim as dreams, and the crystal river seems
Like that River of Life from out the Throne where the blessèd
　　　walk in white.

O the weird northern twilight, which is neither night nor day,
When the amber wake of the long-set sun still marks his west-
　　　ern way:

And but one great golden star in the deep blue east afar
Warns of sleep, and dark, and midnight—of oblivion and de-
cay.

O the calm northern twilight, when labor is all done,
And the birds in drowsy twitter have dropped silent one by
one :
And nothing stirs or sighs in mountains, waters, skies,—
Earth sleeps—but her heart waketh, till the rising of the sun.

O the sweet, sweet twilight, just before the time of rest,
When the black clouds are driven away, and the stormy winds
suppressed :
And the dead day smiles so bright, filling earth and heaven with
light,—
You would think 't was dawn come back again—but the light is
in the west.

O the grand solemn twilight, spreading peace from pole to
pole !—
Ere the rains sweeps o'er the hillsides, and the waters rise and
roll,
In the lull and the calm, come, O angel with the palm—
In the still northern twilight, Azrael, take my soul.

CATHAIR FHARGUS.

(FERGUS'S SEAT.)

A mountain in the Island of Arran, the summit of which resembles a
gigantic human profile.

WITH face turned upward to the changeful sky,
I, Fergus, lie, supine in frozen rest ;
The maiden morning clouds slip rosily
Unclasped, unclasping, down my granite breast
The lightning strikes my brow and passes by.

There 's nothing new beneath the sun, I wot :
    I, "Fergus" called,—the great pre-Adamite,
Who for my mortal body blindly sought
    Rash immortality, and on this height
Stone-bound, forever am and yet am not,—

There 's nothing new beneath the sun, I say.
    Ye pigmies of a later race, who come
And play out your brief generation 's play
    Below me, know, I too spent my life's sum,
And revelled through my short tumultuous day.

O, what is man that he should mouth so grand
    Through his poor thousand as his seventy years ?
Whether as king I ruled a trembling land,
    Or swayed by tongue or pen my meaner peers,
Or earth's whole learning once did understand,—

What matter ?   The star-angels know it all.
    They who came sweeping through the silen night
And stood before me, yet did not appal :
    Till, fighting 'gainst me in their courses bright,*
Celestial smote terrestrial.—Hence my fall.

Hence, Heaven cursed me with a granted prayer ;
    Made my hill-seat eternal : bade me keep
My pageant of majestic lone despair,
    While one by one into the infinite deep
Sank kindred, realm, throne, world : yet I lay there.

There still I lie.   Where are my glories fled ?
    My wisdom that I boasted as divine ?
My grand primeval women fair, who shed
    Their whole life's joy to crown one hour of mine,
And lived to curse the love they coveted ?

Gone—gone.   Uncounted æons have rolled by,
    And still my ghost sits by its corpse of stone,

---

* "The stars in their courses fought against Sisera."

And still the blue smile of the new-formed sky
 Finds me unchanged. Slow centuries crawling on
Bring myriads happy death :—I cannot die.

My stone shape mocks the dead man's peaceful face,
 . And straightened arm that will not labor more ;
And yet I yearn for a mean six-foot space
 To moulder in, with daisies growing o'er,
Rather than this unearthly resting-place ;—

Where pinnacled, my silent effigy
 Against the sunset rising clear and cold,
Startles the musing stranger sailing by,
 And calls up thoughts that never can be told
Of life, and death, and immortality.

While I ?—I watch this after world that creeps
 Nearer and nearer to the feet of God :
Ay, though it labors, struggles, sins, and weeps,
 Yet, love-drawn, follows ever Him who trod
Through dim Gethsemane to Calvary's steeps. .

O glorious shame ! O royal servitude !
 High lowliness, and ignorance all-wise !
Pure life with death, and death with life imbued ;—
 My centuried splendors crumble 'neath Thine eyes,
Thou Holy One who died upon the Rood !

Therefore, face upward to the Christian heaven,
 I, Fergus, lie : expectant, humble, calm ;
Dumb emblem of the faith to me not given ;
 The clouds drop chrism, the stars their midnight
   psalm
Chant over one, who passed away unshriven.

" *I am the Resurrection and the Life.*"
 So from yon mountain graveyard cries the dust
Of child to parent, husband unto wife,
 Consoling, and believing in the Just :—
Christ lives, though all the universe died in strife.

Therefore my granite lips forever pray,
  "O rains, wash out my sin of self abhorred :
O sun, melt thou my heart of stone away,
  Out of Thy plenteous mercy save me, Lord."
Aud thus I wait till Resurrection-day.

A TRUE HERO.

James Braidwood, of the London Fire Brigade : Died June 22, 1861.

OT at the battle front,—writ of in story ;
  Not on the blazing wreck steering to glory ;

Not while in martyr-pangs soul and flesh sever,
Died he—this Hero new ; hero forever.

No pomp poetic crowned, no forms enchained him,
No friends applauding watched, no foes arraigned him :

Death found him there, without grandeur or beauty,
Only an honest man doing his duty :

Just a God-fearing man, simple and lowly,
Constant at kirk and hearth, kindly as holy :

Death found—and touched him with finger in flying :—
Lo! he rose up complete—hero undying.

Now, all men mourn for him, lovingly raise him
Up from his life obscure, chronicle, praise him ;

Tell his last act, done midst peril appalling,
And the last word of cheer from his lips falling ;

Follow in multitudes to his grave's portal ;
Leave him there, buried in honor immortal.

So many a Hero walks unseen beside us,
Till comes the supreme stroke sent to divide us,

Then the LORD calls His own,—like this man, even,
Carried, Elijah-like, fire-winged, to heaven.

———

AT THE SEASIDE.

SOLITARY shining sea
   That ripples in the sun,
  O gray and melancholy sea,
O'er which the shadows run;

O many-voiced and angry sea,
  Breaking with moan and strain,—
I, like a humble, chastened child,
  Come back to thee again;

And build child-castles and dig moats
  Upon the quiet sands,
And twist the cliff-convolvulus
  Once more, round idle hands;

And look across that ocean line,
  As o'er life's summer sea,
Where many a hope went sailing once,
  Full set, with canvas free.

Strange, strange to think how some of them
  Their silver sails have furled,
And some have whitely glided down
  Into the under world;

And some, dismasted, tossed and torn,
  Driven back to port once more,
Thankful to ride, with freight still safe,
  At anchor near the shore.

Stranger it is to lie at ease
  As now, with thoughts that fly

More light and wandering than sea-birds
　Between the waves and sky :

To play child's play with shells and weeds,
　And view the ocean grand
Dwindled to one small wave that whelms
　A baby-house of sand :

And not once look, or look by chance,
　With old dreams quite supprest,
Across that mystic wild sea-world
　Of infinite unrest.

O ever solitary sea,
　Of which we all have found
Somewhat to dream or say,—the type
　Of things without a bound—

Love, long as life, and strong as death ;
　Faith, humble as sublime ;
Eternity, whose large depths hold
　The wrecks of this small Time ;—

Unchanging, everlasting sea !
　To spirits soothed and calm
Thy restless moan of other years
　Becomes an endless psalm.

FISHERMEN—NOT OF GALILEE.

(After reading Renan's " Vie de Jésus.")

T HEY have toiled all the night, the long weary night,
　They have toiled all the night, Lord, and taken
　　nothing :—
The heavens are as brass, and all flesh seems as grass,
　Death strikes with horror and life with loathing.

Walk'st Thou by the waters, the dark silent waters,
  The fathomless waters that no line can plumb?
Art Thou Redeemer, or a mere schemer—
  Preaching a kingdom that cannot come?

Not a word say'st Thou: no wrath betray'st Thou:
  Scarcely delay'st Thou their errors to lull;
On the shore standing, mutely commanding,
    " Let down your nets!"—And they draw them up,
      —full!

⁂

Jesus, Redeemer,—Thou sole Redeemer!
  I, a poor dreamer, lay hold upon Thee:
Thy will pursuing, though no end viewing,
  But simply doing as Thou biddest me.

Though Thee I see not,—either light be not,
  Or Thou wilt free not the scales from mine eyes,
I ne'er gainsay Thee, but only obey Thee;
  Obedience is better than sacrifice.

Though on my prison gleams no open vision,
  Walking Elysian by Galilee's tide,
Unseen, I feel Thee, and death will reveal Thee
  I shall wake in Thy likeness, satisfied.

———

THE GOLDEN ISLAND: ARRAN FROM AYR.

DEEP set in distant seas it lies;
  The morning vapors float and fall,
  The noonday clouds above it rise,
Then drop as white as virgin's pall.

And sometimes, when that shroud uplifts,
　The far green fields show strange and fair:
Mute waterfalls in silver rifts
　Sparkle adown the hillside bare.

But ah! mists gather, more and more;
　And though the blue sky has no tears,
And the sea laughs with light all o'er,—
　The lovely Island disappears.

O vanished Island of the blest!
　O dream of all things pure and high!
Hid in the deep, as faithful breast
　Hides loves that have but seemed to die,—

Whether on seas dividing tossed,
　Or led through fertile lands the while,
Better lose all things than have lost
　The memory of the morning Isle!

For lo! when gloaming shadows glide,
　And all is calm in earth and air,
Above the heaving of the tide
　The lonely Island rises fair;

Its purple peaks shine, outlined grand
　And clear, as noble lives nigh done;
While stretches bright from land to land
　The broad sea-pathway to the sun.

He wraps it in his glory's blaze,
　He stoops to kiss its forehead cold;
And, all transfigured by his rays,
　It gleams—an Isle of molten gold.

The sun may set, the shades descend,
　Earth sleep—and yet while sleeping smile;
But it will live unto life's end—
　That vision of the Golden Isle.

FALLEN IN THE NIGHT!

IT dressed itself in green leaves all the summer long,
    Was full of chattering starlings, loud with throstles'
        song,
Children played beneath it, lovers sat and talked,
Solitary strollers looked up as they walked.
O, so fresh its branches! and its old trunk gray
Was so stately rooted, who forbode decay?
Even when winds had blown it yellow and almost bare,
Softly dropped its chestnuts through the misty air;
Still its few leaves rustled with a faint delight,
And their tender colors charmed the sense of sight,
Filled the soul with beauty, and the heart with peace,
Like sweet sounds departing—sweetest when they cease.

Pelting, undermining, loosening, came the rain;
Through its topmost branches roared the hurricane;
Oft it strained and shivered till the night wore past,
But in dusky daylight there the tree stood fast,
Though its birds had left it, and its leaves were dead,
And its blossoms faded, and its fruit all shed.

Ay, and when last sunset came a wanderer by,
Watched it as aforetime with a musing eye,
Still it wore its scant robes so pathetic gay,
Caught the sun's last glimmer, the new moon's first ray;
And majestic, patient, stood amidst its peers
Waiting for the spring-times of uncounted years.

But the worm was busy, and the days were run;
Of its hundred sunsets this was the last one:
So in quiet midnight, with no eye to see,
None to harm in falling, fell the noble tree!

Says the early laborer, starting at the sight
With a sleepy wonder, "Fallen in the night!"

O thou Tree, thou glory of His hand who made
Nothing ever vainly, thou hast Him obeyed!
Lived thy life, and perished when and how He willed;—
Be all lamentation and all murmurs stilled.
To our last hour live we—fruitful, brave, upright,
'T will be a good ending, "Fallen in the night!"

A LANCASHIRE DOXOLOGY.

" Some cotton has lately been imported into Farringdon, where the mills have been closed for a considerable time. The people, who were previously in the deepest distress, went out to meet the cotton; the women wept over the bales and kissed them, and finally sang the Doxology over them." *Spectator* of May 14, 1863.

RAISE God from whom all blessings flow."
Praise Him who sendeth joy and woe.
The Lord who takes,—the Lord who
gives,—
O praise Him, all that dies, and lives.

He opens and He shuts his hand,
But why, we cannot understand :
Pours and dries up his mercies' flood,
And yet is still All-perfect Good.

We fathom not the mighty plan,
The mystery of God and man ;
We women, when afflictions come,
We only suffer and are dumb.

And when, the tempest passing by,
He gleams out, sun-like, through our sky,
We look up, and through black clouds riven,
We recognize the smile of Heaven.

Ours is no wisdom of the wise,
We have no deep philosophies:
Childlike we take both kiss and rod,
For he who loveth knoweth God.

YEAR AFTER YEAR

A LOVE SONG.

YEAR after year the cowslips fill the meadow,
    Year after year the skylarks thrill the air,
    Year after year, in sunshine or in shadow,
Rolls the world round, love, and finds us as we were.

Year after year, as sure as birds' returning,
    Or field-flowers' blossoming above the wintry mould,
Year after year, in work, or mirth, or mourning,
    Love we with love's own youth, that never can grow old.

Sweetheart and ladye-love, queen of boyish passion,
    Strong hope of manhood, content of age begun;
Loved in a hundred ways, each in a different fashion,
    Yet loved supremely, solely, as we never love but one.

Dearest and bonniest! though blanched those curling tresses,
    Though loose clings the wedding-ring to that thin hand of
        thine,—
Brightest of all eyes the eye that love expresses!
    Sweetest of all lips the lips long since kissed mine!

So let the world go round with all its sighs and sinning,
    Its mad shout o'er fancied bliss, its howl o'er pleasures past:
That which it calls love's end to us was love's beginning:
    I clasp my arms about thy neck and love thee to the last.

"UNTIL HER DEATH."

I.

NTIL her death!" the words read strange yet real,
  Like things afar off suddenly brought near :—
  Will it be slow or speedy, full of fear,
Or calm as a spent day of peace ideal?

II.

Will her brown locks lie white on coffin pillow?
  Will these her eyes, that sometime were called sweet,
  Close, after years of dried-up tears, or meet
Death's dust in midst of weeping?   And that billow,—

III.

Her restless heart,—will it be stopped, still heaving?
  Or softly ebb 'neath age's placid breath?
  Will it be lonely, this mysterious death,
Fit close unto her solitary living,—

IV.

A turning of her face to the wall, nought spoken,
  Exchanging this world's light for heaven's;—or will
  She part in pain, from warm love to the chill
Unknown, pursued with cries of hearts half-broken?

V.

With fond lips felt through the blind mists of dying,
  And close arms clung to in the struggle vain;—
  Or, these all past, will death be wholly gain,
Unto her life's long question God's replying?

VI.

No more.   Within his hand, divine as tender,
  He holds the mystic measure of her days;

And be they few or many, His the praise, —
In life or death her Keeper and Defender.

VII.

Then, come He soon or late, she will not fear Him ;
Be her end lone or loveful, she'll not grieve ;
For He whom she believed in—doth believe—
Will call her from the dust, and she will hear Him.

THE LOST PIECE OF SILVER.

A PRAYER.

OLY Lord Jesus, Thou wilt search till Thou find
This lost piece of silver,—this treasure en-
shrined
In casket or bosom, once of such store ;
Now lying under the dust of Thy floor.

Gentle Lord Jesus, Thou wilt move through the room—
So empty—so desolate! and light up its gloom :
The lost piece of silver that no man can see,
Merciful Jesus! is beheld clear by Thee.

Defaced and degraded, trampled in the dust,
Its superscription Thou knowest still we trust ·
And Thou wilt uplift it and make it re-shine,
For it *was* silver—pure silver of Thine.

Loving Lord Jesus, Thou wilt come through the dark,
When men are all sleeping and no eye can mark.
Though " clean forgotten, like a dead man out of mind,"
This lost piece of silver Thou wilt search for—*and find.*

OUTWARD BOUND.

OUT upon the unknown deep,
  Where the unheard oceans sound,
  Where the unseen islands sleep,—
Outward bound.
Following towards the silent west
  O'er the horizon's curved rim,—
Or to islands of the blest,
  —He with me and I with him—
Outward bound.

Nothing but a speck we seem
  In the waste of waters round,
Floating, floating like a dream,—
  Ontward bound.
But within that tiny speck
  Two brave hearts with one accord
Past all tumult, grief, and wreck,
  Look up calm,—and praise the Lord,—
Outward bound.

A PICTURE—COVERED.

DEAD, dead, dead, dead! and half my life
  Is buried dumb with thee.
  No more I sing thee; 'twixt us twain
Sweeps the great soundless sea.

Thy place is vacant at the hearth,
  And through the garden wide
Thy little children shout and play—
  No mother at their side.

The boys will grow up into men,
 The girls to women fair,
And never know that sacred sight,
 A mother's silver hair.

And I—I go my daily ways,
 And seldom speak thy name
Who sitt'st among the angels;—Dear,
 Remember! All the same

I too remember: our child-dawn;
 Our girlhood bright and free:
Our busy noon of happy hope
 For the eve—which will not be.

And often when the world seems hard,
 And life grows sad and strange,
I sit alone and talk to thee
 As if there were no change:

Or ask thee of that Other Land
 On which in soft surprise
All suddenly, a year ago,
 Opened thy dear brown eyes,—

That aye were seeking—seeking! Now
 For ever they have found:
—*What?* Tell me!—April wind steals past,
 But on it comes no sound.

Ah, silent—silent: dead—dead—dead.
 Yet o'er that mystic sea
The unseen Hand which thee did guide
 Waits to be guiding me.

I too shall follow; where we know
 All things, and all things prove:
But oft I think that even there
 I shall not better love.

A DREAM-CHILD.

"All is nothing, and less than nothing. The children of
Alice call Bartrum father."
CHARLES LAMB'S *Dream-Children.*

ITTLE one, I lie i' the dark
With thy sweet lips pressed to mine;
My hot restless pulses meeting
Thy still heart's unnoticed beating,
In a calm divine.

On my breast thy dear hair floats;
Well its memoried hue I know!
And thine eyes, if thou wert raising,
They would answer to my gazing
Looks of long ago.

Fairy hand, that on my cheek
Falls, with touch as dove's wing soft,
I can feel its curves, resembling
One that like a young bird trembling
Lay in mine so oft.

Thou wilt spring up at my feet
Flower-like—beautiful and wild:
Gossips too on me bestowing
Flattery sweet, will say, thou'rt growing
Like thy father, child.

No, I would not have my face
Imaged, happy one! in thine;
I—who crushed out all my being
In one cup, and poured, clear-seeing,
My heart's blood like wine.

I have given thee a name,—
What name, none shall ever know:

When I say it, there comes thronging
A whole life-time's aim and longing,
    And a life-time's woe.

Ah—that name! I wake—I wake,
    And the light breaks, bleak and bare,—
Sweet one, never born, yet dying,
To my love all unreplying,
    Dream-child, melt to air!

Eyes no wife shall ever kiss,
    Arms no child shall ever fill,
Lift I up to heaven, beseeching
Him who sent this bitter teaching :—
    I will learn it still.

Not as we see, seeth God :
    Not as we love, loveth He :
When the tear-spent eyes are closing,
And the weary limbs reposing,—
    Lo—eternity !

THE FLYING CLOUD.

CLOUD, following sunwards through this evening sky,
    Take thou my soul upon thy folds, and fly
    Swifter than light, invisible as air,
Fly—where, ah where?

Stay—where my heart would stay, then melt and fall
In dews like tears—tears shed, unseen of all,
By some sad spirit which came wandering round
The garden's bound.

Wandering, yet never finding rest or calm ;
Wounded and faint, yet never asking balm :

Sick with dull fear that joy's fast-closèd gate
May ope too late.

Cloud, sailing westward tinged with sunset dye,
As if to mock me, who so helpless lie,
Ah cloud, my longing erred! for me were best
A deeper rest.

Then lift me with thee to those fields of light,
Till earth's fair meads appear no longer bright;
And angels meet us with their wings of fire
That never tire.

Then standing meekly at the golden door,
Filled where I hungered, rich where once so poor,
I may forget—ah, only, only pain—
Love will remain.

And often, sweeping down on wings unfurled
To bear heaven's messages about the world,
A happy spirit may come wandering round
The garden's bound:

Dropping—not tears but blessings;—holy-willed,
Fulfilling all things here left unfulfilled;
Since from the death-change, with fresh wings unworn,
Life sprang new-born.

SLEEP ON TILL DAY.

For a Highland tune—" Sleep on till day."

LEEP on till day, my love, sleep on till day!
No trouble assail thee, nor danger affray!—
But sleep on till day, my love, sleep on till day.
    Airs round thee trembling
    Love sighs resembling,

Linger a moment and vanish away—
Vanish till day, my love, vanish till day.

The pale stars set hourly in western sky gray;
The kind hours, they laugh as they hurry away;
They know 't will be day soon, ah, beautiful day!
    Crownèd to-morrow—
    End of my sorrow!
Meeting with never a farewell to say—
O sleep on till day, my love, sleep on till day!

Yet life's but a vision too lovely to stay:
Morn passes, noon hastens, and pleasures decay;
And evening approaches and closes the day:
    Then laid with praises
    Under the daisies:
Smiling we'll creep to one pillow of clay,
And sleep on till **Day**, my love, sleep on till **Day**.

TO ELIZABETH BARRETT BROWNING ON HER LATER SONNETS.

1856.

 KNOW not if the cycle of strange years
    Will ever bring thy human face to me,
    Sister!—I say this, not as one of thy peers,
But like as those who their own grief can see
In the large mirror of another's tears.

Comforter! many a time thy soul's white feet
    Stole on the silent darkness where I lay
With voice of distant singing—solemn sweet—
    " Be of good cheer, I too have trod that way;"
And I rose up and walked in strength complete.

Oft, as amidst the furnace of fierce woe
    My own will lit, I writhing stood, yet calm

I saw thee moving near me, meek and low,
　　Not speaking,—only chanting the one psalm,
"God's love suffices when all world-loves go."

Year after year have I, in passion strong,
　　Clung to thy garments when my soul was faint,—
Touching thee, all unseen amid the throng;
　　But now, thou risest to joy's heaven—my saint!
And I look up—and cannot hear thy song.

Or hearing, understand not; save as those
　　Who from without list to the bridegroom-strain
They might have sung—but that the dull gates close—
　　And so they smile a blessing through their pain,
Then, turning, lie and sleep among the snows.

So, go thou in, saint—sister—comforter!
　　Of this, thy house of joy, heaven keep the doors.
And sometimes through the music and the stir
　　Set thy lamp shining from the upper floors,
That we without may say—"Bless God—and her!"

INTO MARY'S BOSOM.

A. N.　Died February, 1867.

It was a mediæval superstition that women dying in child-bed did no
enter purgatory, but were carried straight into the bosom of the Mother
of God.

MARY, mother of all mothers,
　　First in love and grief; on earth
　　Having known above all others
　Mysteries of death and birth—
Take, from travail sore released,
One more mother to thy breast.

She like thee was pure and good,
 Happy-hearted—young and sweet—
Given to prayer—of Dorcas mood,
 Open hand and active feet—
Nought missed from her childless life
In her full content as wife.

But God said—though no one heard,
 Neither friend nor husband dear,
"Be it according to My word,
 Other lot awaits thee here.
One more living soul must be
Born into this world—for Me."

So as glad as autumn leaf
 Hiding the small bud of spring,
She without one fear or grief
 Her Magnificat did sing—
And His wondrous ways adored,
Like the handmaid of the Lord.

Nay, as neared her solemn day
 Which brought with it life or death,
Still her heart kept light and gay,
 Still her eyes of earnest faith
Smiled, with deeper peace possessed—
"He will do what seems Him best."

And He did. He led her, brave
 With a blindfold childlike trust
To the entrance of the grave—
 To His palace-gate! All just
He must be, or could not here
 Thus so merciless appear.

He must see with larger eyes :
 He must love with deeper love ;
We, half loving, scarce half wise,
 Snatch at those He does remove—

See no cause for—struggle long
With our sharp mysterious wrong.

But for her, dear saint! gone up
 "Into Mary's bosom" straight,
All the honey of her cup
Yet unspilled,—not let to wait
Till her milky mother breast
Felt the sword-thrust like the rest,—

Eight sweet days she had—full stored
 With the new maternal bliss
O'er her man-child from the Lord;
 Then—He took her.   So to this
Melt her seven and twenty years
Like the night when dawn appears.

Let the February sun
 Shining on the bursting buds,
On that baby life begun,
 On the bird-life in the woods,
O'er her grave still calmly shine
With a beauty all divine.

Though we cannot trace God's ways
 They to her may plain appear,
And her voice that sang His praise
 May still sing it, loud and clear,
O'er this silence of death sleep,
Wondering at those who weep.—

Thus, Our father, one by one
 Into thy wide house we go,
With our work undone or done,
 With our footsteps swift or slow—
Dark the door that doth divide—
But, O God! the other side!

AT A TABERNACLE.

So here we strike our moving tents,
A day's march nearer home.
                              Baptist Hymn.

 FAMISHED, foot-sore, panting flock
    Uncertainly they go:
    ⁃ The howling wolves upon their flank,
The precipice below ;
Around them the bleak wilderness—
    And O, they faint for food ?
Have pity, Shepherd of the sheep,
    Upon this multitude.

Seven thousand hungry souls : like those
    Once seated at Thy feet :
But here are stones instead of bread,
    And bitter herbs for meat :
Loud bellowing of beasts without,
    Within, the frantic cries
Of "miserable sinners," shrieked
    Up to Thy silent skies.

O God, we are sinners, well we know;
    And on Thy mercy call ;
But shall we flaunt our filthy rags
    To Thee, who seest them all ?
Ourselves, ourselves, our constant **cry**—
    "*Me* let Thy light illume ;
Save *me*, though half the universe
    May in Thy wrath consume."

Shall we not rather mutely gaze
    On Thee, whence love begins ;
Until Thy sunlike righteousness
    Drinks up our stagnant sins ?

Until the hunger stings no more,
    The rags are all forgot:
Heaven unto us is—where Thou art,
    And Hell—where Thou art not?

The preacher stops. The gas-lamps glare
    Through misty veils: loud, strong,
Melodious, rises like one voice
    The mighty cloud of song,
Seven thousand living souls at once
    Shout to the lofty dome,
"So here we strike our moving tents,
    A day's march nearer home."

Alas, and 't is the truth they sing
    These pilgrims sad and sore,
Who crowd in gaping multitudes
    Round any new church door:
Who cry for ever " Give us bread:
    Show us the way towards home."
And who is there to feed them? Who
    To march first, and say, Come !

O, only Pastor of the flock,
    Who knowest them all by name,
And call'st them out of many folds
    Differing, and yet the same:
O Shepherd of Thy chosen sheep—
    Chosen by Thee alone,—
Have pity on this multitude
    That pasturage have none.

At tables in the wilderness
    Make them sit down and feed:
Send them apostles bold and true
    To serve the meat they need.
And when the ministers shall fail,
    The baskets empty be,
Give them Thyself, the living bread,
    And let them feed on Thee !

REQUIEM.

Lux æterna luceat eis:
Dōna eis requiem.

 THE hour, the hour supernal,
    When they met the Light Eternal—
    These, laid down at last to sleep
In such longed-for silence deep:
    Waking—Lo, the night 's away—
All is light, and light eternal,
    Full, soul-satisfying day!

Eyes of mine, thus eager gazing
Into the June concave, blazing
With a dazzling blueness bright—
Ye are blind as death or night,
    Whilst my dead, their opened eyes
Mute up-raising, past all praising,
    Pierce into God's mysteries.

O their wisdom, boundless, holy,
O their knowledge, large as lowly:
O their deep peace after pain,
Loss forgotten, life all gain :
    And O God, what great love moves
Them, now wholly nourished solely
    By Thee—infinite Love of loves!

Ye our dead, for whom we pray not:
Unto whom wild words we say not,
Though we know not but ye hear,
Though we often feel ye near,
    Go ye into eternal light ;
You we stay not, and betray not
    Back into our dim half night.

Well we trow ye fain would teach us,
And your spirit hands would reach us
Tenderly from farthest heaven,—
But to you this is not given :
    Humble faith the lesson sole
Ye can preach us, all and each, us
    Travellers to the self-same goal.

Lesson strange, hard of discerning !
Dimly caught with awful yearning
At grave-sides, or taught in throes
Of our utmost joys and woes.
    But one day will come the call,
And thus earning the last learning,
    Like our dead, we shall know all.

THE HUMAN TEMPLE.

" Know ye not that ye are the temple of God, and that the Spirit of God
dwelleth in you ?"

THE TEMPLE IN DARKNESS.

DARKNESS broods upon the temple,
    Glooms along the lonely aisles,
    Fills up all the orient window,
  Whence, like little children's wiles,
Shadows—purple, azure, golden—
  Broke upon the floor in smiles.

From the great heart of the organ
  Bursts no voice of chant or psalm ;
All the air, by music-pulses
  Stirred no more, is deathly calm ;
And no precious incense rising,
    Falls, like good men's prayer, in balm.

Not a sound of living footstep
  Echoes on the marble floor;
Not a sigh of stranger passing
  Pierces through the closèd door;
Quenched the light upon the altar:
  Where the priest stood, none stands more.

Lord, why hast Thou left Thy temple
  Scorned of man, disowned by Thee?
Rather let Thy right hand crush it,
  None its desolation see!
List—" He who the temple builded
  Doth His will there. Let it be!"

A LIGHT IN THE TEMPLE.

Lo, a light within the temple!
  Whence it cometh no man knows:
Barred the doors: the night-black windows
  Stand apart in solemn rows,
All without seems gloom eternal,
  Yet the glimmer comes and goes—

As if silent-footed angels
  Through the dim aisles wandered fair,
Only traced amid the darkness
  By the glory in their hair,
Till at the forsaken altar
  They all met, and praised God there.

Now the light grows—fuller, clearer;
  Hark, the organ 'gins to sound,
Faint, like broken spirit crying
  Unto Heaven from the ground;
While the chorus of the angels
  Mingles everywhere around.

See, the altar shines all radiant,
  Though no mortal priest there stands,

And no earthly congregation
   Worships with uplifted hands :
Yet they gather, slow and saintly
   In innumerable bands.

And the chant celestial rises
   Where the human prayers have ceased :
No tear-sacrifice is offered,
   For all anguish is appeased,
Through its night of desolation,
   To His temple comes the Priest.

THE MOON IN THE MORNING.

BACK, spectral wanderer ! What dost thou here ?
   Are not the streets all thrilled with morning beams,
   While the fair city bathes in misty streams,
Of living gold : and ever and anear
The fresh breeze from the sea sweeps coldly clear ?

It *shall* be morning ! I step forth as one
   Who bears youth's royalty on heart and eye ;
   As if those pale years at my feet did lie
Like dead flowers, and I crushed them ! passing on
Boldly, with looks turned forwards—backward, none !

O breeze and sun of morn ! O castled steep,
   And distant hills that dream in still rejoice !
   O infinite waves, that with unceasing voice
I know are thundering on the bay's curv'd deep,
Wake ye my spirit fom its palsied sleep !

Yes, I will grasp it—life's fair morning-time :
   I will put strength into these pulses dull,
   And gaze out on God's earth so beautiful,
And change this dirge into a happy chime,
That to His footstool may arise sublime.

I look up into heaven. Art thou still there,
 Dim, waning moon! watched, a bright thread, at eve:
 Then fuller, till one night thy beams did weave
A magic light o'er hill and castle fair.
Back, thou pale ghost! haunt not the morning air!

Blank thing, would I could blot thee from the sky!
 Why troublest thou the brightness of the morn?
 " I do but as all things create or born
Serve my appointed course, and then—I die,"—
This answer falleth downwards like a sigh.

I have said ill. Hail, pallid crescent, hail!
 Let me look on thee, where thou sitt'st for aye
 Like memory—ghastly in the glare of day,
But in the evening, light. Grow yet more pale,
Till from the face of heaven thine image fail.

Then rise from out earth's gloom of midnight tears
 A new-born glory. So I know 't will be
 When that pale shade now ever following me—
The unexorcisèd phantom of dead years—
Grows an orbed angel, singing in the spheres.

GREEN THINGS GROWING.

THE green things growing, the green things grow
  ing,
The faint sweet smell of the green things growing!
I should like to live, whether I smile or grieve,
Just to watch the happy life of my green things
  growing.

O the fluttering and the pattering of those green
  things growing!
How they talk each to each, when none of us are
  knowing;

In the wonderful white of the weird moonlight
Or the dim dreamy dawn when the cocks are crow-
    ing.

I love, I love them so—my green things growing:
And I think that they love me, without false show-
    ing ;
For by many a tender touch, they comfort me so
    much,
With the soft mute comfort of green things grow-
    ing.

And in the rich store of their blossoms glowing
Ten for one I take they 're on me bestowing :
Oh, I should like to see, if God's will it may be,
Many, many a summer of my green things grow-
    ing !

But if I must be gathered for the angels's sowing,
Sleep out of sight awhile, like the green things
    growing,
Though dust to dust return, I think I'll scarcely
    mourn,
If I may change into green things growing.

———

JESSIE.

HE little white moon goes climbing
    Over the dusky cloud,
    Kissing its rugged fringes,
  With a love-light, pale as a shroud—
Where walks this moon to-night, Jessie?
Over the waters bright, Jessie ?
  Does she smile on your face as you lift it,
    proud ?
Let her look on thee—look on thee, Jessie !
  For I shall look never more !

One steady white star stands watching
   Ever beside the moon ;
Hid by the mists that veil her,
   And hid by her light's mid-noon :
Yet the star follows all heaven through, Jessie,
As my soul follows after you, Jessie,
  - At moon-rise and moon-set, late and soon :
Let it watch thee, watch thee, my Jessie,
   For I shall watch never more !

The purple-black vault folds softly,
   Over far sea, far land ;
The thunder-clouds, swept down eastward,
   Like a chain of mountains stand,
Under this July sky, Jessie,
Do you hear waves lapping by, Jessie ?
   Do you walk, with the hills on either hand ?
Farewell, O farewell, my Jessie,
   Farewell for evermore !

THE COMING OF THE SPRING.

THE coming of the Spring—
   Oh, the coming of the Spring!
   Now the Winter wears away,
And we thirst, and yearn, and pray,
As a sick man prays for day,
   For the coming of the Spring.

How we dream, 'twill surely bring
Some new delightsome thing ;
Some wondrous bliss that nears
Comet-like, from unknown spheres,
Crowning *this* year of all years
   With the promise of the Spring.

But it comes not, or does wear
A strange horror in its hair;
Or goes on its meteor way
Till it fades in ether gray,
And its glories all decay,
  Like the glories of the Spring.

Then, our May-buds drop o'erhead,
And our primroses lie dead;
And our violets on the moor
Bloom unplucked, in nooks obscure,
And the dull heart shuts its door
  On the beauty of the Spring.

O vain and selfish grief!
O sullen unbelief!
When each bird on each hedge-side,
Where snow lay all winter-tide,
Sings aloud, "God will provide,
  He has sent us back the Spring!"

When each flower the children hold
Smiles—"This life-germ I enfold,
See how safely I can keep!
For I die not—only sleep;
And, through all the Winter deep,
  Wait the coming of the Spring."

THE MORNING WORLD.

E comes down from Youth's mountain-top:
    Before him Manhood's glittering plain
    Lies stretched;—vales, hamlets, towers, and
        towns,
Huge cities, dim and silent downs,
  Wide unreaped fields of shining grain.

All seems a landscape fair as near ;
  So easy to be crossed and won!
No mist the distant ocean hides,
And overhead majestic rides
  The wondrous, never-setting sun.

Gaze on, gaze on, thou eager boy,
  For earth is lovely, life is grand ;
Yet from the boundary of the plain
Thy faded eyes may turn again
  Wistfully to the morning-land.

How lovely then o'er wastes of toil
  That long-left mountain height appears !
How soft the lights and shadows glide !
How the rough places, glorified,
  Transcend whole leagues of level years !

And standing by the sea of Death,
  With anchor weighed and sails unfurled,
Blessed the man before whose eyes
The very hills of Paradise
  Glow, colored like his morning world.

———

COMING HOME.

THE lift is high and blue,
  And the new moon glints through
    The bonnie corn-stooks o' Strathairly :
My ship's in Largo Bay,
And I ken it weel—the way
  Up the steep, steep brae o' Strathairly.

When I sailed ower the sea,
A laddie bold and free,—
  The corn sprang green on Strathairly ;
When I come back again,

'T is an auld man walks his lane,
 Slow and sad through the fields o' Strathairly.

Of the shearers that I see,
Ne'er a body kens me,
 Though I kent them a' at Strathairly;
And this fisher-wife I pass,
Can she be the braw lass
 That I kissed at the back of Strathairly?

O the land 's fine, fine!
I could buy it a' for mine,
 My gowd 's yellow as the stooks o' Strathairly;
But I fain yon lad wad be,
That sailed ower the salt sea
 As the dawn rose gray on Strathairly.

THE DEAD.

NDERNEATH the nodding plumes,
 Black in dolorous pride,
 All along the busy streets
 Curiously eyed;
While anon the mourners follow
In feigned calmness, grief as hollow,
 Some few idly glancing wide—
 How quietly *they* ride!

Underneath the artillery's tramp
 Charging, fiend-possest,
Storms of rattling fiery hail
 Sweeping each safe breast,
Till the kind moon—battle over—
Kiss their faces like a lover,
 Calm boy-faces, earthward prest—
 How quietly *they* rest!

Underneath the pitiless roar
  Of the hungry deep,
Crossed the gulf from life to—life,
  In a single leap ;
Hundreds in a moment knowing
The one secret none is shewing,
  Though the whole world rave and weep—
  How quietly *they* sleep !

Life, this hard and painful Life,
  With a yearning tongue
Calls unto her brother Death :
  "Brother, dear, how long?"
Lays her head upon his shoulder—
Softer than all clasps, scarce colder!—
  In his close arms, safe and strong,
  Slips with him from the throng.

A MARINER'S BRIDE.

"AH me, my dream!" pale Helen cried,
  With hectic cheeks aglow :
  "Why wake me? Hide that cruel beam !
I'll not have such another dream
On this side heaven, I know.

"I almost feel the leaping waves,
  The wet spray on my hair,
The salt breeze singing in the sail,
The kind arms, strong as iron-mail,
  That held me safely there.

"I'll tell thee : On some shore I stood,
  Or sea, or inland bay,
Or river broad, I know not—save
There seemed no boundary to the wave
  That chafed and moaned alway.

"The shore was lone—the wave was lone—
  The horizon lone ; no sail
Broke the dim line 'twixt sea and sky,
Till slowly, slowly one came by
  Half ghostlike, gray and pale.

" It was a very little boat,
  Had neither oars nor crew ;
But as it shoreward bounded fast,
One form seemed leaning by the mast—
  And Norman's face I knew !

" He never looked nor smiled at me,
  Though I stood all alone;
His brow was very grave and high
Lit with a glory from the sky—
  The vessel bounded on.

" I shrieked : 'O take me with thee, love !
  The night falls dark and dread.'—
'My boat may come no nearer shore ;
And, hark ! how mad the billows roar !
  Art thou afraid ? ' he said.

" 'Afraid ! with thee ? '—' The wind sweeps fierce
  The foamy rocks among ;
A perilous voyage waiteth me.'—
' Then, then, indeed, I go with thee,'
  I cried, and forward sprung.

"All drenched with brine, all pale with fear—
  Ah no, not fear ; 't was bliss !—
I felt his strong arms draw me in :
If after death to heaven I win,
  'T will be such joy as this !

"No kiss, no smile, but aye that clasp—
  Tender, and close, and brave ;—

The boat, and o'er her deck there swept,
   Wave thundering after wave.

"I looked not to the stormy deep,
   Nor to the angry sky
Whether for life or death we wrought,
My whole world dwindled to one thought—
   Where he is, there am I!

"On—on—through leaping waves, slow calmed,
   With salt spray on our hair,
And breezes singing in the sail,
Before a safe and pleasant gale,
   The boat went bounding fair:

"But whether to a shore we came,
   Or seaward sailed away,
Alas! to me is all nnknown:
O happy dream, too quickly flown!
   O cruel, cruel day!"

Pale Helen lived—or died: dull time
   O'er all that history rolls;
Sailed they or sunk they on life's waves?—
I only know earth holds two graves,
And heaven two blessed souls.

MOUNTAINS IN SNOW.

COLD—O deathly cold—and silent, lie the white hills
    'neath the sky,
   Like a soul whom fate has covered with thy snow,
    Adversity!
Not a sough of wind comes moaning; the same outline, high
    and bare,
As in pleasant days of summer, rises in the murky air.

Very quiet—very silent—whether shines the mocking sun
Through the wintry blue, or lowering drift the feathery snow-
        clouds dun :
Always quiet, always silent, be it night or be it day,
With that pale shroud coldly lying where the heather-blossoms
        lay.

Can they be the very mountains that we looked at, you and I ?
One long wavy line of purple painted on the sunset sky ;
With the new moon's edge just touching that dark run, like
        dancer's foot,
Or young Dian's, on the hill-side for Endymion waiting mute.

O how golden was that evening ! —O how soft the summer air !
How the bridegroom sky bent loving o'er its earth so virgin
        fair !
How the earth looked up to heaven like a bride with joy op-
        pressed,
In her thankfulness half-weeping that she was thus over blest !

Ghostly mountains ! " Silence—silence ! " now is aye your
        soundless voice,
Lifted in an awful patience o'er the world's uproarious noise ;
O'er its jarring and its greetings—o'er its loving and its hate—
" Silence ! Bare thy brows submissive to the snows of heaven,
        and wait ! "

A RHYME ABOUT BIRDS.

SAID to the little Swallow :
    "Who 'll follow ?
  Out of thy nest in the eaves
   Under the ivy leaves ;
Yet my thought flies swifter than thou :
My thought has a softer nest,
Where it fold its wings to rest,
In a pure-hearted woman's breast ;

While its sky is her cloudless brow."
Swallow—swallow,
Who 'll follow ?

I said to the brown, brown Thrush:
  "Hush—hush!
Through the wood's full strains I hear
Thy monotone deep and clear,
  Like a sound amid sounds most fine;
And so, though the whole world sung
To my love with eloquent tongue,
However their voices rung,
  She would pause and listen to mine."
    Brown, brown thrush,
    Hush—hush!

I said to the Nightingale:
  " Hail, all hail!
Pierce with thy trill the dark,
Like a glittering music-spark,
  When the earth grows pale and dumb;
But mine be a song more rare,
To startle the sleeping air,
And to the dull world declare
  Love sings amid darkest gloom."
    Nightingale,
    Hail, all hail!

I said to the sky poised Lark:
  " Hark—hark!
Thy note is more loud and free,
Because there lies safe for thee
  A little nest on the ground.
And I, when strong-winged I rise
To chant out sweet melodies,
Shall know there are home-lit eyes
  Watching me soar, sun-crowned."
    Poet-lark,
    Hark—hark!

AT THE WINDOW.

NLY to listen, listen and wait,
  For his slow firm step down the gravel
        walk :
To hear the click-click of his hand on the gate
  And feel every heart-beat thro' careless talk :
For love is sweet when life is young ;
And life and love are both so long.

"Only to watch him about the room :
  Lighting it up with his quiet smile,
That seems to lift the world out of gloom
  And bring heaven nearer me, for awhile
A little while, since love is young,
And life seems beautiful as long.

"Only to love him : nothing more :
  Never a thought of his loving me.
Proud of him, glad in him, though he bore
  My heart to shipwreck on the smooth sea.
Love's faith sees only grief, not wrong,
And life is daring when 't is young.

"But yet, what matter ! The world goes round
  And bliss and bale are but outside things !
I never can lose what in him I found,
  Though love be sorrow with half-grown wings,
And should love fly when we are young,
Why, life is still not long—not long.

"And heaven is kind to the faithful heart
  And if we are patient and brave and calm
Our fruits will last when our flowers depart.—
  Some day, when I sleep with folded palm
No longer fair, no longer young,
Life may not seem so bitter long."

The tears dried up in her shining eyes,
　Her parted lips took a saintly peace;
Then, his shadow across the doorway lies;—
　Will her doubts gather, darken, or—cease?
When hearts are pure, and bold, and strong,
True love as life itself is long.

———

JUPITER, AN EVENING STAR.

ULER and hero, shining in the west
　　　With great bright eye,
　　Rain down thy luminous arrows in this
　　　breast
With influence calm and high,
And speak to me of many things gone by.

Rememberest thou—'t is years since, wandering
　　　star—
　Those eves in June,
When thou hung'st quivering o'er the tree-tops far,
　Where, with discordant tune,
Many-tongued rooks hailed the red-rising moon?

Some watched thee then with human eyes like mine,
　Whose boundless gaze
May now pierce on from orb to orb divine
　Up to the Triune blaze
Of glory—nor be dazzled by its rays.

All things they know, whose wisdom seemed obscure;
　They, sometime blamed,
Hold our best purities as things impure;
　Their star-glance downward aimed,
Makes our most lamp-like deeds grow pale and shamed

Their star-glance?—what if through thy rays there
　　　gleam
　Immortal eyes

Down to this dark ?   What if these thoughts, that
    seem
  Unbidden to arise,
Be souls with my soul talking from the skies ?

I know not.   Yet awhile, and I shall know !—
  Thou to thy place
Slow journeying back, there startlingly to show
  Thy orb in liquid space,
Like a familiar death-lost angel face.—

O planet ! thou hast blotted out whole years
  Of life's dull round :
The Abel-voice of heart's blood and of tears
  Sinks dumb into the ground
And the green grass waves on with lulling sound.

ON HIS NINETIETH BIRTHDAY.

W. L.—Oct. 20, 1866.

INETY years, ay, ninety years !
  We, smooth travelling 'mongst our peers
  With a level onward tread
Look at you, so far ahead,
And wonder how life's road appears
At ninety years, at ninety years.

  If the journey has seemed long,—
  If the days when you were young,
  —Near a century ago—
  Ever come in silent show
With their forgotton smiles and tears
To the still heart of ninety years.

  Little the young mother knew
  On the day she welcomed you

To our new, old, wondrous world,
That your pretty ringlets curled
Would whiten 'neath the joys and fears
Of ninety years, full ninety years!

Yet that long dead lady sweet
Who once guided your small feet,
Watched the dawning soul arise
In your laughing infant eyes,
Might smile content from happier spheres
Upon her " child " of ninety years.

Gentle spirit, brave as true,
Freshened still with youth's best **dew**;
Merry heart, that can enjoy,
Simply, fully, as a boy,—
Fear not, though close the shadow nears,
At ninety years, at ninety years.

For when he at last shall come,—
The good Friend who whispers "Home!"
May he come as peacefully
As babe's sleep on mother's knee!
And after (so prays Love with tears)
Not ninety but a hundred years!

IN EXPECTATION OF DEATH.

CONSTANTIA.

WHEN I was young, my lover stole
One of my ringlets fair:
I wept—" Ah no! Those always part,
Who having once changed heart for heart,
Change also locks of hair.

"And mystic eyes, they say, have seen
   The spirits of the dead,
Gather like motes in silent bands
Round hair once reft by tender hands
   From some now shrouded head.

" If "—Here he closed my quivering mouth,
   And where the curl had lain,
Laid payment rich for what he stole :—
Could I to one hour crush life's whole,
   I'd live that hour again !

My golden curls are silvering o'er—
   Who heeds ?   The seas roll wide ;
When one I know their bounds shall pass,
There 'll be no tresses—only grass—
   For *his* hands to divide ;

Where I shall lie, low, deep, a-cold,
   And never hear his tread :
Whether he weep, or sigh, or moan,
I shall be passive as a stone,
   He living, and I—dead !

And then he will rise up and go,
   With slow steps, looking back,
Still—going : leaving me to keep
My frozen and eternal sleep,
   Beneath the earth so black.

Pale brow—oft leant against his brow :
   Poor hand—where his lips lay ;
Dim eyes, that knew not they were fair,
Till his praise made them half they were—
   Must all these pass away ?

Must nought of mine be left for him
   Except the curl he stole ?
Round which this wildly-loving *me*
Will float unseen continually,
   A disembodied soul.

A soul! Glad thought, that lightning-like
  Leaps from this cloud of doom:
If, living, all its load of clay
Keeps not my spirit from his away,
  Thou canst not, cruel tomb!

The moment that these earth-chains burst,
  Like an enfranchised dove
O'er seas and lands to him I fly,
Whom only, whether I live or die,
  I loved, love, and shall love.

I'll float around him—he shall breathe
  My life instead of air;
In glowing sunbeams o'er his head
My visionary hands I'll spread,
  And kiss his forehead fair.

I'll stand, an angel bold and strong,
  Between his soul and sin;
If grief lie stone-like on his heart,
I'll beat its marble doors apart,
  To let peace enter in.

He never more shall part from me,
  Nor I from him divide;
Let these poor limbs in earth find rest!
I'll live like Love within his breast,
  Rejoicing that I died.

STRAYED FROM THE FLOCK.

"Strayed from the Flock.—B. RIVIERE."
          Royal Academy Catalogue. 1867.

HE wind goes sobbing
          Over the moor:
    Far is the fold and shut its door:
But white and safe, beyond terror or shock

Lies the silly lamb that strayed from the flock;
And overhead from a frozen branch
With a tender pity, true and staunch,
    Carols the Robin.

" The blast comes heavy
    With death and sorrow :
To-day it is thee—may be me to-morrow:
Yet I 'll sing one song o'er the silent wold,
For the poor little lamb that never grew old,
Never lived long winters to see
Chanting from empty trees like me,
    Trees once so leafy.

" The snow-flakes cover
    The moorland dun ;
My song trills feebly, but I'll sing on.
Why did God make me a brave bird soul
Under warm feathers, red as a coal,
To keep my life merry, cheery and bright,
To the very last twinkle of wintry light,
    While thine is all over ?

" Why was I given
    Bold strong wings
To bear me away from hurtful things?
While thy poor feet were so tender and weakly
And thy faint heart yielded all so meekly,
Till it bent at last 'neath the silent hand
That bade thee lie down, nor try to stand—
    Was it hand of heaven ?

" The wind goes sobbing,"
    (Thus sang the bird,
Or else in a dream its voice I heard,)
" Nothing I know and nothing can,
Wisdom is not with birds but man :
Yet some, snow-white, snow-soft, not snow-cold,
May be singing o'er the lamb strayed from the fold,
    Besides poor Robin."

THREE MEETINGS.

THE happy meeting from over the sea,
When I love my friend and my friend loves
  me:
And we stand face to face, and for letters read
There are endless words to be heard and said:
With a glance between whiles, shy, anxious, half strange,
As if asking—" Say now, is there any change ?"
Till we settle down just as we used to be,
For I love my friend and my friend loves me.

———

O the blessed meeting of lovers true
Against whom Fate has done all that Fate could do,
And then dropped vanquished; while over those
  slain
Dead weeks, months, years, of parting and pain,
Hope lifts her banner, gay, gallant and fair,
Untainted, untorn, in the balmy air:
And the heaven of the future, golden and bright,
Arches above them—God guards the right.

———

But O for the meeting to come one day,
When the spirit slips out of its house of clay:
When the standers-by with a gentle sign
Shall kindly cover this face of mine,
And I leap—whither?—ah who can know ?
But outward, onward, as spirits must go,
Till eye to eye without fear I see
God—and my lost—as they see me.

APRIL.

"And He that sat upon the throne said: Behold, I make all things new."

GO forth in the fields to meet thee, Spring.
By hanging larch-woods, through whose brown there
    runs
A trembling under-gush of faintest green,
As daily sun-bursts strike adown the hills;
By hedgerows, budding slow in nested nooks,
Where primroses look up with childish smile
From Mother Earth's rich breast; she laughs aloud
"I am young again! It is the April-time."

Sweet April-time—O cruel April-time!
Year after year returning, with a brow
Of promise, and red lips with longing paled,
And backward-hidden hands that clutch the joys
Of vanished springs, like flowers. Cast them not
    down;
Let them not root again! Go by—go by,
Young April; thou art not of us nor ours.

Yet April-time, O golden April-time,
Stay but a little! Hast thou not some spell
In the fresh youth o' the year to make us young?
Thou, at whose touch the rich sap leaps i' the veins
Of dead brown boughs that moaned all winter long,
Roll back the shroud from this our life's lost day,
Setting in showers—and in thy glowing arms
Lift dead morn out o' the west, and bid her walk
Like a returned ghost through upper air:
Canst thou do this? wilt answer?

                                            " Vain, all vain."
The larch wood sighs unto the darkening sky,
The silent sky replies in pitying tears
As the slow rain-cloud trails adown the hills.

"There is a time to be born, a time to die,"
For all things.   The-irrevocable Hand
That opes the year's fair gate, doth ope and shut
The portals of our earthly destinies;
We walk through blindfold, and the noiseless doors
Close after us, for ever.
                               Pause, my soul,
On these strange words—*for ever*—whose large sound
Breaks flood-like, drowning all the petty noise
Our human moans make on the shores of Time.

O Thou that openest, and no man shuts;
That shut'st, and no man opens—Thee we wait!
More longingly than the black frost-bound lands
Desire the budding green.   Awakener, come!
Fling wide the gate of an eternal year,
The April of that glad new heavens and earth
Which shall grow out of these, as spring-tide grows
Slow out of winter's breast.

                             Let Thy wide hand
Gather us all—with none left out (O God!
Leave Thou out none!) from the east and from the
           west.
Loose Thou our burdens: heal our sicknesses;
Give us one heart, one tongue, one faith, one love.
In Thy great Oneness made complete and strong—
To do Thy work throughout the happy world—
Thy world, All-merciful—Thy perfect world.

LAYING A FOUNDATION-STONE.

St. Mary's ; Shortlands.—Oct. 5, 1867.

" The Holy Church throughout all the world doth acknowledge Thee."

FTER harvest dews and harvest moonshine
  Lay the stone beneath this autumn sunshine :
  Ere the winter frosts the leaves are thinning,
Let the workmen see the work's beginning.
Let the slender windows rising higher
Catch new glimpses of the sunset fire,
And the sheltering walls, fresh beauty shewing,
Day by day be strengthening and growing :
Though full many a daily task be meted
Ere the perfect fabric is completed.

Work in faith, good neighbor beside neighbor,
Work, and trust heaven's smile upon your labor :
Ay, though we who in the sunshine stand here,
Joining voice to voice and hand to hand here,
Ere the moss has grown o'er wall and column
Shall be sleeping in a silence solemn,
Or in clearer light and purer air
Busy about His business—*other-where.*

Ay, though in that mystery of mysteries
Lying underneath our sad life-histories,
Midst of labor, earnest, brave, and fervent,
The good Master may call on many a servant,
Sudden rest may fall on wearied sinews,
Though the workers cease—the work continues.

God names differently what we judge failing,
In a glory-mist His purpose veiling,
One by one He moves us, hands anointed
By His hands, to do our task appointed.

But the dimness of our earthly prison
Hides the total splendor of the vision.

Grant us, Lord, behind that veil to feel Thee;
In our humble labors to reveal thee,
Doing what we can do—well believing
One, with Thee, are giving and receiving.

So, this happy sunshine the act gilding,
Lay the stone—and may heaven bless the building.

HEADINGS OF CHAPTERS.

(From ' Christian's Mistake.")

HEN ye 're my ain gudewife, lassie,
    What 'll ye bring to me ?
    A hantle o' siller, a stockin' o' gowd ?—
" I haena ae bawbee."

When ye are my ain gudewife, lassie,
    And sit at my fireside,
Will the red and white meet in your face ?—
    " Na ! ye 'll no get a bonnie bride !"

But gin ye 're my ain gudewife, lassie,
    Mine for gude and ill,
Will ye bring me three things, lassie,
    My toom, toom house to fill ?

A temper sweet, a silent tongue,
    A heart baith warm and free ?
Then I 'll marry ye the morn, lassie,
    And loe ye till I dee.

THE little griefs—the petty wounds,
   The stabs of daily care,—
" Crackling of thorns beneath the pot,"—
As life's fire burns—now cold, now hot,
   How hard they are to bear !

But on the fire burns, clear and still ;
   The cankering sorrow dies :
The small wounds heal ; the clouds are rent,
And through this shattered mortal tent
   Shine down the eternal skies.

———

HE stands a-sudden at the door,
   And no one hears his soundless tread,
   And no one sees his veilèd head,
Or silent hand, put forth so sure,

To snatch us from all mortal sight,
   Or else benignly turn away,
   And let us live our little day,
And tremble back into the light.

But though thus awful to our eyes
He is an Angel in disguise.

———

Love that asketh love again,
Finds the barter nought but pain ;
Love that giveth in full store,
Aye receives as much, and more.

Love, exacting nothing back,
Never knoweth any lack ;
Love, compelling love to pay,
Sees him bankrupt every day,

"AND do the hours slip fast or slow,
      And are ye sad or gay ?
And is your heart with your liege lord, lady,
      Or is it far away ? "

The lady raised her calm, proud head,
      Though her tears fell one by one :
" Life counts not hours by joys or pangs,
      But just by duties done.

"And when I lie in the green kirkyard,
      With the mould upon my breast,
Say not that ' She did well—or ill,'
      Only, ' She did her best ! ' "

A WARM hearth, and a bright hearth, and a hearth swept clean,
Where the tongs don't raise a dust, and the broom is n't seen ;
Where the coals never fly abroad, and the soot does n't fall,
O that 's the fire for a man like me, in cottage or in hall.

A light boat, and a tight boat, and a boat that rides well,
Though the waves leap around it and the winds blow snell :
A full boat and a merry boat, we 'll meet any weather,
With a long pull, and a strong pull, and a pull altogether.

FORGIVE us each his daily sins,
      If few or many, great or small ;
And those that sin against us, Lord,
      Good Lord, forgive them all.

Judge us not as we others judge ;
      Condemn us not as we condemn ;
They who are merciless to us—
      Be merciful to them.

And if the cruel storm should pass,
   And let Thy heaven of peace appear ;
Make not our right the right—or might,
   But make Thy right shine clear.

—

" Peace on earth and mercy mild,"
Sing the angels, reconciled ;
Over each sad warfare done,
Each soul-battle lost and won.

He that has a victory lost,
May discomfit yet a host ;
And, it often doth befal,
He who conquers loses all.

—

It may be under palace roof,
   Princely and wide ;
No pomp foregone, no pleasure lost,
   No wish denied ;
But if beneath the diamonds' flash
   Sweet, kind eyes hide,
A pleasant place, a happy place,
   Is our fireside.

It may be 'twixt four lowly walls,
   No show, no pride ;
Where sorrows ofttimes enter in,
   But ne'er abide.
Yet, if she sits beside the hearth,
   Help, comfort, guide,
A blessed place, a heavenly place,
   Is our fireside.

THE GOLDEN GATE.

 LADY stood at the golden gate,—
　　The golden gate shut close and lorn;
The little spring-birds chirped merry and
　　sweet,
The little spring-flowers grew up at her feet;
She smiled back a spring-smile, gay and young—
　　"'T will open, open to me, ere long!
　Wait," said the lady—" wait, wait:
　　There never was night that had no morn."

The lady sat at the golden gate;
　　The May had withered from off the thorn:
Warm July roses crushed cheek to cheek
In a rapturous stillness, faint and weak;
And a languid love-air filled the breeze,
And birds ceased singing in nest-hung trees
"Wait," said the lady—"wait, wait:
　　There never was night that had no morn."

The lady knelt at the golden gate,—
　　The fast-barred gate—forlorn, forlorn;
The sun laid on her his burning hand,
The reapers' song came over the land,
And the same round moon that lighted the sheaves,
Shewed at her feet dead, drifted leaves:
"Alas!" sighed the lady.　"Yet, wait, wait:
　　There never was night that had no morn."

The lady crouched at the golden gate,
　　With steadfast watch—but so lorn, so lorn!
The earth lay whitening in one shroud,
The wind in the woods howled long and loud;
Till the frosty stars shot arrowy rays;

And fixed forever her death-strong gaze.
A soul rose singing : " No more I wait :
On earth was night—in heaven is morn."

A FAREWELL.

For a Swedish Air.

OOK in my face, dear,
　　Openly and free :
　　Hold out your hand, dear,
　Have no fear of me !
Thus as friends old loves should part ;
Each one with a quiet heart—
　O my Mary—my lost Mary,
Say farewell—and go !

Never to meet more,
　While day follows day :
Never to kiss more,
　Till our lips are clay.
Angry hearts grieve loud awhile ;
Broken hearts are dumb—or smile.
　O my Mary—my lost Mary,
Say farewell—and go !

HIGHLAND CATTLE.

OWN the wintry mountain
　　Like a cloud they come,
　Not like a cloud in its silent shroud
　　When the sky is leaden and the earth all·
　　　dumb,
But tramp, tramp, tramp,

With a roar and a shock,
And stamp, stamp, stamp,
  Down the hard granite rock,
With the snow-flakes following fair
Like an army in the air,
Of white-winged angels leaving
Their heavenly homes, half-grieving,
And half glad to drop down kindly upon earth so
  bare :
With a snort and a bellow
Tossing manes dun and yellow,
Red and roan, black and gray,
In their fierce merry play,
Though the sky is all leaden and the earth all dumb—
Down the noisy cattle come !

Thronèd on the mountain
  Winter sits at ease :
Hidden under mist are those peaks of amethyst
  That rose like hills of heaven above the amber
    seas.
While crash, crash, crash,
  Through the frozen heather brown,
And dash, dash, dash,
  Where the ptarmigan drops down
And the curlew stops her cry
And the deer sinks, like to die—
And the waterfall's loud noise
In the only living voice—
With a plunge and a roar
Like mad waves upon the shore,
Or the wind through the pass
Howling o'er the reedy grass—
In a wild battalion pouring from the heights unto
  the plain.
Down the cattle come again !

O silent peaks : O golden Isle :
That still I see in its last smile,
Dear as dead face, yet unforbid
By the slow-closing coffin lid ::
And lovely as the dreams that come
To exiled men of distant home ;
Shine on—though I behold not ; bear
To happy hearts all thoughts most fair—
To the young, of hope and sweet desire
Bright as your morning crown of fire,—
To the old, of settled peace, hard-won,
But perfect as at set of sun
Ye sit—enrobed in purple light—
Before ye vanish into night.

O sacred glens—gray rocks—dear hills—
Whose very thought my full heart stills—
Whose very name works like a spell,
My Golden Isle, farewell, farewell !

THE FISHER-MAID.

IF I were a noble lady,
    And he a peasant born,
    With nothing but his good right hand
'Twixt him and the world's scorn—
O I would speak so humble,
    And I would smile so meek,
And cool with tears this fierce, hot flush
    He left upon my cheek.
Sing heigh, sing ho, my bonnie, bonnie boat,
    Let's watch the anchor weighed :
For he is a great sea-captain,
    And I a fisher-maid.

" If I were a royal princess,
  And he a captive poor,
I would cast down these steadfast eyes,
  Under this bolted door,
And walking brave in all men's sight
  Low at his feet would fall :
Sceptre and crown and womanhood,
  My love should take them all !
Sing heigh, sing ho, my bonnie, bonnie boat,
  Alone with sea and sky,
For he is a bold sea-captain,
  A fisher-maiden I.

" If I were a saint in heaven
  And he a sinner pale,
Whom good men passed with face avert,
  And left him to his bale,
Mine eyes they should weep rivers,
  My voice reach that great Throne,
Beseeching—'O be merciful !
  Make Thou mine own Thine own ! '
Sing heigh, sing ho, my bonnie, bonnie boat,
  Love only cannot fade :
Though he is a bold sea-captain,
  And I a fisher-maid."

Close stood the young sea-captain,
  His tears fell fast as rain,
"If I have sinned, I'll sin no more—
  God judge between us twain ! "
The gold ring flashed in sunshine,
  The small waves laughing curled-
" Our ship rocks at the harbor bar,
  Away to the under world."—
" Farewell, farewell, my bonnie, bonnie boat !
  Now Heaven us bless and aid,
For my lord is a great sea-captain,
  And I was a fisher-maid."

YOUNG AND OLD.

E were but foolish, dear,
    When we were young;
    Hasty and ignorant,
Daring and strong;
Clutching the red grapes
    Of passion or power—
Ah, they were wild grapes,
    Cankered and sour!
Would we call back those years,
    Strange, ghostly throng?
No. Yet be tender, love,
    We were but young!

Now, growing wiser, dear,
    While growing old,
No pure thought perished yet,
    No warm hope cold,
We'll reap, who sowed in tears;
    Scattering abroad;
Living for all mankind,
    Living to God:
Holding each other safe
    In a firm fold:—
We shall be happy, love,
    Now we are old.

THE MULBERRY TREE.

HEN the long hot days are nearly gone,
    And the fields lie misty in early dawn,
    And the spider-webs hang from blade to
        blade,
Heavy with rain and dun with shade,

Till the lazy sun rises late from his bed,
Large and solemn and round and red,
And changes them all into diamonds bright,
Like common things, glorified in love's light,—
   O then is the prime, the golden prime,
   Of the patient mulberry-tree.

O the mulberry-tree is of trees the queen!
Bare long after the rest are green :
But as time steals onwards, while none perceives
Slowly she clothes herself with leaves—
Hides her fruit under them, hard to find,
And, being a tree of steadfast mind,
Makes no show of blossom or berry
Lures not a bird to come and make merry
   Under her boughs, her dark rough boughs—
   The prudent mulberry-tree.

But by and by, when the flowers grow few
And the fruits are dwindling and small to view—
Out she comes in her matron grace
With the purple myriads of her race :
Full of plenty from root to crown,
Showering plenty her feet adown.
While far overhead hang gorgeously
Large luscious berries of sanguine dye,
   For the best grows highest, always highest,
   Upon the mulberry-tree!

And so she lives through her fruitful season,
Fairest tree that blows summer breeze on ;—
Till the breeze sharpens to fierce wind cold,
And the sun himself sickens, worn and old,
And sudden frosts the green lawn cover
And the day of the mulberry-tree is over.
Her half-ripe treasures strew all the grass
Or wither greenly aloft. We pass
   Like summer friends when her beauty ends.
   Not a sigh for the mulberry-tree!

Yet stands she in the October sun
Her fruits departed—her joys all done,
And lets the wind rave through her emptied boughs,
Like a mother left lone in a childless house;
Till, some still night under frosty skies
She drops her green clothing off—and dies:
Without a blight, or mildew, to taint,
Uncomplaining as some sweet saint
   Who, her full life past, dies, calm to the last—
The grand old mulberry-tree!

LEBEWOHL.

UT into the wilderness
   We apart are going;
    Loosed the joined hands' caress,
   Quenched the fond eyes' glowing;
Gone our happy dream of life
   Like a dried up river;
I no husband, thou no wife,
   Thus we part—for ever!

But the desert quickly ends,
   Whether journeyed over
Sad and slow, as parted friends,
   Or as maid and lover.
Those whom God made spouse and wife
   Let no man dare sever!
In the eternal land of life
   Thou art mine—for ever!

THE PASSING FEAR.

OTHER, I shall not die," she said,
   Calm lying, open-eyed,
    Still smiling when the morning rose,
   Smiling at even-tide,

"Mother it was not Death whose hand,
    Above my eyelids drawn,
Put back my seventeen childish years
    And made a new world dawn.

"O golden world! O wondrous world!
    My heart looks in amaze
Back on those gone-by years, and forth
    Into the future days.

"O mother, mother! was it thus,
    That when my father came
You hid your burning face, and cowered
    Blushing, but not with shame?

"And, mother, was it thus, ay, thus,
    That when my father said
Those words—it seemed an angel's voice
    Wakening the newly dead?

"No death—sweet life! Shall I arise,
    And walk, serene and strong,
My mother's household ways, and sing
    My mother's household song?

"Shall I stand by him, as you stand
    By my dear father's side,
And hear, as you heard yesternight,
    'Dearer the wife than bride?'

"And—strange—O passing strange, to think,
    If ever there should be
For me, grown old, a young arm's clasp,
    Mother, as mine clasps thee?

"O mother, mother, hold me close,
    Until these tears run dry,
God, Thou wert very merciful,
    Who wouldst not let me die!"

AMONG THE TOMBS.

"Ci rivedremo !"

THINK I never saw this place so fair ;—
For, entering, a sea of sunshine pale
Rolled over us, and breaking on the edge
Of an October rain-cloud, wide outspread
In a great flood o'er all the land of graves.

"Look—those far headstones ! How they seem to
      rest
Like lambs upon June meadows ; or snow-sails
Each dropped upon the black sea like a smile ;
Or groups of white-clad children, suddenly
Upstarting in a sunny moor at play :
You would not think this was a field of graves ? "

Ah no ! for with our footsteps entered Life—
Life, staggering underneath her burden sore ;
Life, thrilling with strange touches at her heart ;
Life, with her sad eyes looking up to God ;
Life, with her warm hands clinging still to man ;
Life, blindfold, wondering, gay, despairing, glad,
Gazing at Death with a soft ignorant smile,
That said : "What doest thou here ? "
                          Ay, what doest here
Thou Terror—thou Divider ? We i' the sun
Walk meekly, saying unto Care, "Go by !
Thou art but one—we two ; " and unto Pain,
"God loves all those who suffer, doing no wrong :
And Time, the equal-handed, levels all."

Therefore, O Life, that laugh'st beside these tombs
Hiding behind the splendors grim of Death,

As a child hides behind a murderer's robe ;
Therefore, O Death, that throwest thy garment cool
And wide over this Life, who maniac wild
Runs to and fro, and wrings her bleeding hands,
O Life, the healer, sanctifier of Death,
O Death, which art Life's end, and aim, and crown,
Here be ye reconciled, like parted friends,
Who, shrinking, feared to meet each other's brows,
And read "foe" written there.   Gaze long and
               calm,
Like these who, gazing, know no possible hand
Save that which looses all things, e'er can bind
Them closer.   And gaze tenderly, as those
Who through all chance, all change of place or time,
All glory, all dishonor, all delight,
And all despair, walk constant night and day
Each in the other's shadow—face to face—
Waiting the supreme hour that makes of both
(Life merged in Death, and Death in Life divine)
An indivisible and perfect one,
Married for ever.

RETROSPECTION.

For a Swedish Air.

INDS in the trees
    Chant a glad song ;
    O'er fields the bees
Hum all day long :
Night lulls the breezes, the bees' hum is o'er—
Nature, like thee, changes ever more.

But sunshine bright
    Wakens the bees :
Airs warm and light

Stir the young trees :
Morn is returning with joy-laden store—
Thou wilt return to me—never more !

THE HIGH MOUNTAIN.

For a Welsh Air.

N yonder high mountain the dawn rested first,
 On yonder high mountain the risen sun burst,
 To yonder high mountain I turned thro' the
  day,
Though o'er it mists hovered and rain-clouds hung
  gray.

The rain fell impetuous, the stormy winds blew,
The mists slow descended and hid it from view,
No foot of man trod on its summit dew-pearled,
Yet the dream of it followed me over the world.

Still yonder high mountain sits silent and grand,
And looks like a king over ocean and land,
And when evening purples its heathery breast,
In sight of yon mountain I 'll go to my rest.

. A CHRISTMAS BLESSING.

1867.

EAREST friends of all the rest !
 Let my heart, in peace possessed,
 With its quivering wings safe furled,
No more beat about the world,—
This strange world, so sad. so wide,—
Fly to you this Christmas tide.

Fly—or call you each and all
With the low mysterious call
Of sweet fancy, steadfast love,
Faith that mountains can remove,
Memory that backward turns
Smiling o'er her green wreathed urns;
Hope, uprising like a sun
In child-faces one by one,
Glad to fare as we once fared,
Strong to do what we but dared :
By these spells of magic awe
You unto my heart I draw.

Shepherd of the household flock,
   Righteous father, husband fond
Honor-based as on a rock,
   Seeing the right—and nought beyond :
Veering not with fortune's breath,
   By no selfish currents driven ;—
As we sail through life towards death
   Bound unto the same port—heaven,—
Friend, what years could us divide ?
God thee bless this Christmas tide '.

Mother—made for motherhood,
   Wife most fit, most true, most rare—
Busy after others' good,
   For herself the last to care,
Chosen Mary not more pure,
   Like her, brave and strong of heart,
Bright to enjoy, brave to endure,
   As is wife's and mother's part,—
God guide thee, the home's best guide—
This—and every Christmas tide.

Then, the little nest of doves;
   The delight of heart and eyes;
—My girl-queen of coming loves,

Childish sweet and woman-wise,
—Boys—to all the future heir,
   Statesmen, soldiers yet—who knows?
Opening petals fresh and fair
   Of the glowing household rose;—
Proud I wear you in my breast,—
   Dear I hold you, every one,
Treasure of the years possessed—
   Comfort of the years unknown;
Whatsoe'er those years may hide—
God bless all this Christmas tide.

POEMS FOR CHILDREN.

VIOLETS.

IOLETS, violets, sweet March violets
    Sure as March comes, they'll come too,
    First the white and then the blue—
Pretty violets!

White, with just a pinky dye;
Blue, as little baby's eye,—
So like violets.

Though the rough wind shakes the house,
Knocks about the budding boughs,
There are violets.

Though the passing snow-storms come,
Frightening all the birdies dumb,
Up spring violets:

One by one among the grass,
Saying " Pluck me ! " as we pass, —
Scented violets.

By and by there 'll be so many,
We'll pluck dozens nor miss any :
Sweet, sweet violets!

Children, when you go to play,
Look beneath the hedge to-day : —
Mamma likes violets.

YOUNG DANDELION.

OUNG Dandelion
 On a hedge-side,
 Said young Dandelion,
"Who'll be my bride?

"I'm a bold fellow
 As ever was seen,
With my shield of yellow,
 In the grass green.

"You may uproot me
 From field and from lane,
Trample me, cut me,—
 I spring up again.

"I never flinch, Sir,
 Wherever I dwell;
Give me an inch, Sir,
 I'll soon take an ell.

"Drive me from garden
 In anger and pride,
I'll thrive and harden
 By the road-side.

"Not a bit fearful,
 Showing my face,
Always so cheerful
 In every place."

Said young Dandelion,
 With a sweet air,

"I have my eye on
  Miss Daisy fair.

"Though we may tarry
  Till past the cold,
Her I will marry
  Ere I grow old.

"I will protect **her**
  From all kinds of harm,
Feed her with nectar,
  Shelter her warm.

"What'er the weather,
  Let it go by ;
We'll hold together,
  Daisy and I.

"I'll ne'er give **in,**—no !
  Nothing I fear :
All that I win, O !
  - I'll keep for **my dear.**"

Said young Dandelion
  On his hedge-side,
"Who'll me rely on ?
  Who'll be my bride ? "

RUNNING AFTER THE RAINBOW.

HY thus aside your playthings throw,
  Over the wet lawn hurrying so ?
  Where are you going, I want to know ? "
" I'm running after the rainbow."

"Little boy, with your bright brown eyes
Full of an innocent surprise,
Stop a minute, my Arthur wise,
    What do you want with the rainbow ? "

Arthur paused in his headlong race,
Turned to his mother his hot, young face,
"Mother, I want to reach the pláce
    At either end of the rainbow.

"Nurse says, wherever it meets the ground,
Such beautiful things may oft be found
Buried below, or scattered round,
    If one can but catch the rainbow.

"O, please don't hinder me, mother dear,
It will all be gone while I stay here ; "
So with many a hope and not one fear,
    The child ran after the rainbow.

Over the damp grass, ankle deep,
Clambering up the hilly steep,
And the wood where the birds were going to sleep,
    But he could n't catch the rainbow.

And when he came out at the wood's far side,
The sun was setting in golden pride,
There were plenty of clouds all rainbow dyed,
    But not a sign of the rainbow.

Said Arthur, sobbing, as home he went,
"I wish I had thought what mother meant ;
I wish I had only been content,
    And not ran after the rainbow."

THE BLACKBIRD AND THE ROOKS.

 SLENDER young Blackbird built in a thorn-tree:
A spruce little fellow as ever could be;
His bill was so yellow, his feathers so black,
So long was his tail, and so glossy his back,
That good Mrs. B., who sat hatching her eggs,
And only just left them to stretch her poor legs,
And pick for a minute the worm she preferred,
Thought there never was seen such a beautiful bird.

And such a kind husband! how early and late
He would sit at the top of the old garden gate,
And sing, just as merry as if it were June,
Being ne'er out of patience, or temper, or tune.
"So unlike those Rooks, dear; from morning till
        night
They seem to do nothing but quarrel and fight,
And wrangle and jangle, and plunder—while we
Sit, honest and safe, in our pretty thorn-tree."

Just while she was speaking, a lively young Rook
Alit with a flap that the thorn-bush quite shook,
And seizing a stick from the nest—"Come, I say,
That will just suit me, neighbor"—flew with it away.
The lady loud twittered—her husband soon heard:
Though peaceful, he was not a cowardly bird:
And with arguments angry enough to o'erwhelm
A whole Rookery—flew to the top of the elm.

"How dare you, you—" (thief he was going to say;
But a civiller sentiment came in the way:
For he knew 't is no good, and it anyhow shames
A gentleman, calling strange gentlemen names:)
"Pray what is your motive, Sir Rook, for such tricks,
As building your mansion with other folks' sticks?
I request you 'll restore them, in justice and law."
At which the whole colony set up a—caw!

But Blackbird, not silenced, then spoke out again ;
" I've built my small nest with much labor and pain.
I'm a poor singing gentleman, Sirs, it is true,
Though cockneys do often mistake me for you ;
But I keep Mrs. Blackbird, and four little eggs,
And neither e'er pilfers, or borrows, or begs.
Now have I not right on my side, do you see ? "
But they flew at and pecked him all down the elm-
    tree.

Ah ! wickedness prospers sometimes, I much fear ;
And virtue's not always victorious, that 's clear :
At least, not at first : for it must be confessed
Poor Blackbird lost many a stick from his nest ;
And his unkind grand neighbors with scoffing caw-
    caws,
In his voice and his character found many flaws,
And jeered him and mocked him ; but when they 'd
    all done,
He flew to his tree and sang cheerily on.

At length May arrived with her garlands of leaves ;
The swallows were building beneath the farm-eaves,
Wrens, linnets, and sparrows, on every hedge-side,
Were bringing their families out with great pride ;
While far above all, on the tallest tree-top,
With a flutter and clamor that never did stop,
The haughty old Rooks held their heads up so high,
And dreamed not of trouble—until it drew nigh !

I don't say 't was cruel—I can't say 't was kind—
On the subject I have n't quite made up my mind:
But those guns went pop-popping all morning, alas!
And young Rooks kept dropping among the long grass,
Till good Mr. Blackbird, who watched the whole thing,
For pity could scarcely a single note sing,
And in the May sunset he hardly could bear
To hear the returning Rooks' caw of despair.

"O, dear Mrs. Blackbird," at last warbled he,
" How happy we are in our humble thorn-tree;
How gaily we live, living honest and poor,
How sweet are the may-blossoms over our door."
"And then our dear children," the mother replied,
And she nestled them close to her warm feathered side,
And with a soft twitter of drowsy content,
In the quiet May moonlight to sleep they all went.

JACK-IN-THE-GREEN.

H what a miserable May!
       Too cold to ride or walk or play,
         You children stayed in doors all day,
    Not *too* good, that's soon seen!
Well, well, what 's past we 'd best forget;
Papa 's come home out of the wet,
And, children, what do you think he met ?—
    Jack-in-the-green.

Jack-in-the-green 's a moving bower
Decked with green bough and paper flower;
Within it walks for many an hour
    Under his leafy screen,
Some poor sweep lad, while others, gay
In tattered finery, round him play;
For 't is the sweep's one holiday,
    Jack-in-the-green.

And after Jack there always goes
A tawdry lass with pinched-up toes,
Bright painted cheeks like cabbage-rose,
    And frock of spangled sheen,
Who dances, dances as she can,
And half-pence begs from boy or man;
And her they call "Maid Marian"
    To Jack-in-the-green.

As o'er the fire we cheerful sit,
And, our warm feet encircling it,
Though the rain pelts, care nŏt a bit
    That May like March has been,—
Children, shall father tell to you
A little tale, perhaps as true
As many a book-tale, and as new,
    Of what to-day he has seen?

He stopped to watch the sweeps advance,
Maid Marian began her dance
('T was by Snow Hill, where horses prance,
And cabs drive headlong down).
A child she was, thin, small of size,
With an old face, too sharp and wise
For any child, and heavy eyes,
    And long curls hanging brown.

Across the full street moves the show,
Jack-in-the-green first, staggering slow,
The fife and Pan's-pipes after go,
    Maid Marian skips between:
Up comes policeman with a frown;
Away flies Marian's flaunting gown,
The horses rear—ah! they 've knocked down
    Poor Jack-in-the-green.

*

My little children, snug and warm,
And sheltered from all kinds of harm,
I 'm glad you did not see that form
　　Papa picked up to-day
Out of the street, and carried where
Kind people of sick folk take care,—
A hospital, they call it,—there
　　At last the poor lad lay,

Quiet, upon his tidy bed,
With pale Maid Marian at his head,
In yellow gauze and tassels red,　　　　～
　　And white frock drenched with rain;
Hardly a word she said, until
The doctors went away, and still
He never stirred; then "Brother Will!"
　　She whispered; but in vain.

Half doubtfully my face she scanned,
And touched me with a timorous hand—
"Sir, you 're a doctor—understand
　　So much—please will you tell
A poor girl who 's no father got,
To whom no creature gives a thought;
I mean no harm, sir—whether or not
　　Poor Will may soon be well?

"There 's only brother Will and me,
And he sweeps chimneys, sir, do you see?
And very, very kind is he;
　　Does all that lad can do:
By being Jack-in-the-green this May,
He thought he 'd get "—she stopped to lay
Her hand on his—and drew it away—
　　"O Will, this can 't be you!"

But Will (perhaps he heard the child,
Though he was dying, children) smiled,

As dying people do—so mild
　　His face, so bright and clear.
" Bessy ! "—it sounded far away—
Like voices heard in evening gray :
" Tell Bessy "---What he meant to say,
　　Bessy must wait to hear.

Must wait, my children, till God call
Both rich and poor, and great and small,
Into His presence one and all :
　　Ending both death and pain ;
Where, howe'er old on earth she grow,
And he in heaven be changed also,
I think, poor Bessy sure will know
　　Her brother Will again.

And so, my children, do not weep,
For Will is only gone to sleep ;
And Bessy—why we 'll Bessy keep.
　　To sweep our nursery clean :
And after all her tears are dried,
Learn good things at mamma's dear side ;
Till he 'd be almost glad he died—
　　Poor Jack-in-the-green !

WATERLOO-DAY.

"NOW what is all this ? " cried Sir Richard bold,—
　　Little Sir Richard, twelve years old,
　　As he stood by his grandmother's easy chair,
His hand on his hip with a manly air :
" What is all this I hear them say,
No bells to be rung on Waterloo-day ? "

Grandmother turned and fondly eyed
The sword that hung on the wall beside.

And the bright June sunshine lay full and fair
On her widow's cap and her smooth gray hair:
" Grandfather wished ere he went away
That we should no longer keep Waterloo-day."

" What ? "—and Sir Richard grew hot and red,
And tossed indignant his curly head—
"Forget the day when we beat the French,
We—grandfather brave and uncle Trench ?
Forget the battle—what will folks say !
Grandfather's own great Waterloo-day ?

"And I, who shall be a soldier too,
And all that he did may some time do,
Killing the French by the dozen or score,
Getting a peerage perhaps, and more ;
When I am a man whom all must obey,
I *will* have the bells rung on Waterloo-day."

Grandmother smiled a soft, sad smile,
You could see a tear in her eye the while ;
"Richard, my boy, when you are a man,
If Sir Richard does all Sir Richard can
To be like Sir Robert—the folk will say
And think but little of Waterloo-day.

" Shall I tell you a story—it is not long—
About Sir Robert when he was young :
His fame in all mouths ;—and I liked to hear,
For I was a soldier's wife, my dear ;
And my heart leaped up with pride alway
At the very mention of Waterloo-day.

"But once, when people began to forget
The battle, the peace, and the island set
In the far-away sea where that Emperor died,
Whom nobody feared now—I beside
Your father's cradle sat singing gay :
It was five full years after Waterloo-day.

"Your grandfather, for he liked to be
Somewhere not far from the child and me,
Sat writing his letters; when sudden came
A change in his face I could hardly name,
'The Frenchman!' he said, and no more would say:
Till he told me what happened on Waterloo-day.

"It was a Frenchman—of many more
Whom you say we killed by the dozen or score,
Who dropped like the ranks of standing corn
That our troops gallopped thro', that fresh June morn,
By Hougoumont farm, as they passed that way
On the glorious charge of Waterloo-day.

"Only a Frenchman—dead, or showed
Like dead; so on your grandfather rode,
Rode over him—as troops *must* ride then
Over dead or dying or wounded men,
When a field 's to be won. 'Strike, charge and obey,'
Were the only words upon Waterloo-day.

" The horse trod heavy—the man shrieked.—Dear,
Your grandfather said he still could hear
The shrill, sharp cry, as the Frenchman prayed,
That he who *his* children had orphans made
Might never have living child to say,
'My father fought upon Waterloo-day.'"

"But he had!" cried Richard with eager eyes.
"Ay, because God answers not prayers that rise
Out of mad despair or ferocious wrong;
But your grandfather said he was haunted long
By the dying curse of this Jean Grosset,
Who was trampled to death on Waterloo-day."

Grandmother's voice sank faint and weak;
Little Sir Richard tried to speak—
"Jean Grosset! Is it"—"Hush, and hear!
Grandfather buried him. Many a year

Grandfather sought with vain essay
For his children, orphaned on Waterloo-**day**.

"But when dear grandfather was quite old,
And our son lay sleeping in churchyard mold,
And a tiny grandchild—Richard his name—
Was all that was left unto us, there came
A queer old lady called Ma'mselle Grosset,
To teach the boy French, one Waterloo-day.

"As Ma'mselle told her sorrowful tale,
I watched your grandfather's cheek turn pale,
As if—although forty years had fled—
The white, wan face of the soldier dead
Rose up before him, and seemed to say,
  This was the end of your Waterloo-day.' "

*   *   *   *   *

"Ma'mselle Grosset—dear Ma'mselle Grosset,
I will never more vex her in work or play;
But am I not grandfather's sword to get,
And fight for my queen and country yet?
Is all his glory to rust and decay?
Are we not to remember Waterloo-day?

"And what if the French grow proud and grand,
And threaten us over sea and land,
Are we English lads to stay meek at home,
And wait at our doors till the foe shall come;
Then take to our heels and run away
As if there had never been Waterloo-day?"

Grandmother's eyes flashed bright and bold;
"No—Fight, boy, fight! not for glory or gold,
For Honor! Let every hill and glen
Bristle with rifles, and shoot like men.
But until then, let us all of us pray
There may ne'er be another Waterloo-day."

THE MOON-DAISY.*

HO is his auntie's joy?
  Who loves her bonnie boy
    Week-day and Sunday?
Thinks of him night and morn
Ever since he was born—
  He 'll love her one day?

Come now, my wee, wee man!
Clutch as a baby can
  At the moon-daisy:
Pluck off the petals white
One by one—such delight:
  Laugh till you 're crazy.

" He loves me—he loves me not."—
(Poor auntie's quite forgot!)
  "Loves me not—loves me."
Ay, that's the real thing!
Climb up, my little king:
  Kiss, for that moves me.

Eyes, brow, and sunny hair—
I think my boy all fair;—
  Beauty or no beauty,
I'd love my winsome lad
From the top curl he had
  Down to his shoe-tie!

Bright hair, and eyes, and brow,
What—do you trust me now?
  That my best praise is.
" He loves me—he loves me not—
He loves me!" unasked, unbought—
  Throw down the daisies!

*Children pluck this flower petal by petal, saying, " You love me—you love me not," alternately: the last petal being supposed to tell the truth

THE SHAKING OF THE PEAR-TREE.

OF all days I remember,
  In summers passed away,
  Was " the shaking of the pear-tree,"
In grandma's orchard gay.

A large old-fashioned orchard,
  With long grass under foot,
And blackberry-brambles crawling
  In many a tangled shoot.

From cherry time, till damsons
  Dropped from the branches sere,
That wonderful old orchard
  Was full of fruit all year ;

We pick'd it up in baskets,
  Or pluck'd it from the wall ;
But the shaking of the pear-tree
  Was the grandest treat of all.

Long, long the days we counted
  Until that day drew nigh ;
Then, how we watched the sun set,
  And criticised the sky !

If rain—"'T will clear at midnight ; "
  If dawn broke chill and gray,
"O many a cloudy morning
  Turns out a lovely day."

So off we started gaily,
  Heedless of jolt or jar ;
Through town, and lane, and hamlet,
  In old Llewellyn's car.

He's dead and gone—Llewellyn,
   These twenty years, I doubt:
If I put him in this poem,
   He'll never find it out,

The patient, kind Llewellyn—
   Whose broad face smiled all o'er,
As he lifted out us children
   At grandma's very door.

And there stood Grandma's Betty,
   With cheeks like apples red;
And Dash, the spaniel, waddled
   Out of his cosy bed.

With silky ears down drooping,
   And coat of chestnut pale;
He was so fat and lazy
   He scarce could wag his tail.

Poor Dash is dead, and buried
   Under the lilac-tree;
And Betty's old,—as, children,
   We all may one day be.

I hope no child will vex us,
   As we vexed Betty then,
With winding up the draw-well,
   Or hunting the old hen.

And teasing, teasing, teasing,
   Till afternoon wore round,
And shaken pears came tumbling
   In showers upon the ground.

O how we jumped and shouted!
   O how we plunged amid
The long grass, where the treasures,
   Dropped down and deftly hid;

Long, slender-shaped, red-russet,
　　Or yellow just like gold ;
Ah ! never pears have tasted
　　Like those sweet pears of old !

We ate—I 'd best not mention
　　How many : paused to fill
Big basket after basket ;
　　Working with right good-will ;

Then hunted round the orchard
　　For half-ripe plums—in vain ;
So, back unto the pear-tree,
　　To eat, and eat again.

I 'm not on my confession,
　　And therefore need not say
How tired, and cross, and sleepy,
　　Some were ere close of day ;

For pleasure has its ending,
　　And eke its troubles too ;
Which you 'll find out, my children,
　　As well as we could do.

But yet this very minute,
　　I seem to see it all—
The pear-tree's empty branches,
　　The gray of evening-fall ;

The children's homeward silence,
　　The furnace fires that glowed,
Each mile or so, out streaming
　　Across the lonely road ;

And high, high set in heaven,
　　One large, bright, beauteous star,
That shone between the curtains
　　Of old Llewellyn's car.

IN SWANAGE BAY.

WAS five and forty year ago,
 Just such another morn,
  The fishermen were on the beach,
 The reapers in the corn ;
My tale is true, young gentlemen,
 As sure as you were born.

" My tale 's all true, young gentlemen,"
 The good old boatman cried
Unto the sullen, angry lads,
 Who vain obedience tried ;
" Mind what your father says to you,
 And don't go out this tide.

" Just such a shiny sea as this,
 Smooth as a pond, you'd say,
And white gulls flying, and the crafts
 Down Channel making way ;
And Isle of Wight, all glittering bright,
 Seen clear from Swanage Bay.

" The Battery point, the Race beyond,
 Just as to-day you see :
This was, I think, the very stone
 Where sat Dick, Dolly, and me ;
She was our little sister, sirs,
 A small child, just turned three.

"And Dick was mighty fond of her :
 Though a big lad and bold,
He 'd carry her like any nurse,
 Almost from birth, I 'm told ;
For mother sickened soon, and died
 When Doll was eight months old.

"We sat and watched a little boat,
  Her name the Tricksy Jane,
A queer old tub laid up ashore;
  But we could see her plain;
To see her and not haul her up
  Cost us a deal of pain.

" Said Dick to me, 'Let's have a pull;
  Father will never know,
He's busy in his wheat up there,
  And cannot see us go:
These landsmen are such cowards, if
  A puff of wind does blow.

" 'I've been to France and back three times—
  Who knows best, Dad or me,
Whether a craft's seaworthy or not?—
  Dolly, wilt go to sea?'
And Dolly laughed, and hugged him tight,
  As pleased as she could be.

" I don't mean, sirs, to blame poor Dick:
  What he did, sure I'd do:
And many a sail in Tricksy Jane
  We'd had when she was new.
Father was always sharp; and what
  He said, he meant it too.

"But now the sky had not a cloud,
  The bay looked smooth as glass;
Our Dick could manage any boat,
  As neat as ever was;
And Dolly crowed, ' Me go to sea!'
  The jolly little lass!

" Well, sirs, we went; a pair of oars,
  My jacket for a sail;
Just round ' Old Harry and his Wife'—

Those rocks there, within hail—
And we came back.—D 'ye want to hear,
   The end o' the old man's tale?

"Ay, ay, we came back, past that point,
   But then a breeze up-sprung;
Dick shouted, 'Hoy! down sail!' and pulled
   With all his might among
The white sea-horses that uprear'd
   So terrible and strong.

"I pulled too; I was blind with fear,—
   But I could hear Dick's breath
Coming and going, as he told
   Dolly to creep beneath
His jacket, and not hold him so:
   We rowed for life or death.

"We almost reached the sheltered bay,
   We could see father stand
Upon the little jetty here,
   His sickle in his hand—
The houses white, the yellow fields,
   The safe and pleasant land.

"And Dick, though pale as any ghost,
   Had only said to me,
'We 're all right now, old lad!' when up
   A wave rolled—drenched us three—
One lurch—and then I felt the chill
   And roar of blinding sea.

"I don't remember much but that—
   You see, I 'm safe and sound;
I have been wrecked four times since then,
   Seen queer sights, I 'll be bound:
I think folks sleep beneath the deep,
   As calm as under ground."

"But Dick and Dolly?" "Well, poor Dick!
 I saw him rise and cling
Unto the gunwale of the boat—
 Floating keel up—and sing
Out loud, ' Where's Doll?'—I hear him yet,
 As clear as any thing.

" ' Where's Dolly?' I no answer made:
 For she dropped like a stone
Down through the deep sea—and it closed:
 The little thing was gone.
' Where's Doll?" three times—then Dick loosed
   hold
 And left me there alone."

" It's five and forty year since then,"
 Muttered the boatman gray
And drew his rough hand o'er his eyes,
 And stared across the bay;
" Just five and forty year!"—And not
 Another word did say.

" But Dolly?" ask the children all,
 As they about him stand;—
'' Poor Doll! she floated back next tide
 With seaweed in her hand.
She's buried o'er that hill you see,
 In a churchyard on land.

" But where Dick lies, God knows! He'll find
 Our Dick at judgment day."—
The boatman fell to mending nets,
 The boys ran off to play;
And the sun shone and the waves danced
 In quiet Swanage Bay.

THE WONDERFUL APPLE-TREE.*

OME here, my dear boys, and I 'll tell you a fable,
Which you may believe as much as you 're able;
It is 'nt all true, nor all false, I 'll be bound—
Of the tree that bears apples all the year round.

There was a Dean Tucker of Gloster city,
Who may have been wise, or worthy, or witty;
But I know nothing of him, the more 's the pity,
Save that he was Dean Tucker of Gloster city.

And walking one day with a musing air
In his Deanery garden, close by where
The great cathedral's west window 's seen,—
" I 'll plant an apple," said Tucker the Dean.

The apple was planted, the apple grew,
A stout young tree, full of leaves not few;
The apple was grafted, the apple bore
Of goodly apples, one, two, three, four.

The old Dean walked in his garden fair,
" I 'm glad I planted that young tree there,
Though it was but a shoot, or some old tree's sucker;
I 'll taste it to-morrow," said good Dean Tucker.

But lo, in the night when (they say) trees talk,
And some of the liveliest get up and walk,
With fairies abroad for watch and warden,—
There was such a commotion in the Dean's garden!

* This tree, known among gardeners by the name of "Winter-hanger"
or " Forbidden Fruit," was planted by Dean Tucker in 1760. It, or an off
shoot from it, still exists in the city of Gloucester.

" I will not be gathered," the apple-tree said
" Was it for this I blossomed so red?
Hung out my fruit all the summer days,
Got so much sunshine, and pleasure and praise?"

"Ah!" interrupted a solemn red plum,
"This is the end to which all of us come;
Last month I was laden with hundreds—but now"—
And he sighed the last little plum off from his bough.

"Nay, friend, take it easy," the pear-tree replied
(A lady-like person against the wall-side),
"Man guards, nurtures, trains us from top down to
    root:
I think 'tis but fair we should give him our fruit."

"No, I'll not be gathered," the apple resumed,
And shook his young branches, and fluttered and
    fumed;
" And I 'll not drop neither, as some of you drop,
Over-ripe: I'm determined to keep my whole crop.

" And I with "—O'er his branches just then *some-
    thing* flew;
It seemed like moth, large and grayish of hue,
But it was a Fairy. Her voice soft did sound,
"Be the tree that bears apples all the year round."

*   *   *   *   *   *   *

The Dean to his apple-tree, came, full of hope,
But tough was the fruit-stalk as double-twist rope,
And when he had cut it with patience and pain,
He bit just one mouthful—and never again.

"An apple so tasteless, so juiceless, so hard,
Is, sure, good for nought but to bowl in the yard;
The choir-boys may have it." But choir-boys soon
    found
It was worthless—the tree that bore all the year
    round.

And Gloster lads climbing the Deanery wall
Were punished, as well might all young thieves
    appal,
For, clutching the booty for which they did sin,
They bit at the apples—and left their teeth in !

And thus all the year from October till May,
From May till October, the apples shone gay ;
But 't was just outside glitter, for no hand was
    found
To pluck at the fruit which hung all the year
    round.

And so till they rotted, those queer apples hung,
The bare boughs and blossoms and ripe fruit among ;
And in Gloster city it still may be found—
The tree that bears apples all the year round.

———

A HARE-HUNT.

(From the Hare's side of the question.)

T WAS an October evening
    So still and clear and cold :
    All red and gray the frosty sun
  Went down behind the wold ;
And far off church-bells faintly pealed.
Across the lonely stubble field.

The rabbits darted in and out,
    The corn-crake hoarsely cried,
The tiny field-mouse came and peered
    And picked a grain beside
The creature that lay panting there,
    Only a solitary hare.

Four hours since, and along the brook
　She watched the huntsmen pass,
And the dogs follow—the scent lost
　In the tall reedy grass,
And still she lay and trembled there,
This little, helpless, tired-out hare.

But when the staring sun had set,
　And earth in shadow grew,
While just one twinkling friendly star
　Peeped at her through the blue,
And fast asleep was every bird—
The little hare her weak limbs stirred.

And creeping, creeping, slow she came
　Unto the furze-bush old,
'Neath which her half-grown leverets
　Had huddled from the cold,
Close by the spot where safe and warm
She reared them in her summer "form."

And what the leverets said to her,
　And what the hare said too,
A little bird has told to me,
　And I'll tell part to you—
Just "make-believe," of creatures weak
Who feel, although they cannot speak.

"My children," sighed the mother hare,
　With short and sobbing breath,
"I have not many words to say,
　I'm hunted unto death—
What can great two-legged creatures see,
In chasing a small thing like me?

"Your father—Ah, he *was* a hare!
　I've thought so, oft and oft:
His ears so long, his fur so gray,

His breast so white and soft:
They coursed him, miles and miles—and then
Killed him—those cruel dogs and men.

"*Why* did they? I, a silly hare,
  Could never understand:
So I stole home alone across
  The wood and the ploughed land,
And in our furze-bush mournfully
Brought up my leverets, one, two, three.

"But as the summer time went past,
  You grew so big and strong,
And frisked so merrily, that I
  Almost forgot my wrong,
And nibbled with a fresh delight
Each dewy morn and moonlight night.

"I did my best to keep you off
  The wire-fenced garden ground,
And bade you never lettuce eat
  While clover might be found;
But fly from guns, and gins, and snares
Like wise and careful little hares.

"We never did them any harm,
  (At least, not that I know),
Those creatures who walk upright and
  Make crick-cracks as they go.
Which if they point at a hare's side,
He dies—even as your father died.

"Well, after that we lived forlorn:
  But we lived peacefully;
Had, on the whole, a pleasant year,
  My leverets and I;
And fed and played together, gay,
Until that sad, sad yesterday.

"I lay within my cosy 'form,'
  As still as sitting bird;
The dread approach of hounds or men,
  I never even heard,
Till the pack neared me in full cry,
Then—off like lightning started I.

"I thought but how far I could run
  From where my leverets played,
And then I should not fear so much
  The cruel noise they made,
Those dogs;—I skimmed on like the wind,
Until I left them far behind.

"I stopped to breathe—my heart beat fast—
  But up again they came;
I doubled—crossed—went on again,
  But it was all the same;
And nearer, louder, fiercer grew
The yelping of the horrid crew.

"The fields and hedges flew along,
  The cows stood strange and still:
And I was torn with briers, and bruised
  Adown the quarried hill;
I almost felt the hounds' sharp teeth,
When lo!—that brook the wood beneath.

"It ran so quiet, dark, and deep:
  I thought—'I can but die:
It will not hurt me quite so much
  As dropping dreadfully
Into those foamy wide-mouthed jaws; —
So, in I plunged without one pause.

"Safe—safe! Pack—hunters—all went by
  I'm here my babes among"—
And while she spoke, up through the air

Went the first bird's first song;
The gray dawn reddened on the hill;
The hare turned—shivered—and was still.

Her pretty limbs grew stiff and stark,
 Her glazed eyes opened wide:
Under the furze-bush many a week
 She lay where she had died:
Until the drifting leaves and snow
Buried her safe that none might know.

But how her little leverets throve,
 How long they lived, and well:—
Were coursed or hunted, shot or snared,
 In truth I cannot tell.
Still, many gentlemen declare
It is grand sport to hunt a hare.

THE TWO RAIN-DROPS.

SAID a drop to a drop, "Just look at me!
 I'm the finest rain-drop you ever did see:
 I have lived ten seconds at least on my pane;
Swelling and filling and swelling again.

"All the little rain-drops unto me run,
I watch them and catch them and suck them up each
  one:
All the pretty children stand and at me stare;
Pointing with their fingers—'That's the biggest drop
  there.'"

"Yet you are but a drop," the small drop replied;
"I don't myself see much cause for pride:
The bigger you swell up,—we know well, my friend,—
The faster you run down, the sooner you'll end.

"For me, I'm contented outside on my ledge,
Hearing the patter of rain in the hedge;
Looking at the firelight and the children fair,—
Whether they look at me, I'm sure I don't care."

"Sir," cried the first drop, "your talk is but dull;
I can't wait to listen, for I'm almost full;
You'll run a race with me?—No?—Then 't is plain
I am the largest drop in the whole pane."

Off ran the big drop, at first rather slow;
Then faster and faster, as drops will, you know:
Raced down the window-pane, like hundreds before,
Just reached the window-sill—one splash—and was o'er.

THE YEAR'S END.

O grows the rising year, and so declines
    By months, weeks, days, unto its peaceful
        end;
Even as by slow and ever varying signs
  Through childhood, youth, our solemn steps we bend
  Up to the crown of life, and thence descend.

Great Father, who of every one takest care,
  From him on whom full ninety years are piled
To the young babe, just taught to lisp a prayer
  About the "Gentle Jesus, meek and mild,"
  Who children loves, being once Himself a child,—

O make us day by day like Him to grow;
  More pure and good, more dutiful and meek;
Because He loves those who obey Him so;
  Because His love is the best thing to seek,
  Because without His love, all loves are weak,—

All earthly joys are miserable and poor,
   All earthly goodness quickly droops and dies,
Like rootless flowers you plant in gardens—sure
   That they will flourish—till in mid-day skies
   The sun burns, and they fade before your eyes.

O God, who art alone the life and light
   Of this strange world to which as babes we come,
Keep Thou us always children in Thy sight :
   Guide us from year to year, thro' shine and gloom
   And at our year's end, Father, take us home.

THE JEALOUS BOY.

WHAT, my little foolish Ned,
   Think you mother's eyes are blind,
   That her heart has grown unkind,
And she will not turn her head,
   Cannot see, for all her joy,
   Her poor jealous little boy ?

What though sister be the pet—
   Laughs, and leaps, and clings, and loves.
   With her eyes as soft as dove's—
Why should yours with tears be wet ?
   Why such angry tears let fall ?
   Mother's heart has room for all.

Mother's heart is very wide,
   And its doors all open stand :
   Lightest touch of tiniest hand
She will never put aside.
   Why her happiness destroy,
   Foolish, naughty, jealous boy ?

Come within the circle bright,
   Where we laugh, and dance, and sing,
   Full of love to everything ;

As God loves us, day and night,
　And *forgives* us.　Come—with joy
Mother too forgives her boy.

———

ST. GEORGE AND THE DRAGON.

"Dieu et mon droit."

HAT, weeping, weeping, my little son,
　　Angry tears like that great commander
　　Alexander—
Because of dragons is left not one
To be a new Cappadocian scourge
For your bold slaying
In grand arraying,
Mounted alone, eh?
On Shetland pony
A knight all perfect, a young St. George?

Come sit at my knee, my little son:
Sit at my knee and mend your wagon:—
Full many a dragon
You'll have to fight with ere life be done.
Come, shall I tell you of three or four—
Villainous cattle!
For you to battle,
When mother's sleeping
Where all your weeping
Will not awaken her any more?

First, there's a creature whose name is Sloth,
Looks like a lizard, creeping on sleekly
Simple and weakly,
Powerless to injure however wroth:
But slay him, my lad, or he'll slay you!

Crawling and winding,
Twisting and binding :
Break from him, tramp on him
And as you stamp on him
You 'll be St. George and the dragon anew.

Then there 's a monster—so fair at first,
Called Ease, or Comfort, or harmless Pleasure ;
Born of smooth Leisure—
On Luxury's lap delicious nurst ;
Who 'd buy your soul if you 'd sell it—just
To catch one minute
With joyance on it
Or ward off sorrow
Until to-morrow—
Trample him, trample him into dust !

One more—the reptile yclept False Shame,
That silently drags its feltered length on,
And tries its strength on
Many a spirit else pure from blame ;
But up and at him your courser urge !
Smite hard, I trow, hard
The moral coward,
At throne or altar,
Nor once, once falter—
And be my own son, my brave St. George !

St. George and the dragon—ah, my boy,
There are many old dragons left, world-scourges,
And few St. Georges—
There 's much of labor and little of joy !
But on with you—on to the endless fight—
Your sword firm buckle,
To no man truckle,
Wave your bold flag on
And slay your dragon.
St. George for ever !   God and my right !

A DYING CHILD.

HOW the trembling children gather round,
   Startled out of sleep, and scared and cry-
      ing:
" Is our merry little sister dying?
Will men come and put her underground

"As they did poor baby, last May-day?
   Or will shining angels stoop and take her
   On their snow-white wings to heaven, and make her
Sit among the stars as fair as they?

" But she 'll have no mother there to kiss!
   We are sorely frightened," say the children
   Thinking of this death, so strange, bewildering—
" Tell us, only tell us, what death is?"

Ah, we cannot, any more than you!
   We are also children—of one Father;
   And we only know that He will gather
All His own, and keep them safely too.

So this death as sweet as sleep is made;
   For where'er we go, we go *together*.
   Father, mother, children: He knows whither.
Since He takes us we are not afraid.

Whether little sister lives or dies,
   She is quite, quite safe. Hush—cease all weeping:
   Christ, who once said " Lazarus is *sleeping*,"
Will awake us all in Paradise.

BIRDS IN THE SNOW.

CHILD.

 WISH I were a little bird
   When the sun shines
   And the wind whispers low,
  Through the tall pines,
I 'd rock in the elm tops,
  Rifle the pear-tree,
Hide in the cherry boughs,
  O such a rare tree!

I wish I were a little bird;
  All summer long
I 'd fly so merrily
  Sing such a song!
Song that should never cease
  While daylight lasted,
Wings that should never tire
  Howe'er they hasted.

MOTHER.

But if you were a little bird—
  My baby-blossom.
Nestling so cosily
  In mother's bosom,—
A bird, as we see them now,
  When the snows harden,
And the wind's blighting breath
  Howls round the garden:

What would you do, poor bird,
  In winter drear?
No nest to creep into,
  No mother near:

Hungry and desolate
   Weary and woeful,
All the earth bound with frost,
   All the sky snow-full?

     CHILD (*thoughtfully*).

That would be sad, and yet
   Hear what I 'd do—
Mother, in winter time
   I 'd come to you!
If you can like the birds
   Spite of their thieving,
Give them your trees to build,
   Garden to live in,

I think if I were a bird
   When winter comes
I 'd trust you, mother dear,
   For a few crumbs,
Whether I sang or not,
   Were lark, thrush, or starling.—

     MOTHER (*aside*).

Then—Father—I trust *Thee*
   With this my darling.

THE STORY OF THE BIRKENHEAD.

Told to two children.

AND so you want a fairy tale,
   My little maidens twain?
Well, sit beside the waterfall,
   Noisy with last night's rain;

On couch of moss, with elfin spears
  Bristling, all fierce to see,
When from the yet brown moor down drops
  The lonely April bee.

All the wide valley blushes green,
  While, in far depths below,
Wharfe flashes out a great bright eye,
  Then hides his shining flow;—

Wharfe, busy, restless, rapid Wharfe,
  The glory of our dale;
O I could of the River Wharfe
  Tell such a fairy tale!

"The Boy of Egremond," you cry,—
  "And all the 'bootless bene:'
We know that poem, every word,
  And we the Strid have seen."

No, clever damsels: though the tale
  Seems still to bear a part,
In every lave of Wharfe's bright wave,
  The broken mother's heart—

Little you know of broken hearts,
  My Kitty, blithe and wise,
Grave Mary, with the woman soul
  Dawning through childish eyes.

And long, long distant may God keep
  The day when each shall know
The entrance to His kingdom through
  His baptism of woe!

But yet 't is good to hear of grief
  Which He permits to be;
Even as in our green inland home
  We talk of wrecks at sea.

So on this lovely day, when spring
　　Wakes soft o'er moor and dale,
I'll tell—not quite your wish—but **yet**
　　A noble "fairy" tale.

                                    * ·

'T was six o'clock in the morning,
　　The sea like crystal lay,
When the good troop-ship Birkenhead
　　Set sail from Simon's Bay.

The Cape of Good Hope on her right
　　Gloomed at her through the noon:
Brief tropic twilight fled, and night
　　Fell suddenly and soon.

At eight o'clock in the evening
　　Dim grew the pleasant land;
O'er smoothest seas the southern heaven
　　Its starry arch out-spanned.

The soldiers on the bulwarks leaned,
　　Smoked, chatted; and below
The soldiers' wives sang babes to sleep,
　　While on the ship sailed slow.

Six hundred and thirty souls held she,
　　Good, bad, old, young, rich, poor;
Six hundred and thirty living souls—
　　God knew them all.—Secure

He counted them in His right hand,
　　That held the hungering seas;
And to four hundred came a voice—
　　"The Master hath need of these."

On, onward still the vessel went,
  Till, with a sudden shock,
Like one that 's clutched by unseen Death,
  She struck upon a rock.

She filled. Not hours, not minutes left;
  Each second a life 's gone:
Drowned in their berths, washed overboard,
  Lost, swimming, one by one;

Till, o'er this chaos of despair
  Rose, like celestial breath,
The law of order, discipline,
  Obedience unto death.

The soldiers mustered upon deck,
  As mute as on parade;
"Women and children to the boats!"
  And not a man gainsayed.

Without a murmur or a moan
  They stood, formed rank and file,
Between the dreadful crystal seas
  And the sky's dreadful smile.

In face of death they did their work
  As they in life would do,
Embarking at a quiet quay—
  A quiet, silent crew.

"Now each man for himself. To the boats!"
  Arose a passing cry.
The soldier-captain answered, "Swamp
  The women and babes?—No, die!"

And so they died. Each in his place,
  Obedient to command,
They went down with the sinking ship,
  Went down in sight of land.

The great sea oped her mouth, and closed
　　O'er them.   Awhile they trod
The valley of the shadow of death,
　　And then were safe with God.

　　　　　　*　　　*

My little girlies—What! your tears
　　Are dropping on the grass,
Over my more than "fairy" tale,
　　A tale that "really was!"

Nay, dry them.   If we could but see
　　The joy in angels' eyes
O'er good lives, or heroic deaths
　　Of pure self-sacrifice,—

We should not weep o'er these that sleep —
　　Their short, sharp struggle o'er—
Under the rolling waves that break
　　Upon the Afric shore.

God works not as man works, nor sees
　　As man sees: though we mark
Ofttimes the moving of His hands
　　Beneath the eternal Dark.

But yet we know that all is well
　　That He, who loved all these,
Loves children laughing on the moor,
　　Birds singing in the trees;

That He who made both life and death,
　　He knoweth which is best:
We live to Him, we die to Him,
　　And leave Him all the rest.

MAGNUS AND MORNA.

A SHETLAND FAIRY TALE.

IN FOUR SCENES.

WITH MUSIC.

CHARACTERS.

MAGNUS	A *Fisherman*	(Tenor.)
FEA	*His Mother*	(Contralto.)
MORNA		(Soprano.)
TWO CHILDREN.		

Six Sea-Maids (MORNA'S *Sisters*), *Fishermen, and Girls, as Chorus.*

SCENE I.

OVERTURE.—*During which the curtain rises upon a wild sea-shore in the Shetland Isles. Stormy night. Moon comes out and makes a pathway across the water, along which are seen gliding seven figures—sea-maids—to elfin music. They disappear behind a rock and the music ceases.*

Then enter MAGNUS, *dejectedly. He sits down on a stone and sings—*

A broken-hearted fisherman I wander to and fro,
My sail flaps idle in the wind, my nets hang loose below,
There is no quiet in the night, no sunshine in the day,
For my love she is married and gone far away—O iero—
My love she is married and gone far away.

Her lips were red as coral, her hair was soft and brown ;
Her voice was like the birds' songs before the sun goes
    down.
I hear it through the silence of heavy night and day,
Though my love she is married and gone far away—O
    iero—
My love she is married and gone far away.

*   [The elfin music is heard beginning again* ; MAGNUS
starts and listens.

MAGNUS.

Is it the song of winds and waters,
Or the voice of the ocean-daughters
That once a year upon Midsummer-night
Come to dance on the sea-sand white,

Clad in their sealskins soft and fair ?
Which if they lose—O deep despair !
They can never return to the sea.—
Hush !—I behold them.   How fair they be !

He hides behind a rock.   Enter seven sea-maids ; one (MORNA)
*being distinguished by very long yellow hair.   They take off
their sealskin robes, lay them in a heap, and join hand-in-
hand singing—*

Dance we, dance we over the strand,
Half on ocean and half on land.
Dance we merrily as we go,
Mimicking mortals—O iero.

Sing we, sing we, all through the night,
Under the dreamy moonshine white,
Till morning glimmers and then we go—
Plunge into ocean—O iero.

The last musical phrase is an echo of MAGNUS's *song. He repeats it from his hiding-place, on which the music stops confusedly, and the sea-maids begin searching for their sealskins. The youngest sister,* MORNA, *who cannot find hers, goes about wringing her hands and singing the same tune, with sorrowful expression.*

MORNA.

I search for my sealskin over the sand,
Half on ocean and half on land,
Singing mournfully as I go—
Where is my sealskin ?—O iero!

MAGNUS *again echoes "O iero"—upon which the seven sea-maid, vanish—and six seals are seen swimming away from behind the rock into the far-away sea.*

MAGNUS (*advancing with a bewildered air*).

Dream of the night, if a dream it be—
Stay, O stay, lovely maids of the sea !—
My eyes are dazzled, my heart beats fast ;

[*He kicks his foot against something, which he picks up
and examines carefully.*

What is this that the wave has cast
At my very feet ?   A sealskin fair ?

MORNA (*behind the scenes*).

Where is my sealskin, where, O where ?

[MAGNUS *hastily hides the sealskin in his breasts
and crouches down again beside the rock, watching.*

Enter MORNA, *weeping and wringing her hands.*

Lost ! lost ! lost !
O the dance on the fatal coast !
O my father and O my mother !
O my dearest sisters and brother !
O my palace beneath the sea !
O my life so merry and free !
Lost ! lost ! lost !

[MAGNUS *comes forward. She tries to escape, but he gently intercepts her. She sinks down on the sand, hiding her face in her hair.*

MAGNUS.

Who art thou ?

MORNA.

No one.

MAGNUS.

Nay, declare
Thy name and race, O thou fairest fair !
I bow before thee on humble knee,
I will not harm—I will worship thee.

[*She puts back her hair, and looks steadily at him ; then stretches out a hand, which he kisses passionately.*

MAGNUS.

The sea is wild, the night is cold,
Come with me to my mother old—
Old and feeble, but kind and dear ;
Come to my mother : have no fear.

[*She looks up comforted.*

MAGNUS (*impetuously*).

I have a cottage small and poor;
Come like sunshine in at the door!
I have a heart most true and warm;
Hide thou in it from every storm!

[MORNA *hesitates; then allows him to lead her for-*
ward.

DUET.

MAGNUS.

Lovely lady from over the sea,
Come to me, O come to me;
Beautiful lady, have no fear;
I am here.
I will serve thee, I will defend thee.
I will work for thee, I will tend thee;
Lovely lady from over the sea,
Come to me.

MORNA.

Fisherman with the gentle eyes,
Do not despise me, do not despise,
I have lost my father and mother,
Sisters and brother;
I am lonely, sad, and forsaken,
My heart is broken, my sealskin taken
I can never return to the sea;
Woe is me!

BOTH.

I will serve thee, I will defend thee,
I will work for thee, I will tend thee;
He will serve me, he will defend me,
He will work for me, he will tend me.

MAGNUS.

Beautiful lady from over the sea,
   O come to me.

MORNA.

I can never return to the sea—
   I come to thee.

                                        [*Scene closes.*

SCENE II.

Interior of a fisherman's cottage. FEA, an old woman, sits knit-
ting. MORNA, dressed like a fisherman's wife, rocks the
cradle with one child in it: an elder boy lies asleep on the
floor beside her.

MORNA.

Sleep, my baby, beside the fire,
   Sleep, child, sleep;
Winds are wailing, nigher and nigher,
Waves are rising, higher and higher,
   Sleep, child, sleep;
While thy father, out on the sea,
Toils all night for thee and me.

FEA.

While thy father, out on the sea,
Toils all night for her and thee.

MORNA.

Sleep, my baby, content and blest,
   Sleep, child, sleep;
Whether the heart in thy mother's breast
Is light or heavy—so best! so best!

Sleep, child, sleep;
While thy father, out on the sea,
Toils all night for thee and me.

FEA.

While thy father out on the sea,
Toils all night for her and thee.

Interlude of soft music, during which FEA *drops asleep. Then is heard the same mysterious elfin tune as in Scene I.* MORNA *springs up and listens.*

MORNA.

Seven long years have I left my home,
Down in the depth of the ocean foam ·
Still, O still, come my sisters sweet,
Across the waves on their silvery feet.
Once a year, upon Midsummer-night,
I see them all in the moonshine white;
I hear them dance unto music low—
I hear, I hear, but I cannot go.

[*She listens.*

Is it the wail of the wind I hear?
Or is it your voices, sisters dear?

[*A gust of wind suddenly bursts the door open and six white figures are seen in the moonlight*

CHORUS.

Sister, sister, here we stand;
We have left the bright sea for the dreary land;
We have come from the deep to our sister sweet,
And we gaze and gaze, but cannot meet.

[MORNA *rushes to the doorway, and makes desperate efforts to induce them to cross it, but they always shrink back.*

CHORUS.

Sister, sister, here we stand;
Only an innocent mortal hand
Can lead us over thy threshold stone.
Sister, give us thy little one.

After some hesitation MORNA *fetches the elder child, who leads the
first sea-maid across the door-stone. The rest follow, and burst
into a wild dance, with mysterious elfin lights flitting about on
the cottage floor.* FEA *wakes up, and looks on horrified; then
drops on her knees with a shriek. Immediately the six sea-maids
fly through the door, which closes with a blast of wind, and the
cottage is left in darkness.*

FEA.

Where art thou, witch-wife?

MORNA.

Mother, dear,

Be patient—there is nought to fear.
Gone—all are gone! and I left here.

> [*She sobs and sinks into an attitude of deep despair.*
> FEA *stands over her, with a threatening
> aspect.*

FEA.

Accursed be the fatal day
When Magnus found thee in the bay.
Cursed the hour throughout his life,
When thee he took for wedded wife.
Cursed thy children twain—and thee,
For thou didst lure my child from me.

MORNA!

Pity and pardon!

FEA.

Never! Go—.
Back to thy sea-depths.

MORNA.

Would 't were so!
Would I could take my babes and fly!
Would I could die!—but we cannot die;
We live as long as the rocks and stones!
Ah, hush, my little one, hush thy moans!

[*She takes the child out of the cradle and sits rocking
it on her breast,* FEA *watching her.*

FEA (*song*).

When we are young our boys are sweet,
They climb our knees and lie at our feet;
When we are old they are hard to please,
Cold as the rock and wild as the breeze
They kiss us kindly and speak us fair,
But we know their hearts are otherwhere.
    O my son's my son till he gets him a wife,
    But my daughter's my daughter all her life.

When we are young our days are bright,
And full of hope from morn till night;
When we are old we sit alone,
And think of pleasant days long gone,
When the house was full of the children's noise,
The wilful girls and the naughty boys.
    O my son's my son till he gets him a wife,
    But my daughter's my daughter all her life.

MORNA (*advancing timidly*)

And all my life I'll try to be,
Mother, a daughter unto thee.

[FEA *turns angrily away.* MAGNUS *is heard*
without, singing.

MAGNUS.

O the fisherman's life is the life for a king,
  Yeo ho, my jolly boys, pull together!
When thro' the taut ropes the winds whistle and sing,
  The moon is up and we 'll get good weather.

[*He enters, but stops suddenly in dismay at sight of*
the two women.

MAGNUS.

So sad? So fierce? My darling wife?
Mother—the comfort of my life?

Song (MAGNUS.)

When a man comes home
  Don't begin to wrangle;
    Better far to sleep
    In the hungry deep,
Neath white sheets of foam,
  And of sea-weed tangle.
  Peace, peace, peace,
  Cease, cease, cease,
When a man comes home
  Don't begin to wrangle.

MORNA.

When a man comes home
  Let him enter smiling;
    Take the children sweet,
    Playing round his feet:
Throw off grief and gloom
  And the world's beguiling
  Peace, peace, peace,

Cease, cease, cease,
When a man comes home
Let him find all smiling.

FEA.

When a man comes home,
He should still remember
'T is not always May,
Either work or play—
Sure as June will come
There will come December.
Peace, peace, peace,
Cease, cease, cease,
Evening brings all home,
And sunshine in December.

[*General reconciliation.* MAGNUS *leads out the two women, each carrying a child; then returns and sits musing over the fire.*

MAGNUS.

Seven years of bliss and yet of fear,
My white sea-maid, my Morna dear;
My children's mother, my own wife,
The crown and glory of my life.
And yet, and yet, that secret old,
Never forgotten, never told.

[*He takes the sealskin out of his breast, and examines it by the fire-light.*

If she could find it, if she could know,
Would she snatch her magic dress and go?
Would she break the ties that bind her here,
And seek her sisters and parents dear?
Would she love us still—her babes and me,
Or go back to her palace beneath the sea?

MORNA (*from within*).

Magnus!

MAGNUS.

My love!—

[*Hurriedly concealing the sealskin as* MORNA *ap
pears.*

The night is wild,
Sleep like the children—sleep, dear child.

[*He tenderly leads her away : then returns to his
place takes out the sealskin and looks at it.*

Who knows what misery dawn may bring?
Where can I hide this accursed thing?
What grave is deep enough? What spot
So safe from her eye that she finds it not?
Ha!—

[*He discovers a hole in the thatch in which he care-
fully hides the sealskin*

There let it bide—there let it bide!
Now—slip our moorings with the tide!

(*Song*) MAGNUS.

The maid that deceived me was fatal and fair
With the curl on her lip and her arrogant air,
The wife I deceive is as tender and true
As the grass on the mountain-slope covered with dew.
Ah! many a storm Love can safely out-ride,
But a secret at home is like rocks under tide.

The maid that forsook me was cruel and cold,
She cared not for love, she cared only for gold.
The wife of my bosom is simple and mild,
With the heart of a woman, the smile of a child.
Ah! many a storm Love can safely out-ride,
But a secret at home is like rocks under tide.

[*He goes out. Scene closes.*

Scene III.

Outside a fisherman's cottage on the sea-shore. Projecting rock and view of distant sea. MAGNUS sits mending nets. MORNA goes in and out with the children; then leaves them and stands gazing dreamily out across the sea. FEA, entering from cottage, points her out to MAGNUS, who calls her sharply.

MAGNUS.

Morna!—

MORNA.

Ay, husband.

MAGNUS.

What dost see?—

MORNA.

Nothing.   They are all gone from me.

[*She stands as if in a dream and then begins singing.*

Song (MORNA.)

Down in the deep, up in the sky,
I see them always, far or nigh,
And I shall see them till I die—
  The old familiar faces.
They may have long forgotten mine—
But I remember, every line,
  The old familiar faces.
  Ah! nothing e'er replaces
  The old familiar faces.

And all day long, so close and near
As in a mystic dream I hear
Their gentle accents kind and dear—

The old familiar voices.
They have no sound that I can reach—
But silence sweeter is than speech
    The old familiar voices!
    Nothing my heart rejoices
    Like the old familiar voices.

MAGNUS (*bitterly.*)

No time for idling or regret—
The wind is fair—the sails are set—
There—take my task till I return—

[*Throwing her the nets.*

Mourn not.   A good wife need not mourn.
Go, tend the children—mind the house—
Women should work and men carouse.

[*Sings.*

A fisherman's life is a life for a king—
    Ho, my jolly boys, pull together.—

[*Stops, seeing enter a marriage procession—the bride on
    horseback, led; and followed by a confused crowd of
    fishermen, girls, etc.*

CHORUS.

Drink, my jolly boys, drink and be merry,
Bonnie the bride is, and brown as a berry;
Soft are her lips, and sweet as red clover,
Drink and be merry, lads, half seas over.

MAGNUS (*clinking glasses with the bridegroom*).

Drink, my jolly boys, drink with discerning,
Wedlock's a lane where there is no turning;
Never was owl more blind than a lover,
Drink and be merry, lads, half seas over.

CHORUS—*Drink, my jolly boys*

MORNA (*to the bride*).

Live and be happy, lass!　Ah, one remembers
How the fire blazed that is now black embers!
Won is the husband, lost is the lover!
Live and be happy, lass!　Wed—and all 's over.

CHORUS—*Drink, my jolly boys.*

[*The procession moves on—*MAGNUS *eagerly following,*
glass in hand.

MORNA (*entreatingly*).

You will not go?　O husband, stay!
This day of all days!　See, the bay
Is glittering in the sunset light—
Midsummer-night—midsummer-night.
Another hour—one little hour,
And they will have me in their power—
My sisters—Stay!　O Magnus, stay?

CHORUS (*mockingly*).

Won is the husband, lost is the lover,
Drink and be merry, lads, half seas over.

MAGNUS *bursts away and follows the procession.* FEA *does the*
*same—at a distance—*MORNA *remains alone, in a mournful at-*
titude, the children clinging to her.

MORNA.

O my salt sea home,
　O my coral dwelling,
O the yellow foam,
　Round about it swelling.

[*Then with a sudden change to tenderness.*

Come, my children dear;
　Come, my baby blossom;

Come and shelter here
　　In your mother's bosom.

O my life of youth
　　Full of mirth and laughter,
Pleasantness and truth,
　　O the dark days after.

Come, my children dear ; etc.

*While she is singing the second verse, the eldest boy, who has escaped
from her, goes scrambling about and finds under the thatch the
sealskin which MAGNUS had hidden.　He brings it to his mother,
who recognizes it and evinces the wildest joy.*

MORNA.

Found—found—found !
　　Above earth's noises
I hear the sea's sound :
　　My whole heart rejoices—
　　Rejoices, rejoices—
For I hear the sea's sound !

[*Then with a sudden remorse she embraces her children.*

Good-by—good-by—
　　Little lips and fingers !
Kiss me—do not cry,
　　Mother lingers—lingers.

[*Again she breaks from them, and clasps the seal-
skin to her breast.　The mysterious elfin music
is heard faintly.*

Found, found, found !
　　I hear the old voices
Around—all around ;
　　My whole heart rejoices—
Rejoices, rejoices,
　　I hear the sea's sound !

Fᴇᴀ *appears. At sight of her* Mᴏʀɴᴀ *rushes to the projecting rock and is seen to leap from it into the sea. Scene closes.*

Scene IV.

Sea-shore, same as in Scene I. Enter Mᴀɢɴᴜs, *wandering aimlessly with a child in either hand. He sits down on the stone where he had watched the sea-maids dancing and singing.*

MAGNUS.

She has gone and left me
On her dreary shore
I seek her vainly
Forever more :
Morna—Morna—
I seek her vainly forevermore.

She has gone and left me
A year and a day :
My heart is broken,
My head is gray.
Morna—Morna—
My heart is broken, my head is gray.

By lonely fireside
I sit and weep ;
Her little children
Sob in their sleep.
Morna—Morna—
Come back to us, Morna, from the cruel deep.

Elfin music is heard, and, as in Scene I., the seven sea-maids enter and sing.

CHORUS.

Dance we, dance we, over the strand,
Half on ocean and half on land ;

Dance we merrily as we go,
Mimicking mortals, O iero!

Suddenly MORNA, *distinguishable by her long yellow hair, is seen and recognized by her children. They rush forward, break through the circle of dancers, and cling to their mother. The six sisters vanish.* MORNA *is left alone.*

MAGNUS (*advancing slowly*).

Art thou my wife—my Morna sweet?

[*She makes no answer..*

How beautiful—from silver feet
To golden head! So fresh; so fair;
With not a grief and not a care,
So gay and happy, bright and free,
Forgetting me—forgetting me!

MORNA.

Farewell!

MAGNUS.

Art still my wife?

MORNA.

Farewell!

MAGNUS.

O dearer than all words can tell!
Come home with us, my wife, come home!

MORNA.

I see strange faces on the foam;
They beckon me.

MAGNUS (*opening his arms*).

Here is thy place.

MORNA *(shrinking from him).*

Forget you ever saw my face ;
Forget the dance upon the shore ;
Forget the day so sad and sore ;
Forget all love and all regret.
Husband ! farewell !—Forget ! forget !

Duet ; MAGNUS *and* MORNA.

Farewell and pardon, if thou pardon hast,
Farewell and love me, if thy love can last,
Farewell and mourn me, if thy love be past.

*They solemnly clasp hands and part. The moonlight slowly changes
into dawn, and the chorus of the sea-maids is heard faintly in the
distance.*

MORNA.

Far in the east the morn is gray
I must be gone before 't is day.

MAGNUS.

O stay but till the sunrise bright.

MORNA.

And then—adieu, days of delight !
Among my gorgeous coral halls,
Where never a child's footstep falls,
Never is heard one loving voice,
But all is mirth and mad rejoice.
Must I go back to days of care,
Of weary hands and silvering hair,
Of anxious love and tender pain—
And I live the old days o'er again ?

*While she is singing the stage darkens, and the six sea-maids come
    gliding in, trying to snatch at* MORNA. *Music—a melancholy
    elfish wail.* MORNA *stands motionless, the children clinging
    round her, and* MAGNUS *on his knees beside her clasping her
    hand. The sun begins to rise.*

CHORUS OF SEA-MAIDS.

We must depart,
We that have no heart—
We that all night long
Waste in dance and song.
Wake, foolish mortal; wake—'t is day.
Wake to your work—we only play.

They vanish to elfish music. MORNA *bursts away and follows them:
    then hesitates, turns, and finally is seen standing on the projecting
    rock—dark against the sunrise.*

MORNA.

Depart, depart,
Ye that have no heart,
Ye that all life long
Waste in dance and song.
Depart, depart—but I stay, I stay;
My night is over: 't is day, 't is day!

[*She points to the rising sun; then, dashing her
    sealskin into the waves, comes back to husband
    and children. Tableau.*

Enter CHORUS OF FISHERMEN, *etc.*

By the fireside still the light is shining,
The children's arms round the parents twining.
From love so sweet, O, who would roam?
Be it ever so homely, home is home.

Should we fall out, let us mend ill-doing,
And begin anew a second wooing;
From love so sweet, O, who would roam
Be it ever so homely, home is home.

Curtain falls.

The following Twenty Poems were written for Children.

A LITTLE DEAD PRINCE.

Buried June 1, 1873.

(The child of the Princess Alice of England, Grand Duchess of Hesse-Darmstadt.)

OVER the happy mother's bed
   Gambol three children, loving as gay:
   Ernest strong, and delicate Fritz,
    Pretty baby Victoria.
Two little princes, sans sword, sans crown,
   One little princess, infant sweet,
In the mother's breast, as rich, as full
   As any mother's in lane or street,
They grew, three roses, love-rooted deep—
   Filling, with perfume all their own,
The palace air—oft sharp and keen,
   In the lonely heights too near a throne

The palace windows stand open wide,
   The harmless windows, and through them pass
May winds, to the palace-children dear,
   As to cottage children upon the grass;
Out through the door bold Ernest runs,
   The mother follows with anxious mind
Fearless of fate, for a minute's space
   Leaving the other two behind.

Grand on the bed—a mimic queen,
  Tiny Victoria gravely sits;
While grasping closely his darling toy,
  Up to the window climbs merry Fritz;
It drops—his treasure! He leans and looks,
  Twenty feet down to the stony road—
Hear ye that shriek from the mother's lips?
  Hast thou no mercy, O God, O God?
One ghastly moment he hangs in air
  Like a fledgeling bird from the warm nest thrown
With innocent eyes of mere surprise—
  Then falls—and the bright young life is done.

Mother, poor mother, try to see
  Not the skeleton hand that thrust him there
Out of sunshiny life into silent death,
  But the waiting angels in phalanx fair.
O try to think that the earth's hard breast
  Was the bosom of God, which took him in,
Safe from the clutch of the years unknown,
  Full of sorrow, sickness, peril or sin:
O hear far off the low sound of tears
  Dropping from many an eye like mine,
As we look on our living children sweet,
  And our English mother hearts bleed for thine.

God comfort thee! Under the robe of state
  That hides but heals not wounds throbbing wild,
May'st thou feel the touch of one soft dead hand
  The child, that will always remain a child.
And when long years shall have slipped away
  When gray hairs come and thy pulse beats slow,
May one little face shine star-like out
  O'er the dim descent that all feet must go.
Mother, poor mother! 'neath warm June rain
  Bear to the grave this coffin small;
Oft, our children living are children lost,
  But our children dead—yes, we keep them all,

INDIAN CHILDREN.

ATHER, Mother, o'er the seas—
Seldom, in their careless ease
Do the children think of these,

While, as kings lament a gem
Lost from out a diadem—
How the parents grieve for them!

Missing all their infant ways,
Daily doings, pretty "says"—
Nobody to blame or praise,—

Only gentle Auntie kind!
She with ever-anxious mind,
And wise fondness, never blind,

Gives up all her youth's delights
For tired days and wakeful nights:
Every week long letters writes

All about the little folks:
Innocent learning, baby jokes;
How they grew up like young oaks—

Strong and sturdy, handsome, gay—
Are her pride from day to day :
Her care too, she does not say.

O let the slow years run fast ;
And, the weary absence past,
Parents dear come home at last.

Then, poor Auntie—she will glide
Very quietly aside,
In her sweet contented pride.

She has done her patient part,
And all love her with full heart—
If a lonely tear should start,

Hide it, choke it, let it be
Drowned in the Indian sea!
Hateful, hideous jealousy;

Poison-tree whose branches fill
All our earth with cureless ill,
Nay, whose very roots do kill.

All we do with heart-love free
For His little ones, saith He,
"Ye have done it unto Me."

THE LITTLE COMFORTER·

"WHAT is wrong with my big brother?"
        Says the child;
    For they two had got no mother
And she loved him like no other:
        If he smiled,
All the world seemed bright and gay
To this happy little May.

If to her he sharply spoke,
        This big brother—
Then her tender heart nigh broke;
But the cruel pain that woke,
        She would smother—
As a little woman can;—
Was he not almost a man?

But when trouble or disgrace
        Smote the boy,
She would lift her gentle face—
Surely 't was her own right place

To bring joy ?
For she loved him—loved him so!
Whether he was good or no.

May be he will never feel
    Half her love ;
Wound her, and forget to heal :
Idle words are sharp as steel :
    But above,
I know what the angels say
Of this silent little May.

DON'T BE AFRAID.

(To a timid child.)

ON'T be afraid of the dark,
    My daughter, dear as my soul !
    You see but a part of the gloomy world,
  But I—I have seen the whole.
And I know each step of the fearsome way,
Till the shadows brighten to open day.

Don't be afraid of pain,
  My little tender child :
When its smart is worst there comes strength to bear
  And it seems as if angels smiled,—
As *I* smile, dear, when I hurt you now
In binding up that wound on your brow.

Don't be afraid of grief,
  'T will come—as night follows day;
But the bleakest sky has tiny rifts
  When the stars shine through—as to say
"Wait, wait a little—till night is o'er
And beautiiul day come back once more."

O child, be afraid of sin,
   But have no other fear,
For God 's in the dark, as well as the light;
   And while we can feel Him near,
His hand that He gives, His love that He gave,
   Lead safely, even to the dark of the grave.

GIRL AND BOY.

LFRED is gentle as a girl,
   But Judith longs to be a boy:
   Would cut off every pretty curl
With eager joy !

Hates to be called "my dear"—or kissed :
   For dollies does not care one fig :
Goes, sticking hands up to the wrist
   In jackets big.

Would like to do whate'er boy can ;
   Play cricket—even go to school :
It is so grand to be a man !
   A girl's a fool !

But Alfred smiles superior love
   On all these innocent vagaries.
He 'd hate a goose ! but yet a dove
   Ah, much more rare is !

She 's anything but dove, good sooth !
   But she 's his dear and only sister :
And, had she been a boy, in truth,
   How he 'd have missed her !

So, gradually her folly dies,
   And she 'll consent to be just human,
When there shines out of girlish eyes
   The real Woman.

AGNES AT PRAYER.

"OUR Father which art in heaven,"
Little Agnes prays,
Though her kneeling is but show,
Though she is too young to know
All, or half she says.
God will hear her, Agnes mild,
God will love the innocent child.

"Our Father which art in heaven."
She has a father here,
Does she think of his kind eyes,
Tones that ne'er in anger rise—
"Yes, dear," or "No, dear."
They will haunt her whole life long
Like a sweet pathetic song.

"Our Father which art in heaven,"
Through thy peaceful prayer,
Think of the known father's face,
Of his bosom, happy place;
Safely sheltered there;
And so blessed—long may He bless!
Think too of the fatherless.

———

GOING TO WORK.

COME along for the work is ready—
Rough it may be, rough, tough and hard—
But—fourteen years old—stout, strong and
steady,
Life's game 's beginning, lad!—play your card—
Come along.

Mother stånds at the door-step crying;
    Well but she has a brave heart too:
She 'll try to be glad—there 's nought like trying,
    She 's proud of having a son like you.
        Come along.

Young as she is, her hair is whitening,
    She has ploughed thro' years of sorrow deep,
She looks at her boy, and her eyes are brightening,
    Shame if ever you make them weep!
        Come along.

Bravo! See how the brown cheek flushes!
    Ready to work as hard as you can?
I have always faith in a boy that blushes,
    None will blush for him, when he 's a man.
        Come along.

MY LITTLE LADY.

Y little lady all in white
        Do you want to know—do you want
            to know,
Why 1 sit at the tree-foot out of sight,
My crutch beside me—a pitiful sight?
    Are you sorry for me? God made me so;
    My grand little lady!

Are you grieved that you can jump and run,
    In your pretty frock and your dainty shoes,
Just as you like, in or out of the sun,
With lightsome feet and heart full of fun,
    While I sit still, as I cannot choose
    But sit still, my lady!

My old black frock burns hot on my back;
  My worn old frock, for it's long ago
Since mother died, and trade is slack;
And I'd rather dress in any old sack
  Than stint the little ones. Do you know
  What hunger is, lady?

Ah, I beg your pardon. Those gentle eyes
  Are filling with tears, fast filling with tears;
You have left your swans unfed :—surprise
Is melting to pity. You're not too wise;
  But you'll be wiser when at my years;
  And you're kind, my lady.

Yes, I'm older, graver—sadder too—
  O I've had my share, I've had my share—
Of things unknown to the like of you.
God sees us both. What He bids me do,
  I'll try to do. What He bids me bear,
  I'll bear, my lady.

It's hard sometimes, the hunger and pain,
  And the children's crying—that's worst of all;
But I do my best and I don't complain,
There—I'm glad to see you smile again.
  Give me my crutch—No, I shall not fall,
  Still—thank you, my lady.

And though I crouch at the foot of the tree,
  And you o'er the meadow can run and shout,
There's the same bright sun for you and me,
The same birds singing out merrily;
  It is good to see you dancing about
  My bright little lady.

'T would not make me happy to make you sad;
  And I don't like pity, and God is kind;
If I your park and your castle had,

But no little sisters to make me glad,
   No father to work for—to my mind
   'T would be dull, my lady.

So let each of us go our appointed way;
   Safe to the end—safe to the end;
Good at our work, and good at our play,
Should you pass, my dear, again some day
   I 'll be glad to see you, my grand young friend
   My sweet little lady.

DICK AND I.

E 'RE going to a party, my brother Dick and I
   The best, grandest party we ever did try;
   And I 'm very happy—but Dick is *so* shy!

I 've got a white ball-dress, and flowers in my hair,
And a scarf, with a brooch too, mamma let me wear:
Silk stockings and shoes with high heels, I declare!

There is to be music—a real soldier's band:
And *I* mean to waltz, and eat ice, and be fanned
Like a grown-up young lady, the first in the land.

But Dick is so stupid, so silent and shy;
Has never learnt dancing, so says he won't try—
Yet Dick is both older and wiser than I.

And I 'm fond of my brother—this darling old Dick:
I 'll hunt him in corners wherever he stick,
He 's bad at a party—but at school he 's a brick!

So good at his Latin, at cricket, football,
Whatever he tries at. And then he 's so tall!
Yet at play with the children he 's best of us all.

And his going to the party is just to please *me*,
Poor Dick! so good-natured.　How dull he will be!
But he says I shall dance "like a wave o' the sea."

That's Shakspere, his Shakspere, he .worships him so,
Our Dick he writes poems, though none will he show;
I found out his secret, but I won't tell: no, no.

And when he's a great man, a poet, you see,
O dear! what a proud little sister I'll be;
Hark! there comes the carriage.　We're off, Dick and
　　me.

MY LITTLE BOY THAT DIED.

OOK in his pretty face for just one minute;
　　His braided frock and dainty buttoned shoes,
His firm-shut hand, the favorite plaything in it,
Then tell me, mothers, was it not hard to lose
　　And miss him from my side,
　　My little boy that died?

How many another boy as dear and charming,
　　His father's hope, his mother's one delight,
Slips through strange sicknesses, all fear disarming,
　　And lives a long, long life in parents' sight;
　　Mine was so short a pride;
　　And then—my poor boy died.

I see him rocking on his wooden charger,
　　I hear him pattering through the house all day,
I watch his great blue eyes grow large and larger,
　　Listening to stories whether grave or gay,
　　Told at the bright fire-side,
　　So dark now, since he died.

But yet I often think my boy is living,
　　As living as my other children are.
When good-night kisses I all round am giving,

I keep one for him though he is so far.
  Can a mere grave divide
  Me from him—though he died?

So, while I come and plant it o'er with daisies
  (Nothing but childish daisies all year round),
Continually God's hand the curtain raises,
  And I can hear the merry voice's sound,
    And feel him at my side,
    My little boy that died.

———

OUR BLACK BROTHER.

On board an English ship.

BRING him forward to the light,
    Our black brother—
  Knock his chains off, horrid sight!
Though we cannot make him white,
    We can smother
Every thought unkind or ill,
Is he not our brother still?

Though he has an ugly face,
    Our black brother—
Or we deem so, proud white race!
Sure, in his own swampy place,
    · His poor mother
Thought him as he walked or ran,
All that 's beautiful in man.

Lift him from the noisome hold—
    Wretched brother,
Cruelly thus bought and sold:
Clasp his hand in kindly fold
    Like another,
Lads, what matter, white or black?
Wipe the blood-drops from his back.

Though his brain be dull and dark,
    Hapless brother !
Light in it one little spark
—Knowledge—love, perhaps : then mark,
    Soon, another—
One by one each feeble ray
Broadens into beauteous day.

KISSING THROUGH THE CHAIR.

EEP-BO, peep-bo!
    Kissing through the chair;
    Mamma has kissed baby
Twice I declare !
Like a little poker
    Stiff, baby stands :
Stamps with his tiny feet
    Pushes with his hands.

Peep-bo, peep-bo !
    What a funny chair !
Baby is as tall as
    Mamma, standing there.
Quite upon a level—
    And so very grand ;
Baby might be Prince of Wales,
    Or king of Eng-land.

Peep-bo, peep-bo !
    Just another kiss !
Then he may run away,
    After some new bliss.
So wide his world is !
    So long his year !
Baby has no end of joys,
    Mamma's joy is—here.

GRANDPAPA.

GRANDPAPA lives at the end of the lane,
His cottage is small and its furniture plain;
No pony to ride on, no equipage grand,
A garden, and just half an acre of land;
No dainties to dine off, and very few toys,—
Yet is grandpapa's house the delight of the boys.

Grandpapa once lived in one little room,
Grandpapa worked all day long at his loom:
He speaks with queer accent, does dear grandpapa,
And not half so well as papa and mamma,
The girls think his clothes are a little too rough,
But the boys all declare they can't love him enough.

A man of the people in manners and mind,
Yet so honest, so tender, so clever, so kind;
Makes the best of his lot still, where'er it be cast,
A sturdy old Englishman, game to the last,
Though simple and humble and unknown to fame,
It 's good luck to the boys to bear grandpapa's name!

MONSIEUR ET MADEMOISELLE.

DEUX petits enfants Français,
Monsieur et Mademoiselle.
Of what can they be talking, child?
Indeed I cannot tell.
But of this I am very certain,
You would find naught to blame
In that sweet French politeness—
I wish we had the same.

Monsieur has got a melon,
   And scoops it with his knife,
While Mademoiselle sits watching him :
   No rudeness here—no strife :
Though could you only listen,
   They 're chattering like two pies—
French magpies, understand me—
   So merry and so wise.

Their floor is bare of carpet,
   Their curtains are so thin,
They dine on meagre *potage*, and
   Put many an onion in !
Her snow-white caps she irons :
   He blacks his shoes, he can ;
Yet she 's a little lady
   And he 's a gentleman.

O busy, happy children !
   That light French heart of yours,
Would it might sometimes enter at
   Our solemn English doors !
Would that we worked as gaily,
   And played, yes, played as well,
And lived our lives as simply
   As Monsieur et Mademoiselle.

————

A FRENCH NUN.

SHE sits upon her pallet bed ;
   Her heavy eyes down bending lowly,
   Sad thoughts may rack her weary head,
But never thoughts unholy :
And though she murmurs Latin prayers,
To say that she prays *not*—who dares ?

She has no husband and no child,
  Is half forgot by mother, father :
Yet, won by her sweet aspect mild,
  Round her the convent scholars gather ;
Though shut is every kindred door,
She is the sister of the poor.*

Les Petites Sœurs des Pauvres are well known throughout France, and well-beloved, deservedly.

We serve not as she serves—good sooth !
  We live not as she lives—half dying :
We think our truth the only truth,
  But God forbid we call hers lying ;
Or doubt that Mary's holy Son
Has comfort for the lonely nun.

THE YOUNG GOVERNESS.

I MEAN to be a governess
    And earn my daily bread ;
  For we have many mouths to feed,
  And O ! they must be fed—
Anne, Emily, Will, Tom, and I,
  And little baby Ned.

And though I am but just fourteen,
  I 'm stout andbig and tall,
And I can learn my lessons best,
  They say, among us all.
Strong girls like me must never thrust
  The weak ones to the wall.

So I 'm to be a governess,
  And to do my busy part
Outside, while others work at home ;

Down tears ! they must not start !
Who 'd tell the children mother died—
. Died of a broken heart ?

My heart it will not break, I think,
   For I am young and bold ;
Much bolder than our Emily,
   Though she 's eighteen years old :
I bore all father's angry words
   And looks unkind and cold.

He 's gone ; and none will hurt us now,
   Young birds in lonely nest,
Trying to keep each other warm,
   Without a mother's breast ;
But Tom and I, we 're nearly fledged,
   And we shall help the rest.

I will be such a governess !
   Not cross, as you will see ;
I 'll make my children love their books,
   Just for the love of me—
And work just for the sake of work,
   To reach the top o' the tree.

I 'll teach them how to scorn a dunce,
   An idle dunce, I mean :
Those that will learn and those that won't,
   What difference between ?
Why, just a wise man and a fool—
   A beggar and a queen !

So I will be a governess
   And earn my daily bread,
Honest and happy, holding high
   My independent head ;
O what a merry house we 'd be
   If mother were not dead !

THE LAST LOOK OF ENGLAND.

HE last look of England—as the ship in full sail
    Glides past Dover pier in the moonlight so
      pale.
Dover town is all sleeping, and the long curve of lights
Stretches shoreward below the dark line of the Heights.

But, a dozen miles inland the sailor-boy sees
A hop-covered cottage and three hives of bees
Just under the window, where lies fast asleep,·
Ah no, she is waking, and waking to weep.

"O mother, O mother!" the sailor-boy sighs·
And 't is not the salt spray that's blinding his eyes!
"O mother, my mother, I 'll be good, I 'll be brave,
And I 'll never forget the last kiss that you gave."

Not a bit of a coward is the sailor-boy true,
With his bright open eye and his jacket of blue,
He can work like a Briton, fight too, if needs be,
Yet the last look of England is a sad sight to see.

But when he comes back after years four and five
And finds the dear home safe, the mother alive,
As the white Dover cliffs gleam afar on his lee
O the first sight of England is a glad sight to see.

BLIND.

LIND, blind, blind,
    She never beholds the sun;
    Nor the white clouds fly o'er the deep
      blue sky,
Nor the shining rivers run.

Long, long ago,
  When she was a little child,
All these she seems to have seen in **dreams,**
  With her dear dead mother mild.

Then fell the cloud;
  And her life grew dark with awe;
She ceased to trace any form or face,
  And she felt instead of saw.

Dark, all dark.
  The children left her alone,
She could not play, but sat still all **day,**
  And her heart sank like a stone.

Dark, so dark;
  In the busy, noisy **day,**
Or the silent night without sound **or sight,**
  To her it was dark alway.

Sighing she 'd mourn,
  From all happy life exiled,
"As well be dead, with a stone at my head
  As be a living child."

Till, one strange morn,
  She was touched by a gentle hand;
"I am blind like you, yet my work **I do,**
  Come, and you shall understand."

So she went home,
  To a Home where all were blind,
But each sang in the dark as a lark,
  And worked with contented mind.

Work, happy work;
  And play, O such merry play!
They could read and write and their dreary
      night
  Was turned into cheerful day.

Blind, blind, blind,
    But the darkness is all gone—
She can work and play as happy as they,
    And her life is but begun.

Blind, still blind,
    But the lamp in her soul shines bright,
Till in Paradise her dear shut eyes
    Shall open to God's own light.

(The sight of the happy children at the Royal Normal School for the
Blind, Norwood, London, suggested this poem.)

THREE COMPANIONS.

 E go on our way together,
    Baby, and dog, and I ;
    Three merry companions,
    'Neath any sort of sky ;
Blue as her pretty eyes are,
    Or gray, like his dear old tail ;
Be it windy, or cloudy, or stormy,
    Our courage does never fail.

Sometimes the snow lies thickly,
    Under the hedge-row bleak ;
Then baby cries " Pretty, pretty,"
    The only word she can speak.
Sometimes two rivers of water
    Run down the muddy lane ;
Then dog leaps backwards and forwards
    Barking with might and main.

Baby 's a little lady,
    Dog is a gentleman brave :
If he had two legs as you have
    He 'd kneel to her like a slave ;

As it is he loves and protects her,
　　As dog and gentleman can ;
I'd rather be a kind doggie
　　I think, than a brute of a man.

———

THE MOTHERLESS CHILD.

HE was going home down the lonely street,
　　A widow-woman with weary feet
　　And weary eyes that seldom smiled:
She had neither mother, sister, nor child.
She earned her bread with a patient heart,
And ate it quietly and apart,
In her silent home from day to day,
No one to say her "ay," or "nay."

She was going home without care to haste;
What should she haste for?　On she paced
Through the snowy night so bleak and wild,
When she thought she heard the cry of a child.
A feeble cry, not of hunger or pain,
But just of sorrow.　It came again.
She stopped—she listened—she almost smiled—
"That sounds like the wail of a motherless child."

A house stood open,—no soul was there—
Her dull, tired feet grew light on the stair;
She mounted—entered.　One bed on the floor,
And Something in it: and close by the door,
Watching the stark form, stretched out still,
Ignorant, knowing not good nor ill,
But only a want and a misery wild,
Crouched the dead mother's motherless child.

What next? Come, say, what would you have ,
    done,
Dear children, playing about in the sun,
Or sitting by pleasant firesides warm,
Hearing outside the howling storm ?
The widow went in, and she shut the door,
She stayed by the dead an hour or more—
And when she went home through the night so wild,
She had in her arms a sleeping child.

Now she is old, and feeble, and dull,
But her empty heart is happy and full,
If her crust be hard and her cottage poor,
There's a young foot tripping across the floor,
Young hands to help her that never tire,
And a young voice singing beside the fire ;
And her tired eyes look as if they smiled,—
Childless mother and motherless child.

BORN AT JERUSALEM.

(Gladys Mulock Holman Hunt. Sept. 18, 1876.)

NGLISH child of Eastern birth:
    Welcome to our wondrous earth—
    Welcome, innocent blue eyes,
Opening upon Syrian skies:
Welcome, feet that soon will stand
On Judea's sacred land:
Bud from honorable stem,
Babe; born at Jerusalem.

Were I of the ancient faith
That smote Paynims here to death,
I should say, the virgin mild
Specially on thee had smiled;
That the Mother of all mothers
Had loved thine beyond the others,
Sending such a priceless gem
To her, in Jerusalem.

Or, if of that older creed
Ere the world of Christ had need,
I should dream of Rachel fair,
Hannah, who child Samuel bare,
Hebrew women grand and calm,
Whose pure lives roll like a psalm
Down the centuries.—Who like them,
Mothers of Jerusalem?

Little sweet god-daughter mine !
Thy small unknown face will shine
Like the stars which shepherds see
Still, o'er plains of Galilee :
And thy unheard voice will fill
Silence, like Siloam's rill,
Where the hills with purple hem
Stand about Jerusalem.

Babe, thy future who can see ?
But we bless thee full and free ;
Walk, where walked Christ's stainless feet,
In the temple and the street,
" Holy, harmless, undefiled,"
Yet to parents human child—
Till thou walk with Him and them
In the New Jerusalem.

THE ARCTIC EXPEDITION.

From the Woman's Side.

LET me smile a little, I pray,
Just a little and while I may,
Even as a child smiles.   After to-day
I shall have whole years to weep in.
O let me talk like a child, unchid :
After to-day 't will all be hid—
No hand will lift up the coffin-lid
Of the silence I shall sleep in.

In Portsmouth harbor the good ship rides,
Rocked safely upon the placid tides,
As love in a happy heart abides—
Moving with each emotion ;
With voices and hands alive all o'er.
To-morrow—haply for evermore
I shall look out from a desolate shore
Upon an empty ocean.

O love, my hero and my saint!
This woman's heart turns sick and faint,
Although I utter no complaint,
    Although my firm lips fail not.
I see the rocks 'neath smiling seas,
I hear a storm in every breeze,
I feel the icebergs as they freeze,
    In deeps where ships can sail not.

O love, my love, so brave, so young,
Strong arms, pure heart, and silent tongue,
O lonely years that stretch out long!
    One cry, as of lost existence,
And I sit me down before my doom,
As a white ghost sits at the door of its tomb,
No moan, no cry, no tears, no gloom,
    Only a dumb persistence.

Be of good cheer. Sail on, sail on,
Unto life—or death; for both are one
To the infinite faith in sweet days gone,
    To the infinite Love that folds thee:
These woman-arms are weak, I know,
But my heart is strong as a well-bent bow,
And whither thou goest I will go,
    In my spirit that upholds thee.

Sail on, sail on, through whatever seas ·
God leads thee, whether to toil or ease.
Come back triumphant if He so please,
    Or with un-won crown, inglorious.
Only come back! No! Should God say
That He will crown thee another way,
Love, see beyond our night, His day!
    And we are still victorious.

AT ST. ANDREWS.

THE air is light, the sea is bright, the sky without a
    cloud,
    The elder folk look on content, the children laugh
       aloud,
And all along St. Andrew's bay and by Balcarras hill
The stooks lie yellow in the sun, the leaves drop brown and
    still.
The rowan-berries shine instead of the flowers that used to
    blow
In the days when we went gipsying, a long time ago!

The young old earth is just the same, as pleasant and as
    kind,
But in the light of happy eyes our happiness we find;
The hills look as they used to look, far set in purple air—
Perhaps the hills of Paradise will hardly shine more fair!
And thus we live them o'er again, with a strange reflected
    glow,
The days when we went gipsying, a long time ago!

ON A SILVER WEDDING.

OUR silver wedding, our silver wedding!
    Has old Time unnoticed treading,
    Stamped out five-and-twenty years?
Brought us all these girls and boys,
Household sorrows, household joys,
Hopes and fears—
    And a silver wedding?

Our silver wedding, our silver wedding,
Shall we still, life's current heading,
Some day safely drift ashore,

After more years—twenty and five—
Living, glad to be alive,
As of yore,
    At our golden wedding?

This silver, wedding, this silver wedding,
We the merry dances treading,
In our fireside circle stand.
Then, mayhap, we'll stand alone,
Nest all empty, nestlings flown—
Hand-in-hand,
    At our golden wedding.

That golden wedding, that golden wedding,
May it find us, without dreading,
At the foot of the dark stair
Which leads up, as earth's sounds cease,
Into silence, into peace:
Love still there,
    Waiting eternal wedding.

BROTHER AND SISTER.

A. T. and M. C.

ROTHER and sister walk not any more
    In life's calm gloaming down the twilight shore,
    But suddenly all separated stand,
While stretched between them lies the strange, sad, silent
    Land.
Ye dead—ye living—diverse though your road,
Both are as one beneath the eye of God:
And faith beholds, not distant, a safe shore:
Brother and sister there shall meet for evermore.

UNDER THE STARS.

September 1, 1875.

O YOUTH, rose-crowned, yet full of strife,
 Craving half-comprehended joys,
Hearing the desperate fight of life
 But as a far-off pleasant noise,
Come, e'er on thy bold path thou start,
 While not a cloud thy future mars,
And still that wildly-beating heart
 Under the stars.

O stormy prime, yet beautiful,
 With fierce delight, ecstatic pain,
Spending and being spent ; no lull,
 No rest, no counting loss or gain :
Pause, ere with weary feet thou tread
 The blood-stained field of ended wars,
And bow the glories of thy head
 Under the stars.

O heavy time of brows discrowned,
 Of hanging hands and feeble knees,
With piteous pale ghosts haunted round,
 And longings for impossible ease.
Nay, beat no more, poor wounded bird,
 Against Fate's iron prison-bars,
When earth-sounds cease, God's voice is heard
 Under the stars.

Soon, soon will come the supreme hour
 When like a painted show life seems,
Or perfume of remembered flower,
 Or dear dead faces seen in dreams.
Clasp hands beneath this silent night,
 That heals all wounds and hides all scars.
God, Thou alone art Love—and Light—
 Beyond the stars.

THE BOAT OF MY LOVER.

For a Gaelic air—Fhir a Bhata.

 BOAT of my lover, go softly, go safely,
    O boat of my lover that bears him from
      me!
Past the homes of the clachan, past the burn singing
    sweetly,
Past the loch and the mountain that he 'll never more
    see.

O boat of my lover, go softly, go safely;
    Thou bearest my soul with thee over the tide:
I said not a word, but my heart it was breaking,
    For life is so short, and the ocean so wide.

O boat of my lover, go softly, go safely:
    Though the dear voice is silent, the kind hand is gone:
But, O love me, my lover! and I 'll live till I find thee;
    Till our parting is over, and our dark days are done.

THE BOAT OF MY BROTHERS.

(Written for a young reader who complained that the foregoing song was
"too lover-y.")

 BOAT of my brothers, go softly, go safely:
    For the whale* is behind us, all of us know;
    Fred, Victor, and Randy, with Ernest so
      handy,
And Diarmid our captain. Then row, brothers, row.

* Which had been seen in the loch.

O boat of my brothers, go softly, go safely,
  For there are the little kids waiting below;
Sweet Lora and Dolly, with the family folly,
  "King" Donald, and Callum—so row, brothers, row.

O boat of my brothers, go softly, go safely,
  The top of the Cobbler is all in a glow,
On the loch there is chaffing, and daffing, and laughing,
  But we all pull together, so row, brothers, row.

DEEP IN THE VALE.

AIR.—Waters of Elle.

EEP in the vale, afar from every beholder,
  In the May morning my true love came to
    me,
Silent we sate, her head upon my shoulder,
Fondly we dreamed of days about to be;
Softly we talked of days about to be.

Deep in the vale the rain falls colder and colder,
Safely she sleeps beneath the kirkyard tree;
Yet still I feel her hand upon my shoulder,
Still, still I dream of days that could not be,
Still, still, I weep for days too sweet to be.

THE ELECT KNIGHT.

"I could not love thee, dear, so much,
Loved I not Honor more."

ERE boy and girl, mere boy and girl—
    Yet belted knight and ladye pure;
  Just entering life's gates of pearl,
    They hear the summons, "Fight," "Endure."
  At once, obedient to the word,
  She buckles on his shining sword.

Her cheek is blanched with anguish dumb,
  But her fair hands the weapon bind;
Her heart bleeds inly—no tears come—
  She keeps for him an equal mind;
Therefore, however sore the fight,
In midst of darkness there is light.

O unknown years, what may ye yield
  Unto these twain, now heart to heart?
Swift death upon the battle-field,
  A whole life's loss, apart, apart?
Or halcyon days, love-shared, love-worth,
Bringing all heaven down to earth?

Thou, God, seest all!   Thy will be done;
  What Thou layest on them, help to bear!
Give them the joy of conflicts won,
  The peace of well-endured despair.
And when it seemeth to Thee best,
Take them to Thy eternal rest.

BESIDE A TOMB.

Francois Pierre Guillaume Guizot, né le 4 Octobre, 1797; décédé le 12 Sep-
tembre, 1874.

" Je suis la Résurrection et la Vie."

IKE a sweet face all soiled with tears,
  Rain-sodden the " rich valley" lies;
  The sky, once blue as children's eyes,
Gray, blank—so unlike heaven! appears.

While up and down the wintry earth
  The wind goes, like a human cry;
  "Why live, since soon we all must die?
What is the use of death or birth?"

Beside these wooden crosses poor
    His granite tomb stands, strong and still,
    Emblem of that unconquered will,
And spirit steadfast to endure.

That calm, great heart and equal mind.
    Whether blind Fortune smiled or frowned—
    And is all hidden underground?
Is nothing—*nothing*—left behind?

If to the fireside turn we back,
    What find we? Ah, an empty chair—
    A silent absence everywhere,
A bitter universal lack.

Do our dead know we love them yet?
    When we stretch out vain hands and weep
    Smile they, as we o'er our child's sleep
Whose eyes with foolish dreams are wet?

Dreams that we know will end with morn—
    Soul, well-beloved, is it thus with thee?
    La Résurrection et la Vie:
We die. Is it thou who art newborn?

Can our dead hear us when we cry?
    Thou, landed on the further shore,
    Couldst thou across the ocean's roar.
Send back clear answer, " It is I.

"The Resurrection? it is found.
    The Life! I live it, in His light
    Who out of darkness bringeth light
And flowers from seed hid underground.

"I have believed, and now I know.
    Believe ye! "—Who would not believe?
    Who would for death a moment grieve
If we were *certain* it was so ?

But God Himself this silence deep
    Has made, and so—His will be done!
    We trust Him, in or out o' the sun.
We love Him, waking or asleep.

He must be Love, whence all loves flow.
    Our faith He could not falsify,
    When His saints leave us, let us cry,
"Whither thou goest I will go."

HER BIRTHDAY.

Henriette Guizot De Witt.

August 8, 1873.

BRING no gifts of precious store,
    Nor homage wrapped in gorgeous
        rhyme;
I only love you—nothing more,
    With love that owes small help from time.

Love, born full-grown although full late,
    That sits at rest with folded wings,
Watching you in your fair estate,
    And as he watches, softly sings:

No song of youth—only a psalm
    Sweet sounding through the year's decline.
All peace and patience, strength and calm,
    Such as you give, dear friend of mine.

Contented Love, that gives and takes
    All mutual help, in life's rough track:
In others' joy its sunshine makes,
    And feels no pain and finds no lack.

Admiring Love, that smiles to see
   In daughter, sister, mother, spouse,
The centre of felicity,
   The living Heart of all the House.

There have been those who walked, they say,
   With angels, like as friend with friend.
Thus friend or angel, dear, I pray
   To walk with you until the end.

AN EVERY-DAY STORY.

MY old love, whom I loved not—
   Is this your friendly hand?
   Your very voice with a tremble in it,
   None else could understand?
My old love, whom I loved not,
   After so many years!
Parting in silence and in pain—
   To meet with smiles, not tears.

My old love, whom I loved not,
   Do you regret—not I!—
That all died out which best were dead,
   All lived, which could not die?
Till at the end we meet here,
   And clasp long empty hands;
Keeping the silent secret safe
   That no one understands.

You will leave a name behind you—
   A life pure, calm and long;
But mine will fade from human ear
   Like a forgotten song.
You have lived to smile serenely
   Over a grief long done:
You shall die with children round your bed
   But I shall die alone.

O kind love whom I loved not!
  O faithful, firm and true!—
Did one friend linger near my grave
  I think it would be you.
Could I wish one heart to hold me
  A little, unforgot,
I think, 't would be that heart of yours
  My love—whom I loved not!

———

FOUND DROWNED.

SHE searches, searches, everywhere,
  As she would treasure find,—
Old Susan with the wandering eye,
  And long-bewildered mind.

All up and down the shining sands
  With eager step she goes,
And speaks with hesitating voice,
  Not knowing friends from foes.

"O have ye seen my pretty boy,
  My little baby-brother?
I never murdered him, indeed,
  He was too like his mother;—

"My mother—she frowns out of heaven,
  As once on me she smiled:
And bids me wander night and day,
  Until I find the child.

"It is not many months ago"—
  (She has lost count of years)
"I laid him on the sunny sand,
  Asleep, and had no fears.

"I only went a little way,
　And sat behind a stone,
Writing to William Beverley
　That is to India gone;

"But he'll come back and marry me,
　He says, in two years more:
I shall be then scarce twenty-one,
　And he just twenty-four.

"But can he marry me?"—She starts—
　"Me that was hanged!—I mean
They would have hanged me, but perhaps
　Somebody told the Queen.

"And she said—what, I do not know:
　I think I slept, or died,
And woke up in a world of dreams,
　Most horrible and wide.

"I did not kill the boy," she moans,
　"I only left him here;
Just here—and so the tide came in—
　And ebbed out, bright and clear.

"Not guilty,—O my lord, my lord,
　Not guilty!" (shrieking wild)
"I only let him float away
　And drown—my mother's child.

"And so my mother made them shut
　On me the prison door:
And I was dead: yet now it seems
　I am alive once more.

"I walk along the glittering sands,
　I hear his shouts of joy;
I know I'll find him very soon,
　My little darling boy."

So on she goes with cautious tread,
  And eager eyes and wild—
But never, never, will she find
  The little drownèd child.

AN HONEST MAN.

Fletcher Harper, last survivor of the original firm of Harper Brothers,
New York.

NO soldier, statesman, hierophant, or king;
  None of the heroes that you poets sing:
  A toiler, ever since his days began;
Simple, though shrewd; just-judging, man to man:
God-fearing; learned in life's hard-taught school,
By long obedience lessoned how to rule;
Through many an early struggle led to find
That crown of prosperous fortunes—to be kind.
Lay on his breast these English daisies sweet,
Good rest to the gray head, and the tired feet,
That walked this world for seventy steadfast years!
Bury him with fond blessings, and few tears,
Tears only of remembrance, not regret.
On his full life the eternal seal is set
Unbroken, till the resurrection day.
So let his children's children go their way.
Go and do likewise, leaving 'neath this sod
An honest man—"the noblest work of God."

DIED HAPPY.

YOU say, O friends, that I am strangely altered,
  My fading youth has won the calm of age:
Sweet strength has come into my voice that faltered,
  And why? Because my life has turned a page
    After that day.

A page—you could not trace the writing in it,
So blurred and blotted, faded and obscure,
Yet angels, looking down one golden minute,
Can read it all, with smile content and pure,
As mine that day.

Dear sisters, walking in our pleasant garden,
Whiter than lilies, rosier than the rose,
And almost of my pale lot asking pardon,—
Wherefore? When I might pity you, God knows,
After that day.

I have no fear of life and all its noises,
Or silent death, since more than life it brings.
In halcyon nest midst earth's tumultuous noises,
My soul sits quiet, folds her wings, and sings,
After that day.

THE SHADOW OF THE CROSS.

W. Holman Hunt's Picture.

ART Thou half weary of the work of life,
The scarce begun, ne'er to be ended, strife,
O Son of Mary?
Jesus of Nazareth, the carpenter
God-given, twenty years ago, to her,
His mother Mary:
Jesus, the Lord's Anointed, pure from sin,
The Way by which a far-off heaven we win,
The Door through which we all can enter in.
Christ, Son of Mary.

Our days, Thou knowest, are short and full of woes,
Our cross, like Thine, full soon its shadow throws,
Tired Son of Mary.
Our birth-crowns that our mothers treasure up

Are melted oft into one anguish-cup,
     They drink, like Mary.
And with dim, frightened eyes, they also see
The shadow of some strange accursed Tree
Where their dear sons give up the ghost, like Thee,
     Great Son of Mary.

O full of life, with all life's lawful joys
Calling upon Thee in mellifluous voice,
     Fair Son of Mary;
A young man's strength to do God's whole behest,
The noontide labor earning evening rest,
     Sweet Son of Mary:
Yet through it all, love-wise, beyond all these,
The shadow of the Cross Thy mother sees
In its unfathomable mysteries,
     Heart-pierced Mary.

But Thou, with those divine eyes, pure from fear,
Thou seest the rest remaining even here,
     To Thee and Mary,
And all God's people—all his children poor
Who are thy brethren—Thou knock'st at their door,
     Blest Son of Mary.
And by and by, Thy earthly travail done,
Death consummating what Thy life begun,
Thou 'lt say—"Come unto Me, earth-weary one,
     I am Son of Mary."

O Son of God, and still the woman's seed,
Bruise Thou our serpent-sins, although we bleed
     Like Thee—and Mary:
Forgive, should we too, tired ere work is done,
Look forward longingly to set of sun,
     (No mother Mary!)
And in the evil days, with anguish rife
Remember us!   Through all this mortal strife,
Lead us unto Thy everlasting life,
     Christ, Son of Mary.

ST. CHRISTOPHER.

ARRY me across."
 The Syrian heard, rose up, and braced
 His huge limbs to the accustomed toil;
"My child, see how the waters boil—
The night-black heavens look angry-faced,
 But life is little loss.

 " I 'll carry thee with joy,
If needs be, safe as nested dove.
For o'er this stream I pilgrims bring
In service to one Christ—a King,
Whom I have never seen, yet love."
 " I thank thee," said the boy.

 Cheerful, Arprobus took
The burden on his shoulders great,
He stept into the waves once more:
When up they leaped with foaming roar,
And 'neath the little child's light weight
 The tottering giant shook.

 "Who art thou?" cried he, wild
Struggling in middle of the ford;
"Boy, as thou lookest, it seems to me
The whole world's load I bear in thee,
"Yet"——"For the sake of Christ, thy Lord
 Carry me," said the child.

 No more Arprobus swerved,
But gained the further bank, and then
A voice cried "Hence *Christopherus* be,
For, carrying, thou hast carried Me
The King of angels and of men,

And in the moonlight blue
The saint saw—not the wandering boy,
But Him who walked upon the sea,
And o'er the plains of Galilee!
Full-filled with mystic awful joy,
His dear Lord Christ he knew.

O little is all loss,
And brief the space 'twixt shore and shore,
If Thou, Lord Jesus, on us lay
Through the deep waters of our way
The burden that Christopherus bore—
To carry Thee across.

DEAD, YET SPEAKING.

"I have been dying for years, now I shall begin to live." These were almost the last words of the Rev. James Drummond Burns, Minister of the Presbyterian Church at Hampstead, who died of consumption abroad, in 1865, deeply beloved and lamented.

EAD and alive again. Alive to us,
Who through the long, long lapse of years
still mark
The after-glow thy sunset luminous
Threw back upon our dark.

Alive to God, and to His work divine,
Though in what sphere we know not, nor need
know;
Content to follow those dear steps of thine,
And where thou goest, to go.

The blessings of the happy, and at rest,
The sorrowful, and those whose sorrows cease,
Blossom, like April daisies on thy breast;
Sleeping the sleep of peace.

But far beyond all sound of earthly strife,
　　Or silent slumber 'neath this long, green sod,
Thou hast passed, triumphant, into perfect life,
　　The soul's true life in God.

THE NOBLE COWARD.

"Were I a king, I would never make war."—Saying (reported) of the
Crown Prince of Prussia.

M I afraid of man?
　　　　Of swarming armies, death in their van,
　　　　Spreading like locusts over my plains?
Of *mitrailleuess* that sweep like rains
O'er my battalions, firm as a wall;
The iron drops blasting as they fall,
Till that living, moving, wonderful mass
Of souls and bodies, as thick as grass,
Lies prone like the swath when the mowers pass?

Am I afraid? What, I—
Who was born a king, and a king shall die?
Shall the will of another my will control
To make me sin against mine own soul?
To bid me sow my fair land with graves,
I, who rule content over men, not slaves,
I, my people's father, who keeps the keys
Of bliss or mourning, want or increase,
Curses or blessings, war or peace?

But I am afraid of God:
Afraid of His law, written clear and broad,
"Thou shalt do no murder;" and, hear ye dead!
"Who sheddeth man's blood, man his blood shall
　　　　shed."
Be it of one or of thousands, I hear the sound,
Abel-like, of that blood crying out from the ground,

Go to, ye nations!   Bless me, or ban,
I sit in my judgment seat—kings can:
And I rule by the law of God, not man.

I will do no murder, Lord.
I will not go forth with fire and sword
O'er this pleasant earth which thou madest so fair
And man makes hideous—will not tear
Out of poor souls the dear life-breath,
Inventing daily some fierce fresh death,
Till the nations gaze, aghast at first
At the new Aceldama, then athirst
For blood—drink up the cup accurst.

Ye tell me I am "afraid!"
Brute force, false glory, poor ghosts, scarce laid,
Go back to Gehenna and sleep!   I stand,
Holding my honor in my right hand,
Instead of an unsheathed sword, and say,
"I will not fight."   Let them mock who may.
I—"a city set on a hill"—unawed
By smile or sneer, by treason or fraud;
I, a king before man, am the servant of God.

RESPECT THE BURTHEN.

An Incident.

REAT Garibaldi, through the streets one day
Passing triumphant, while admiring throngs,
With acclamations and exultant songs,
For the uncrowned kingly man made way,
Met one poor knave, 'neath heavy burden bowed,
Indifferent to the hero and the crowd.

His zealous followers would have driven aside
The sorry creature, but that good man said,
Laying a kind hand on the suffering head,

"Respect the burthen." Then, majestic-eyed
He paused, and passed on, no man saying him nay;
The heavy-laden also went his way.

Thou happy soul, who journeyest like a king
    Along a rose-strewn road, whate'er thy lot,
      "Respect the burthen." Thou mayst see it, or
        not,
For one heart is to another a sealed thing:
Laughter there is which hideth sobs or moans,
Firm footsteps may leave blood-prints on the stones.

Respect the burthen, whatso'er it be,
    Whether loud outcries vex the startled air,
    Or in dumb agonies of loss, despair
Lifts her still face, so like tranquility;
Though each strained heart-string break, she never
    shrinks;
Says "Let this cup pass from me," stoops and drinks.

O heavy burthen! why 't is borne, or how,
    None know—save those who bear, and He whose
      hand
    Has laid it on, saying, "My beloved, stand
Upright—and take this chrism upon thy brow—
God's own anointed. Sore thy load may be,
But know—within it thou art carrying ME."

PASSING BY.

"And they told him that Jesus of Nazareth passeth by."

 RICH man, from your happy door,
    Watching the old, the sick, the poor,
    Who neither ask, nor sigh, nor weep,
So tired, to them heaven means but sleep,
While you, given good things without measure,

Sometimes can hardly sleep for pleasure.
  Let not the blessed moment fly,
  Jesus of Nazareth passeth by.

O sinners, weary of your sin,
Longing a new life to begin,
When all the gates of help are shut,
And all the words of love are mute.
Earth's joys are sere, like burnt-up grass,
And even the very heavens as brass.
  Turn not away so hopelessly,
  Jesus of Nazareth passeth by.

Self-hardened man, with smooth bland smile,
Woman, whose heart's a desert isle
Set in the sea of household love,
Whom nothing but "the world" can move;
At your white lie, your sneering speech,
Small crimes no punishment can reach,
  See, your child lifts a wondering eye,
  Jesus of Nazareth passeth by.

O all ye foolish ones, who feel
A sudden doubt, like piercing steel,
Strike your dead souls—make your hearts burn
Till conscience sighs, Return, return—
Why let the heavenly impulse fleet,
Love's wave wash back from your worn feet,
  Know ye not Him who comes so nigh,
  Jesus of Nazareth passing by?

He must not pass. Fond, fast, and sure,
Hold Him. In likeness of His poor,
His prodigals by sin beguiled,
Or innocent face of little child,
Clasp Him, quite certain it is He,
In form of earthly misery;
  So, when thou meetest Him on high,
  Believe, He will not pass thee by.

A POSSIBILITY.

(The thought of a mourning mother.)

Y little baby was buried to-day;
   She is gone deep down in the church-yard
      clay,
  And up in the sky so dull and gray.
    Who will take care of my little baby?

Who will kiss her? her waxen feet
That never have walked—her small hand sweet,
Where I left a white lily, as was meet—
    O who will kiss my little baby?

Who will teach her—her wings to try,
Her tender limbs their new work to ply,
Her soft dumb lips to sing gloriously—
    Say, who will teach my little baby?

I have a mother. She died quite young:
All have forgotten her, long and long;
Will she find my pretty one in the blest throng,
    And be glad to see my little baby?

Angels are far off—*she* is near:
Christ, born of a woman, hear, O hear!
Give my child to my mother dear,
    And I 'll cease to weep for my little baby.

Nothing in heaven can be so blest,
Nothing so safe as a mother's breast:
Give her my lamb, and I shall rest
    If my mother takes care of my little baby.

A WINTER WEDDING.

At Chiselhurst Church, January 9, 1873.

T fled away in a clang of bells,
  Marriage bells,
  On the wings of the wind that wailed fare-
    wells,
That bold, ,weak, fate-struck, suffering soul
Whom Christ wash clean and then make whole .
And we stand in the light of two young faces,
Two happy hearts whom our heart embraces :
We hear the peaceful organ's sound,
The angry storm sweeps harmless round,
    Blessed is the bridegroom, though the heavens
        are dun ;
    Blessed is the bride whom no sun shines on.

Mayhap, some wandering angels say,
Stop and say,
As through the gloom they carry away
That bodiless spirit to One who knows
—He only—whither man's spirit goes :
"God give these all that the dead man lacked
(As man dare judge) in thought, word, and act,
Deny them all that to him was given,
Lest earth's doors opened close doors of heaven."
    Blessed is the bridegroom without crown or
        lands :
    Blessed is the bride with her heart in her hands.

Peal, ye marriage-bells, peal through the rain ;
Blinding rain !
God makes happiness, and permits pain ;
Winter and summer do good trees grow ;
And strong souls strengthen through weal and woe.

"Be not afraid!" sighs the wild-sobbing wind.
"Smile," say the clouds, "for blue heaven is behind."
Blessed is the bridegroom under shower or sun;
Blessed is the bride whom love's light shines on.

ALL SAINTS' DAY.

At New College Chapel, Oxford.

I SHALL find them again, I shall find them again,
Though I cannot tell when or where,
My earthly own, gone to worlds unknown,
But never beyond Thy care.

I shall find them again, I shall find them again,
By the soul that within me dwells,
Leaps to them, and Thee, with a rapture free
As this jubilant anthem swells;

"*I heard a voice saying.*" What it says
I hear. So, perchance, do they,
As I stand between my living, I ween,
And my dead, upon All Saints' Day.

And I see all clear—new heavens, new earth,
New bodies, redeemed from pain;
New souls—ah, not so! with the soul that I know
Let me find, let me find them again.

Let me walk with them under any sky,
Beside any land or sea,
In what shape or make Thou will'st us to take
If 't is like unto, near to, Thee.

Let me wander whither Thou bidst me go,
Rest, labor, or even remain
Lulled to long still sleep in the earth or the deep,
If I wake, Lord, to find them again.

Only at times does the awful mist
  Lift off, and we seem to see
For a moment's space the far dwelling-place
  Of these our beloved, and Thee.

Only at times through our soul's shut doors
  Thou passest, in visit brief,
And we cease to grieve and cry " Lord, I believe,
  Help Thou mine unbelief."

O linger, linger, invisible host
  Of the sainted dead, who stand
Not so far off, though men may scoff,
  Touch me with unfelt hand.

But my own, my own, ye are holding me fast
  With the human clasp that I knew :
Through the chorus clear your voices I hear,
  And I am singing with you.   .

Ah, they melt away as the anthem dies,
  Back comes the world's work, hard, plain,
Yet God lifted a space the veil from His face,
  And He smiled, " Thou shalt find them again."

A SEPTEMBER ROBIN.

MY eyes are full, my silent heart is stirred.
        Amid these days so bright
        Of ceaseless warmth and light ;
    Summer that will not die,
    Autumn, without one sigh
    O'er sweet hours passing by—
    Cometh that tender note
    Out of thy tiny throat,
Like grief, or love, insisting to be heard
O little plaintive bird !

No need of word₄
Well know I all your tale—forgotten bird !
    Soon you and I together
    Must face the winter weather,
    Remembering how we sung
    Our primrose fields among,
    In days when life was young ;
    Now, all is growing old,
    And the warm earth's a-cold,
Still, with brave heart we 'll sing on, little bird,
Sing only. Not one word.

BLUE GENTIAN.

 SHALL never be a child
    With its dancing motion wild,
      Or a free-footed maiden any more,
Yet my heart leaps up to see
The new leaf upon the tree ;
And to hear the light winds pass
O'er the flowers in the grass,
    And for very joy brims o'er,
    As I kneel and pluck the store
      Of blue gentian.

I shall never climb thy peak
Great white Alp that cannot speak
    Of the centuries that pass over thee like
      dreams ;
Of all those solemn things,
Sealed to beggars as to kings.
Yet I sit in a world of light,
Color, beauty, sound and sight.
    While at every step, meseems,
    Small, sweet joys spring up, like gleams
      Of blue gentian.

I shall not live o'er again
This strange life, half bliss, half paiu;
    I shall sleep, till Thou call'st me to arise,
Body and soul—with new-born powers.
If Thou wakest these poor dumb flowers,
Wilt Thou not awaken me
Whose soul yearneth after Thee?
So when faith grows dim and dies,
Let me think of Alpine skies,
    And blue gentian.

FORSAKEN.

"Then all the disciples forsook Him and fled."

F even Thee, the righteous and the holy,
    These did forsake,
What wonder human hearts, loving as lowly,
    Do sometimes break?

All stand far off in the dark hour of trial,
    Just before sleep:
'Neath the lip's smile we feel the soul's denial,
    And turn and weep.

Thou weep'st not, Lord. John had thy breast for
    pillow,
    Thou, the hard Cross:
Yet our weak bosoms heave like sobbing billow,
    At each light loss.

Sweet summer friends, farewell. Your flight you've
    taken,
    (Small blame—God wot!)
In the lone hour of death, Thou, once forsaken,
    Forsake us not!

MOTHER AND SON.

In the centre aisle of the church at Budleigh Salterton is a flat stone, underneath which lies buried Mistress Raleigh, a farmer's wife at Hayes close by, and mother of the great Sir Walter. His head, tradition says, was, after his execution, secretly brought here and placed in his mother's coffin.

UNDAY after Sunday, down this church aisle gray,
 Devon men and maidens demurely pass to pray ;
 Sunday after Sunday falls the village tread,
Heavily on the pavement-stone, quaintly letteréd.
No one reads the letters, no one heeds the fame,
 Sighs for love and sorrow, weeps the death of shame.
Love, fame, and shame together are whelmed beneath the wave
Of centuried time that sweeps across this long-forgotten grave.

His tale is told and ended, the little Devon boy,
The courtier-youth, gay sailing adown the stream of joy :
The twelve years captive, breasting hard fortune like a rock—
The old man calmly laying his head upon the block.
And there—you may believe it or believe it not,
Still, the very legend sanctifies the spot—
Some kind hand, nobly fearless, did play Fate's mis-played part,
And placed the tired head, child-like, upon the mother's heart.

She—no one knows her story, and none has carved her face,
She lived, died, and was buried, here, in her native place,
Scarcely a furlong distant from the daisied lea
Where once her baby-hero gambolled at her knee.
Better so.   What record needs to tell us more
Of this Devon woman, mother's lot who bore ?
In the evening shadow and the morning smile
Let them sleep together beneath the gray church aisle.

Take this leaf of laurel, Willie—
  Brighter ones to thee belong;
Yet thou wilt not quarrel, Willie,
  With a sister's greeting song.
I cannot bind with worldly chains,
  I cannot give thee wealth, Willie;
But I can bless thee for thy strains,
  And wish thee Peace and Health, Willie:
And hold thee as a shining one—
Poor, but GOD's high-hearted son.

———◆———

AUTUMN THOUGHTS.

LOOK out, look out; there are shadows about;
  The forest is donning its doublet of brown;
The willow-tree sways with a gloomier flout,
  Like a beautiful face with a gathering frown!
'Tis true we all know that summer must go,
  That the swallow will never stay long in our eaves;
Yet we'd rather be watching the cowslip blow,
  Than be counting the colours of Autumn leaves!

Look high, look high, there's the lace-winged fly,
  Thinking he's king of a fairy realm;
As he swings with delight on the gossamer tie,
  That is linked 'mid the boughs of the sun-tipped elm
Alas! poor thing, the first rustle will bring
  The pillars to dust, where your pleasure-clue weaves;
And many a spirit, like thine, will cling
  To hopes that depend upon Autumn leaves!

Look low, look low; the night gusts blow
  And the restless forms in hectic red
Come whirling and sporting wherever we go;
  Lighter in dancing, as nearer the dead!
Oh! who has not seen rare hearts, that have been
  Painted and panting, in garb that deceives;
Dashing gaily along in their fluttering sheen
  With Despair at the core, like Autumn leaves!

Look on, look on; morn breaketh upon
  The hedgerow boughs, in their withering hue;
The distant orchard is sallow and wan,
  But the apple and nut, gleam richly through.

Oh ! well it will be if our life, like the tree,
　Shall be found, when Old Time of green beauty bereaves,
With the fruit of good works for the planter to see
　Shining out in Truth's harvest, through Autumn leaves !

Merrily pours, as it sings and soars,
　The west wind over the lands and seas ,
Till it plays in the forest and moans and roars,
　Seeming no longer a mirthful breeze !
So music is blest, till it meeteth the breast
　That is probed by the strain, while the mourner grieves,
To think it was sung by a loved one at rest ;
　Then it comes like the sweet wind in Autumn leaves !

Not in an hour are leaf and flower
　Stricken in freshness, and swept to decay ;
By gentle approaches, the frost and the shower
　Make ready the sap-veins for falling away !
And so is Man made to as peacefully fade,
　By the tear that he sheds, and the sigh that he heaves ;
For he's loosened from earth by each trial-cloud's shade,
　Till he's willing to go, as the Autumn leaves !

Look back, look back, and you'll find the track
　Of our human steps strewn thickly o'er
With Joy's dead leaves, all dry and black ;
　And every year still flinging more.
But the soil is fed where the branches are shed,
　For the furrow to bring forth fuller sheaves ;
And so is our trust in the Future spread
　In the gloom of Mortality's Autumn leaves !

———◆———

WILT THOU BE TRUE ?

INSCRIBED TO ———.

" WILT thou be true ?" we ask it of the flower
　That decks our garland in the festive scene ;
But leaves that fall before the parting hour
　Mock us, and tell how vain the words have been,
　　　　　　　" Wilt thou be true ?"

" Wilt thou be true ?" we ask it of the billow,
　And launch our bark upon the crystal tide ;
But many a sea-weed shroud and coral pillow
　Have met the lips that trusted while they cried,
　　　　　　　" Wilt thou be true ?"

Then said the Saint with kinder face
"Since, haply, ye 're a lad o' grace,
   Whom no false flames encumber,
Speer ye in Edinburgh town
For six braw lasses, sent to crown
A good man's board in Terrace Doune :
   Go.   One 's the lucky number."

On wings of love I fly anew,
And enter—for my coat of blue
   Invisible secures me :
There I behold the sisters six ;
Five with eye-arrows me transfix.
The sixth assails me with sweet *kicks*
   "All love," mamma assures me!

Now, who will be this wife of mine?
She with the hair of ebon twine,
   The dark-eyed witch, and fairy—
A Spanish gypsy—Roman belle—
A brown Rebecca at the well?
No.   Being unco black mysel,
   I 'd never do for Mary!

Next comes a sonsie Scottish lass
Who ne'er need care what says her glass,
   Because her heart 's sae bonnie :
I love her frank and smiling face
Her sensible and quiet grace—
Save that I 've not seen all the race,
   I think I 'd marry Annie.

Hiatus—pause in this fair show—
Behold! a Lind in embryo—
   A tiny Saint Cecilia—
Were I an angel, on my wings,
I 'd stoop, and kiss her as she sings,
But being a man of common things
   I dare not woo Amelia.

Ha! here 's a roly-poly sprite.
Pa's plaything, and mamma's delight
   I 'm sure whoever *she* be :
But would it do for me to marry
A wee, wee wife in arms to carry ?
So, as I 'm far too old to tarry,
   My grandson shall have Phœbe.

St. Valentine forgive my sins !
What—had I quite forgot the Twins !
   Come, dearest maid of any,
My own low-voiced, brave-hearted girl,
Of soft blue eyes, and fair brown curl,
My beautiful, my pure white pearl,
   O let me wear you, Jenny !

Miss Jennie shakes her head the while,
And answers with her quiet smile
   So sweet, it drives me dizzy—
(While close beside her laughs at me
Her sister, like as like can be ;)
   "I loe ye weel, but then ye see,
     I couldna part wi' Lizzie."

Now, gentle saint, have pity on me,
Or else this answer has undone me—
   He growls—"Go fetch your brother,
As like yourself as are two peas—
Bid him woo Lizzie on his knees.
If she consent, and Jenny please,
   Why—you can take the other !"

1880.—Mary, married and died; Jenny, died unmarried : Annie, Amelia,
Phœbe, Lizzie, married and living still. "So runs the world away."

FIVE IRISH SONGS.

I.

TO HIS MARY.

Air.—O Mairi is deas do gaire: O Mary thy laugh is sweet.

O MARY, thy laugh was sweet
    In the days Love remembers:
When a fire burns safe, complete,
    There's warmth in its embers.
O Mary, thy voice was clear,
    As song of the lark or linnet;
Even now when its notes I hear
    There's the old tune in it.

O Mary, thy heart was true,
    No change, no surrender:
Many fairer girls I knew,
    None like thee, strong as tender.
O Mary, thy smile is bright:
    A moon thro' the storm clouds driven;
On earth I shall lose its light:
    May I find it in heaven!

II.

THE EMIGRANT.

Air.—O mo chaillin le mise: My girl along with me.

SWEETLY the sunshine was dancing on the sea,
   When we walked out together, my girl along with
      me.
O softly the twilight was melting down the shore,
When I kissed her and told her I 'd love her ever-
      more.

O sadly the white mist is creeping o'er the strand:
We 're leaving dear old Ireland to dwell in a foreign
      land;
But brightly the sunrise is shining on the sea;
And we shall go together, my girl along with me.

III.

THE HAY.

Air.—The Cutting of the Hay.

'M glad to praise the April days,
    And the long bright nights of May:
    But best is June with a sweet new moon
  And the cutting of the hay:
The girls all go in a steady row,
    Tedding the swaths we lay,
And a pleasant noise is the laugh of the boys,
  At the cutting of the hay.

When all is done, the joke and the fun,
　　And the wain carries all away ;
Sure, some must part with a heavy heart,
　　After cutting of the hay.
But I will stand with my girl in my hand
　　Before Father Tom some day ;
And bless this June, with the birds all in tune,
　　At the cutting of the hay.

―――

IV.

A LULLABY.

GOOD-BYE, good-bye, sweet soul !
　　We drop no tear :
　Full early you have reached your goal ;
　　And we stay here.
Your life was like a winter day,
　　Brief, cold, though bright :
And when you wake it will be **May :**
　Good night, good night.

Farewell, farewell, dear heart !
　　Of hearts most true.
With false ones we could lightly part,
　　But death took you.
Good night, and draw the curtains close :
　　Rise, soul new-born ;
Sweet body, sink to kind repose,
　　Until the morn.

V.

LOST KATHLEEN.

Air.—Far beyond yon mountain.

AR, far beyond yon mountain, across the cruel sea,
  She dwells in another country, the girl that was
        born for me :
But I lost her, ah ! I lost her, in the foolish days of yore :
Now—I blind my eyes with weeping for my Kathleen
  Astore.

I will not pass yon mountain, nor sail across that sea ;
My heart is dead within me, for the girl that loved but me :
Is she sighing, is she smiling, as she sits at another's door ?
But mine is shut for ever to my Kathleen Astore.

THE GREAT LOCH LOMOND SCHEME.

A Reminiscence.

ON the seventeenth of August
    Eighteen hundred and seventy-**five,**
    A Noble Family woke up
Glad that they were alive:
And very much alive they were
    As all their doings show,
Said they, "Whether it rains or not
    To the Trosachs we will go."
        So, peace to those that lie and sleep,
        Good luck to them that dream,
        And health to the two Promoters
        Of the Great Loch Lomond scheme.

There were four heads of families
    Two boys, a damsel fair,
And one sweet soul quite unattached,
    "Everybody's body" there.
They hired a splendid car-ri-age,
    And journeyed unafraid,
From Arrochar to Tarbet straight,
    Then sailed for Inversnaid.
        O the waterfall, the shining loch,
        The hills—one golden dream!
        Blest be the two Promoters
        Of the Great Loch Lomond scheme.

They travelled on by glen and loch
    Enjoyed great things and small,
But one another's company
    Enjoyed they most of all—

Until at Stron-na-chlacher
  They deigned to sit and feed:
Blessing the kind and prudent hand
  Which had supplied their need.
    Good appetites to all who eat,
    And drink, by bog and stream;
    But most to the two Promoters
    Of the Great Loch Lomond scheme.

Adown Loch Katrine's silver wave
  They steamed; passed Ellen's Isle
Beneath umbrellas. The skies wept:
  But they the more did smile:
So placid were their thankful hearts;
  Forgetting "might have beens,"
They sat and soaked, and soaked and sat,
  Happy as kings and queens.
    How sweet is rain—that makes the hills
    To vanish like a dream—
    How wise were the Promoters
    Of the Great Loch Lomond scheme.

Ere long the kindly skies grew bright
  As Kandy's merry eyes:
The clouds pass off: the purple peaks
  Like Victor's spirits rise.
And though the Glasgow tourists swarm
  About them, just like bees,
This Noble Family, I say,
. Enjoys itself at ease.
    Success to every drop of rain
    Followed by sunny gleam,
    But most to the Promoters
    Of the Great Loch Lomond scheme.

      *   *   *   *   *

On the thirtieth of November,
  Eighteen hundred and seventy-five

The humble poet sat her down
  And, being still alive,
Though not so very much alive,
  As on that pleasant day,
Began to jog her memory
  To finish up this lay :
      But ah ! she only went to sleep,
      And wrote as in a dream,
      " Good luck to the two Promoters
      Of the Great Loch Lomond scheme."

In clouds across her window pane
  The feathery white snow flies :
And all her brains are frozen up,
  Her soul alone has eyes.
With them she sees the gleaming loch,
  The sunset hues, as clear
As paradise—the silent moon,
  The faces kind and dear.
      And still she says, " 'T is good to sleep,
      And better still to dream
      Long life to the two Promoters
      Of the Great Loch Lomond scheme."

MISSED.

M. C. N. P.   Died September 20, 1879.

" Four corners to my bed,
Four angels round my head ;
One to watch and one to pray,
Two to bear my soul away."

OUR angels, sure, stand round
    That small spot of moonlight ground,
    Where the turf folds safe and sweet
O'er *his* eyes, and hands, and feet.
Hands more meet to gather flowers
Than to strain and toil like ours :
Feet too soft for this world's road,
Eyes that seemed to search for God,—
So, God took him.
           Five years' space—
Just to learn the little face
And remember it : to hear
In the child-voice pure and clear
Words that seemed to teach His ways,
Who " out of babes' mouths perfects praise ;"
Then, this silence.
           Gather here,
Living children, good and dear,
· Let your Christmas mirth arise,
What has youth to do with sighs?
Cluster round the Christmas fire ;
Labor, dream, endure, aspire :
Live your lives as Heaven sees best,
Struggle, conquer, work, and rest.
But he rests already. Done,
All his task, ere heat of sun.
In the five years did he drain,

Every drop, the cup of pain,
With a saintly patience sweet,
Laid it down, and rose complete
Into the perfect life of God.
Moon, shine softly on that sod,
Colder than this household hearth—
Yet the holiest spot on earth
To the hearts, whose lips are dumb.
And each Christmas that shall come
Bringing memòries at flood-tide,
Smiles long faded, tears long dried,
There will come too, unforgot,
One among them who " is not : "
Never changing as they change,
Never growing old or strange.
Creeping, silent and unseen,
Them and the harsh world between:
Entering with noiseless foot
Each heart's door, open or shut:
An angelic influence mild,
Yet eternally a child.

9 781330 456675